Queering the Moderns

Queering the Moderns

Poses/Portraits/Performances

Anne Herrmann

december, 2000

Val —

thanks so much for being
a companion in thinking
about things queer and
theoretical, and for being
committed to the transformation
of ideas. best wishes,

palgrave

QUEERING THE MODERNS

First published 2000 by
PALGRAVE™
175 Fifth Avenue, New York, N.Y. 10010 and
Houndmills, Basingstoke, Hampshire, England RG21 6XS.
Companies and representatives throughout the world.

PALGRAVE™ is the new global publishing imprint of St. Martin's Press LLC Scholarly and Reference Division and Palgrave Publishers Ltd (formerly Macmillan Press Ltd).

ISBN 0-312-23327-2 hardback

Library of Congress Cataloging-in-Publication Data
Herrmann, Anne.
Queering the moderns: poses/portraits/performances / by Anne Herrmann.
p. cm.
Includes bibliographical references (p.) and index.
ISBN 0-312-23327-2 (cloth)
1. English literature—20th century—History and criticism. 2. Homosexuality andliterature—Great Britain—History—20th century. 3. Homosexuality and literature—United States—History—20th century. 4. American literature—20th century—History and criticism. 5. Gays' writings, American—History and criticism. 6. Gays' writings, English—History and criticism. 7. Modernism (Literature)—Great Britain. 8. Modernism (Literature)—United States. I. Title.
PR478.H65 H47 2000
820.9'920664—dc21 00–040487

Design by Letra Libre, Inc.

First edition: September 1, 2000
10 9 8 7 6 5 4 3 2 1

Printed in the United States of America

Permissions

Excerpts from ORLANDO, copyright 1928 by Virginia Woolf and renewed 1956 by Leonard Woolf, reprinted by permission of Harcourt, Inc.

Excerpts from A ROOM OF ONE'S OWN by Virginia Woolf, copyright 1929 by Harcourt, Inc. and renewed 1957 by Leonard Woolf, reprinted by permission of the publisher.

Excerpts from THE DIARY OF VIRGINIA WOOLF, Volume III: 1925–1930 by Virginia Woolf, copyright © 1980 by Quentin Bell and Angelica Garnett, reprinted by permission of Harcourt, Inc.

Excerpts from THE LETTERS OF VIRGINIA WOOLF, Volume III: 1923–1927, copyright © 1977 by Quentin Bell and Angelica Garnett, reprinted by permission of Harcourt, Inc.

Excerpts from WHAT IS REMEMBERED by Alice B. Toklas, © 1963 by Alice B. Toklas, © 1991 by Edward Burns. Reprinted by permission of Henry Holt and company, LLC.

Excerpts from THE AUTOBIOGRAPHY OF ALICE B. TOKLAS by Gertrude Stein Copyright © 1933 and renewed 1961 by Alice B. Toklas. Reprinted by permission of Random House, Inc.

Excerpts from EVERYBODY'S AUTOBIOGRAPHY by Gertrude Stein Copyright © 1937 and renewed 1964 by Alice B. Toklas. Reprinted by permission of Random House, Inc.

Excerpts from THE MEMOIRS OF JOHN ADDINGTON SYMONDS by John Addington Symonds Copyright © 1984 by the London Library. Reprinted by permission of Random House, Inc.

Excerpts from ALONG THIS WAY by James Weldon Johnson, copyright 1933 by James Weldon Johnson, renewed © 1961 by Grace Nail Johnson. Used by permission of Viking Penguin, a division of Penguin Putnam Inc.

Excerpts from WE by Charles A. Lindbergh, copyright 1927, renewed © 1955 by Charles A. Lindbergh. Used by permission of G. P. Putnam's Sons, a division of Penguin Putnam Inc.

Excerpts from WEST WITH THE NIGHT by Beryl Markham. Copyright © 1942, 1983 by Beryl Markham. Reprinted by permission of North Point Press, a division of Farrar, Straus and Giroux, LLC.

Excerpts from "Passing," "Cafe: 3 A.M.," and "Jim Crow Car" from COLLECTED POEMS by Langston Hughes. Copyright © 1994 by the Estate of Langston Hughes. Reprinted by permission of Alfred A. Knopf, a Division of Random House Inc.

Excerpts from THE AUTOBIOGRAPHY OF AN EX-COLOURED MAN by James Weldon Johnson. Copyright © 1927 by Alfred A. Knopf Inc. and renewed by Carl Van Vechten. Reprinted by permission of Alfred A. Knopf, a Division of Random House Inc.

Chapter 1 first appeared as "On Amelia Earhart: The Aviatrix as American Dandy: in the *Michigan Quarterly Review* 39: 1 (Winter 2000) and appears with permission.

". . . there are important senses in which 'queer' can signify only when attached to the first person. One possible corollary: that what it takes—all it takes—to make the description 'queer' a true one is the impulsion to use it in the first person."

—Eve Kosofsky Sedgwick,
"Queer and Now," Tendencies *(1993)*

"There's no such thing as autobiography there's only art and lies."

—Jeanette Winterson,
Art and Lies *(1994)*

"Its image is queer because I queer its relation to other images and bodies."

—Elspeth Probyn, "Queer Belongings:
The Politics of Departure" *(1995)*

Contents

Acknowledgements

I would like to thank the graduate students who have made invaluable contributions as research assistants, in particular Ondine Le Blanc, who combed the archives and inadvertently uncovered my interest in aviation history, and Troy Gordon, my ongoing conversation partner in things modernist and queer, with whom I traveled to Kenya. I likewise remain indebted to Michelle Risdon, Austin Booth, and Virginia Purvis-Smith.

I also extend my thanks to fellow teachers: Michael Awkward, Ross Chambers, Marlon Ross, and Abby Stewart. As friends, colleagues, and fellow travelers, they have made these years in the profession an adventure worth getting ready for. I remain especially grateful for their encouraging responses to the completed manuscript. Martha Umphrey continues to share her enormous gifts as reader of both writer and text in ways that greatly enhance their legibility. In addition, I remain indebted to Adela Pinch, who asked to peruse an early version of the Amelia Earhart chapter, and Larry Goldstein, who sought it out for publication purposes.

B- has helped me wrestle with the material aspects of the manuscript, and, in daily practice, reminds me to remain interested in things outside the academy.

The pleasures of reading and writing are in my case largely solitary ones, which makes them more and more old-fashioned. I thus express my gratitude to an institutional setting that remains confident, in spite of pressures to become increasingly accountable, that with the giving of time and money there will eventually be a product, in this case, hopefully, one worth waiting for.

Prologue

Queer

In a short story by Virginia Woolf entitled "A Society" (1921), a group of young women form "a society for asking questions" in order to judge, rather than just praise, the accomplishments of men. Having learned to read, and thus no longer restricted to producing the men who will produce the books, these women refuse to continue doing their jobs populating the world until they are convinced that men are doing their jobs civilizing it. Three of the women infiltrate the male bastions to conduct their ethnographic research by donning disguises: Rose dresses as an Aetheopian Prince to board a man-of-war; Castalia disguises herself as a charwoman to spend a week at Oxbridge; Elizabeth passes as a male reviewer in order to enter the London literary scene. The answer to the question: "whether we are justified in continuing the human race" remains inconclusive, not just because of men's refusal to answer questions posed by women, but because one question can only lead to another. Five years of attempting to find answers result in a series of digressions that in 1914 was finally brought to a stand-still by the question, "Why do men go to war?"[1]

Between the ready man-of-war and the outbreak of the Great War, there is Oxbridge, where women enter rooms in order to clean them, and the London literary scene, where critics, even women, must dress as men. This leaves the London Library, where Poll has been condemned to read everything, much of which, she discovers, is not worth reading. The Society is founded "when Poll, who had said nothing, burst into tears":

> Poll, I must tell you, has always been queer. For one thing her father was a strange man. He left her a fortune in his will, but on condition that she read all the books in the London Library. We comforted her as best we could; but we knew in our hearts how vain it was. For though we like her, Poll is no beauty; leaves her shoe laces untied; and must have been thinking, while we praised men, that not one of them would wish to marry her.[2]

In an effort to make Poll independent by turning her into a walking library, the will of her father makes Poll forever dependent on him by making her task interminable. She is both the heir of her father's "queerness," manifested by his strange will, and "made queer" by the strangeness of his last testament. Reading too much makes women odd, while only those who are single would consent to so much reading. The state of Poll's shoelaces signals both that she can afford to be untidy because she is economically independent, and that leading a life of the mind can make one absent-minded, that is, unfit for marriage.

The woman who reads too much is not the only sign of "queerness" in this text. Castalia as charwoman at Oxbridge comes across a "queer looking book": an edition of Sappho by Professor Hobkin that is less about her work than about a quarrel between two male scholars concerning her chastity. Rather than entering a discussion about what chastity is or whether it matters, Castalia loses hers to a good-looking student, thereby offering the only conclusive answer to the Society's question of whether the race should be continued. She produces the daughter who will either not be taught to read, or, as founder of the Society of the future, taught to believe, not in man's, but in her own intellect.

"Queerness" means strange, a place like Oxbridge that to a stranger—"it's all so queer"—can provide no answers, but only further questions about whether university professors manage to produce either good people or good books. Queer also means being too much like a man to be desired by one. Queer, for Woolf in 1921, doesn't yet mean gay. It isn't Sappho's sexual object choice that is under discussion, but her chastity. It isn't her chastity that is at issue, as Eve Sedgwick has taught us, but rather the bond between the two male professors.[3] In the erotic triangle, the rivalry "between men" and for the woman is not about the woman, least of all because, as in the case of Sappho, she might be sexually indifferent to men. When Rose, who has disguised herself as an Aetheopian Prince is discovered to be a woman, she engages in mutual caning with the captain of the ship. This is not done to preserve the honor of the British navy, but as a means of preserving male homosociality against the threat of homosexuality. On the one hand, caning suggests a displaced form of sodomy; on the other hand, it punishes both women who cross-dress as men and men who show signs of effeminacy. Women have access to the bonds "between men" either by reading what men have written about women's chastity, by losing theirs outside of marriage, or by passing as men in order to learn what men do when women aren't there. Whichever one it is, heteronormativity—compulsory heterosexuality as normative—has been queered.

The Manx Cat

In Elizabeth Gaskell's *Mary Barton* (1848), in a chapter entitled "A Traveller's Tale," a young sailor offers to return with a Manx cat from his island of origin as a specimen for an amateur natural historian:

> "They look as queer and out o'nature as flying fish, or—," he gulped the words down that should have followed. "Especially when you see'em walking a roof-top, right again the sky, when a cat, as is a proper cat, is sure to stick her tail stiff out behind, like a slack rope dancer a-balancing; but these cats having no tail, cannot stick it out, which captivates some people uncommmonly."[4]

The cat is queer inasmuch as the older man has never heard of, much less seen such a creature, a creature of nature, yet somehow unnatural, like a fish with wings. The lack of a tail makes the cat akin to a circus performer, but unlike the acrobat who defies nature, the Manx cat seems to defy natural law. The sight becomes arresting because of what one can't see—the cat's tail less visible than the acrobat's rope—so that nature becomes more spectacular than an air-borne spectacle. A traveler's tale, like the circus, is meant to captivate its audience, forcing one to imagine what can't be seen, marveling at what seems impossible.

In Virginia Woolf's *A Room of One's Own* (1929), the first person narrator, while having lunch at a women's college, thinks about gender relations before and after the Great War, bursts out laughing, and explains her laughter not by revealing her thoughts, but by pointing at a Manx cat,

> who did look a little absurd, poor beast, without a tail, in the middle of the lawn. Was he really born so, or had he lost his tail in an accident? The tailless cat, though some are said to exist in the Isle of Man, is rarer than one thinks. It is a queer animal, quaint rather than beautiful. It is strange what a difference a tail makes—you know the sort of things one says as a lunch party breaks up and people are finding their coats and hats.[5]

Again the cat is queer because it lacks a tail. But in this case, Woolf wonders whether somewhere tailless cats are not considered queer. What, she asks, is the difference a tail makes? Certainly not the difference between natural and unnatural, or even supernatural, reminiscent of the Victorians, but rather the difference gender makes. For Freud, it is the difference between something to see and nothing to see; for Woolf, it is the difference between pudding and wine at Oxbridge and stewed prunes and water at Newnham and Girton. The natural symmetry of (heterosexual) romance has been permanently disrupted by women driving ambulances and men returning shell-shocked from the trenches. In either case, the queerness of the Manx cat does something to render the speaker inaudible—the sailor "gulping down" his words or the narrator trailing off as she finds her coat and hat.

Women and Airplanes

The point is not that Woolf is queer, but that she queers things in a way that is no longer familiar to us. What she looks at appears strange and is made strange, so much so that the relationship between women and airplanes becomes a queer one. Inasmuch as women get the vote and airplanes fly across the Atlantic at the same time, they enter history together. Together they will disappear: being mere novelties, they will become either obsolete or naturalized. Woolf suggests, again in *A Room of One's Own,* that women enter history not because they invented airplanes, but because, like airplanes, their entrance is remarkable. At the same time, what that entrance means will go unmarked:

> One could not go to the map and say Columbus discovered America and Columbus was a woman; or take an apple and remark, Newton discovered the laws of gravitation and Newton was a woman; or look into the sky and say aeroplanes are flying overhead and aeroplanes were invented by women. There is no mark on the wall to measure the precise height of women.[6]

Like America, like gravity, women have always existed, even if only recently discovered. Like airplanes, women seem newly invented, inasmuch as middle-class women are entering the professions for the first time. Because they are the first, they are modern; even though they are professionals, they are marked by their gender; once they have infiltrated the professions, what will mark them as women? No longer protected as women and not yet the same as men, they will gradually disappear:

> Remove that protection, expose them to the same exertions and activities, make them soldiers and sailors and engine-drivers and dock labourers, and will not women die off so much younger, so much quicker, than men that one will say, 'I saw a woman today,' as one used to say, 'I saw an aeroplane.' Anything may happen when womanhood has ceased to be a protected occupation, I thought, opening the door.[7]

By entering the world of men, women make their appearance not only in a world whose discoveries they didn't make, but in a world where they will be discovered in order to be made redundant. Once women are not the first, to fly the Atlantic or to be aerial elephant scouters in Kenya, that is, they no longer function as signs of modernity, the difference that gender makes will prevent them from flying as fast or being hired at the same rate as male pilots. Entering history means entering dressed as a man, only to be reminded that the red scarf of the aviatrix is not a tie, even as the red tie signals the erotic relations between men, which is what makes it queer.

Flight reconnects Europe and North America by displacing the military conflict of the Great War onto the heroism of the aviator, which is partly diplomatic, partly technological, partly aesthetic. It connects the colonies of the British Empire to one another and to the metropole by displacing the extraction of natural resources and surplus labor onto flight as a form of mobility for aristocrats. The air becomes a place where Jim Crow laws can be abandoned and women are no longer tied to the typewriter. Many flights fail. Some never take off.

On the one hand, the airplane signifies the possibility of a radical elsewhere; on the other hand, that elsewhere is saturated with prior formations. New Negroes move North and sexual inverts head for the nearest big city, without the intervention of flight, following in the footsteps of nineteenth-century migrants. The train becomes a form of transport that both takes one elsewhere and is an elsewhere, where racial segregation is policed, and thus repeatedly disputed. Expatriates take steamers to Europe or East Africa, a symptom of their desire to be elsewhere, as well as the site of the symptom itself—losing one's voice on deck as one embarks on a speaking tour. To be in two places is to be out of place because that other place is still there, making things queer.

Queering

In Nella Larsen's *Passing* (1929), a text from the Harlem Renaissance, Irene Redfield and Felise Freeland are walking down 57th Street when they encounter the husband of Clare Kendry. Clare Kendry's husband is prepared to greet Irene, but she responds coldly:

> Felise drawled: "Aha! Been 'passing,' have you? Well, I've queered that."
>
> "Yes, I'm afraid you have."
>
> "Why, Irene Redfield! You sound as if you cared terribly. I'm sorry."
>
> "I do, but not for the reason you think. I don't believe I've ever gone native in my life except for the sake of convenience, restaurants, theatre tickets, and things like that. Never socially I mean, except once. You've just passed the only person that I've ever met disguised as a white woman."[8]

Irene Redfield is able to pass as white, but chooses to do so only situationally, having done so in the home of Clare Kendry. Clare is married to a white man who, by passing Irene Redfield arm in arm with her friend Felise, has come to understand that Irene is not white, and therefore neither is his wife. Irene describes passing as both "going native" and putting on a "disguise," assuming the role of ethnographer in relationship to white culture by appearing as white in order to facilitate one's role as participant-observer. To queer an instance of racial passing is not the same as to out a queer identity. To look white is not the same as to be not Negro. And to be Negro means walking arm in arm with another Negro, which queers racial passing without necessarily suggesting sexual queerness.

Irene's disapproval of Clare's racial passing becomes a way of disavowing her sexual attraction for Clare. On the one hand, Irene wants to protect Clare's secret even as she wants to protect her from a white-supremacist husband. On the other hand, married to a Negro who longs to transcend racial difference by moving to Brazil, she is attracted not only to a woman, but to a woman who passes as white. Same-sex desire relies on Irene's and Clare's shared ability to pass, while their difference lies with Irene's lack of regret at having been queered. Queering racial identity means setting the record straight, renaming the body that looks white as black and recrossing the color line, even as in modern, urban spaces it can be crossed again and again. Queering sexual identity means failing to disavow one's same-sex desire or outing someone suspected of passing as straight. The glass closet, in contrast to the color line, is about not knowing who knows one is queer and feigning ignorance even when one possesses knowledge. The queerness, then, of the verb to queer, is that it can go either way.

In the modernist period queerness still means "strange, odd, peculiar, eccentric; suspicious, dubious; not in a normal condition, out of sorts; bad, worthless" (Oxford English Dictionary). Queerness is less about object choice than about the recognition on the part of others that one is not like others, a subject out of order, not in sequence, not working. To be not like others can mean both being only one thing, like a bachelor, that is, suspiciously single, or being more than one thing, as in passing for someone of another race. Queerness is something one can inherit, and thus becomes difficult to disavow; queering is something one does, inadvertently, by re-establishing a norm. The multiple ways in which one can be odd or at odds simultaneously recognize and serve as a cover for those who are sexually queer.

Queerness does not rely on the desire for a gendered opposite, as in sexual inversion, where a "man trapped in a woman's body" desires another man as though he were a woman, imagined by the turn-of-the-century sexologists. Nor does it rely on same-sex object choice, as in post-Stonewall lesbian and gay identity politics. Rather, queer as the "resistance to regimes of the normal"[9] means not changing identities to justify desire, but desiring in ways that make strange the relations between identities. As Elspeth Probyn suggests: "through desire I queer images by rendering their relations strange; queer images that become avid for other relations."[10] These other relations are as much about identification as about desire, identification as the product of a psychoanalytic split subject, marked by what Diana Fuss calls "the detour through the other that defines the self."[11] Identifications cross boundaries in unexpected directions, even as they always take the form of "a displacement *upward;* the ego elevates itself through identification, imagines itself always in relation to a higher ideal."[12] Thus identifications do not move predictably from marked to unmarked category, from inferior to superior social status. The man who identifies with the feminine takes a detour through the elevated ideal of male same-sex love in Greek antiquity; the white, female colonizer diverts her identification with black masculinity through the aristocratic lineage of the thoroughbred. The verb to queer can go either way. But the detour it takes on the way to cross-identification will always point in the direction of an imaginary ideal.

The Memoir

The memoir as literary genre is the result of a queering of linguistic gender: in French the masculine *mémoir* regenders the feminine *mémoire,* or memory. The Oxford English Dictionary suggests that the change in gender is "commonly accounted for by the supposition that the word is elliptical for *écrit pour mémoire,*" a writing for, rather than from memory. The memoir as genre refers to both autobiographical and biographical record, as well as to a record of events, understood not as "a complete history, but treating of such matters as come within the personal knowledge of the writer." This distinguishes it from autobiography as "the writing of one's own history" or "the story of one's life written by himself" (OED). The individual life becomes a pretext for disseminating a version of public history from the point of view of an accumulated "personal knowledge." This knowledge produces an autobiographical narrative that begins not with childhood memories like those reactivated by Marcel Proust's *Madeleine* in *Remembrance of Things Past* (1913–27), but begins in the present at the moment when an identity comes into existence for the first time, that is, both as new and as news. The narrative is not about a withdrawal from the sphere of common culture into a sequestered world in which the public no longer plays a significant role, as "high modernism" has so often been constructed. Rather, it is about negotiating the public in the first person because no one has ever seen anything like it. Coming into existence through writing means doing so from the position of an identity that has had no previous existence and doing it in a way that has never been done before in writing.

For Gertrude Stein the moment of the modern begins with the beginning of the twentieth century, in 1901:

> As the peasants always say every year comes to an end, and they like it when the bad weather does not keep them from working, they like to work, it is a pastime for them work is, and so although the last half of the nineteenth century did not interest them they did work. And now the twentieth century had come and it might be more interesting, if it was to be really interesting of course they would not work quite so much, being interested does sometimes stop one from working, work might then be even somewhat disturbing and distracting. So the twentieth century had come it began with 1901.[13]

For Virginia Woolf it begins "on or about December, 1910," with the opening of the "Manet and the Post-Impressionists" exhibit at the Grafton Galleries in London:

> Read the *Agamemnon,* and see whether, in process of time, your sympathies are not almost entirely with Clytemnestra. Or consider the married life of the Carlyles and bewail the waste, the futility, for him and for her, of the horrible domestic tradition which made it seemly for a woman of genius to spend her time chasing beetles, scouring saucepans, instead of writing books. All human relations have shifted—those between masters and servants, husbands and wives, parents and children. And when human beings change there is at the same time a change in religion, conduct, politics, and literature. Let us agree to place one of these changes about the year 1910.[14]

In each case, historical change takes the form of an imaginary moment, chosen for the purpose of telling the story differently. For Stein, the focus is on labor, the fact that work can be both a distraction and distracting, that elite women, like Stein, can now engage in interesting work, like writing. Stein justifies her own work by, on the one hand, seeing it as analogous to the timeless labor of the peasant and, on the other hand, imagining peasants working less, rather than more, or not at all. Woolf situates the question of labor within Victorian marriage, where the woman of genius cannot yet do interesting work. The possibility of writing as work, and of becoming a woman writer, transforms not only individual life histories, but the course of events known as history. In Woolf's case, the division of labor involves the power relations between men and women within the domestic sphere. The co-mingling of autobiography, biography, and history queers the memoir by making personal histories stand in for a knowledge of history now exposed as partial.

These partial histories—of women in aviation, of the avant-garde on the Left Bank, of New Negroes in New York—provide a way of positioning the self not only in history, but in relation to a public in order to generate publicity. Contaminated by modern genres—the newspaper report, the "instant book," the case study—these memoirs at the same time rely on the recirculation of prior texts—Daniel Defoe's *Robinson Crusoe* (1718), Walter Pater's *Marius the Epicurean* (1885), and nineteenth century slave narratives. Whether posing in order to facilitate the distribution of an icon, like Amelia Earhart who looks like Charles Lindbergh, or creating a portrait that redisseminates recognizable names from literary history, like Orlando's, or publicizing a private performance by revealing its sexual secrets in the form of a sexological case history, like the androgyne's, these texts seek cultural accreditation through publication, even as their reception histories are traversed by detour.

The publicity of the private, characteristic of what Roland Barthes calls the "public photograph," is marked by a resistance to conventional divisions between private and public. In the age of photography, the reconstitution of this division takes the form of not just making the private public, but of consuming public images privately: "I want to utter interiority without yielding intimacy."[15] Reminiscent of the simultaneous disavowal and display of the glass closet, it marks the queerness of these autobiographical texts in terms of authorship as the sign of a contested signature. The proper name of the author refers less to a writerly subject than to the authorizing of a subjectivity that has not yet entered into writing. Thus the identity of the author is not necessarily an authentic one, contaminated by the ambiguities of anonymity, the use of pseudonyms, even charges of plagiarism. James Weldon Johnson's anonymous novelistic fiction passes as the authentic autobiography of the "ex-coloured man," enabling someone else to claim authorship. Alice B. Toklas's auto/biography is written by Gertrude Stein, who seeks to reclaim the exclusive affections of her lover by appropriating her voice in order to ensure publication. After Beryl Markham's death, the friend of a former spouse claims that *West With the Night* was written not by her, but by her husband. In each case there are suspicions about, if not disavowals of, the referential accuracy of the signature.

Writing for rather than from memory, these stories appropriate the memoir for purposes of ethnographic record. A personal knowledge of history makes possible the case history of a subculture that takes the form of a translation between cultures in order to recruit those residing elsewhere—literally recruiting women into aviation, enlisting empathy for the plight of androgynes, promoting for the sake of racial uplift the accomplishments of the Talented Tenth. Identities are located geographically—Harlem, Bloomsbury, East Africa—making competing claims for the cultural center of modernism. These auto-ethnographies are written by indigenous ethnographers who either fail to pass as indigenous because, as post-Reconstruction mulatto, their origins lie in the North not the South, or are both native and non-native, inasmuch as the androgyne is at the same time uptown middle-class queer and Bowery fairy. Auto-ethnographers serve as their own informants, vacillating between a resistance to being queered and providing an *apologia* for queer identity. Their texts are as much about the naming of an identity for the first time as they are about the failure of that identity to be simply new, filled with residue, by what came before, or by what resides elsewhere.

I queer my own text by including the transatlantic flight, the nowhere as a sign of modernity that retraces the path of empire even as the means of getting there has been modernized. The solo flier sees nothing, has no witnesses, and, if unsuccessful, will never be seen again. Unlike the fieldwork account that begins, like travel writing, with the story of arrival, the aviator's accomplishment can only be measured by an arrival that marks the end, not the beginning of a journey. The point of arrival is not to stay, but to cash in on the accomplishment in order to commence the next flight. The aviator queers modernism by producing writing that relies neither on literary authorship nor on authenticating documents, but rather on an act of self-authorization.

Modernist Memoirs

"Queering the Moderns: Poses/Portraits/Performances" rethinks British and American modernism by reading at the intersection of several literary and cultural historical narratives that make competing claims for how the geography of identity might be remapped in the early twentieth century: the transatlantic flight; British colonialism in East Africa; Bloomsbury; women on the Left Bank; the Harlem Renaissance; gay New York. By focusing on the memoir, I seek to bypass a developmental model of subjectivity that posits identities as fixed and/or discovered by considering processes of queering not in terms of outing a secret or recuperating a stigmatized identity, but as "resistance to regimes of the normal."

Heteronormativity at this historical moment means, for women, identifying with the masculine as opposed to occupying the role of the feminine in marriage, and for men, interracial homoeroticism and sex between queers and "normal men" as a way of postponing rather than precluding marriage. The processes of identification made possible by the queerness of modernity force one to distinguish between the aviatrix, who flies in order to be able to fly, an enterprise managed by her husband, and the female flyer, an unmarried woman who flies in order to earn a living; to recognize the coexistence of the married lesbian, a woman whose marriage enables her to have a female lover, and the lesbian marriage, heteronormativity as performed by two women; to introduce the New Negro, the male mulatto who marries a white woman, and the fairy, an effeminate man who believes he is a woman. Identities such as these offer contradictions that post-modernists are often too ready to subsume under the "hetero-homosexual binarism," as George Chauncey suggests, "that was consolidated as the hegemonic sexual regime in American culture . . . around 1940."[16]

The first two chapters focus on the female aviator, for whom autobiography is a form of publicity that markets the female flyer as icon posing as aviatrix in order to make money. Amelia Earhart and Beryl Markham were the first women to fly the Atlantic solo: Earhart from West to East in 1932 and Markham from East to West in 1936. "Amelia Earhart: The Aviatrix as American Dandy" discusses her three autobiographical texts, *20 Hrs. 40 Min.* (1928), *The Fun of It* (1932), and *The Last Flight* (1937) in terms of regendering both the aviator—the heroic male solo flyer—and aviation—from military enterprise to commercial industry. In "Beryl Markham: The Female Flyer as *Femme Fatale*" I consider *West With the Night* (1942) in terms of the feminization of Africa by the white female colonialist who identifies with black African boys and wild animals in a landscape she recolonizes for the aristocratic tourist with her airplane.

The second two chapters consider the female writer as auto/biographer, writing either the fictional biography or the auto/biography of her female lover. The pending dissolution of the lesbian couple prompts the production of a literary portrait in order to re-establish the female intimacy that makes possible the woman writer's status as best-selling author. "*Orlando* as 'Imaginary Portrait'" traces a genealogy of the literary portrait from Walter Pater to Oscar Wilde to Lytton Strachey in order to consider how Woolf inserts herself into a gay male literary tradition that enables her in *Orlando* (1928) to construct the portrait of Vita Sackville-West as "new biographer." In "*The Autobiography of Alice B. Toklas* as 'Portrait Narration,'" the focus is on Gertrude Stein's return to narration in both *The Autobiography* (1933) and *Everybody's Autobiography* (1937), as she begins the production of an ongoing autobiographical narrative in order to explain to herself, as well as audiences to whom she lectures in America, what she has been attempting to do in her experimental writing.

The final two chapters examine autobiography as auto-ethnography, in other words, ethnographic case-studies of queer masculinity written for members of the dominant group. Each text is prefaced by authenticating documents—authored by a white patron and a medico-legal professional—authorizing its publication by means of a homosocial relationship that seeks to normalize the performance of a marked, as opposed to unmarked, form of masculinity. "The New Negro as 'Ex-Coloured Man': A Fictional Autobiography" considers James Weldon Johnson's *Autobiography of an Ex-Coloured Man* (1912; 1927) as the representation of a nameless male mulatto whose queer relationship to a white father mediates a homoerotic subtext where white masculinity becomes the object of both desire and identification. "The Androgyne as 'Fairie': A Self-Authored Case History" focuses on two published texts of an imagined trilogy, Earl Lind's *Autobiography of an Androgyne* (1918) and Ralph Werther—Jenny June's *The Female Impersonators* (1922) that describe the life of an androgyne, a man who considers himself to be a woman and who passes as a man by identifying first with the Greek hermaphrodite and then with the turn-of-the-century dandy.

These modernist memoirs represent not just competing cultural contexts, but also reveal queer connections: Earhart and Markham never meet, although they are asked to comment on each other's accomplishments; Woolf and Stein meet, activating Woolf's anti-Semitism, even as the Woolfs' Hogarth Press publishes Stein's "Composition as Explanation"; James Weldon Johnson praises Stein's story "Melanctha" to Carl Van Vechten, who authenticates his autobiographical fiction; and the landing of an airplane becomes the site of a possible homosexual encounter, when Lytton Strachey imagines his attraction for the pilot or when the bleachers set up for Lindbergh's arrival in New York become a site for sexual cruising.

The Aviator

Amelia Earhart standing in front of her plane. With permission from Bettmann/CORBIS.

Amelia Earhart:
The Aviatrix as American Dandy

i. "These pioneers themselves established the aviator's image, partly by their idiosyncratic behavior and partly by their own accounts of it. Since many of their activities were by their nature individual and unwitnessed it was unavoidable that this image, to a very great extent, should be self-created." (David Lance, "Folklore of Aviation," *Journal of the Royal United Services Institute for Defense Studies* 21:1 [1976])

ii. "Lindbergh had the world at his feet, and he blushed like a girl!" (Charles Lindbergh, "*WE*" [1927], 318)

On 13 June 1927, following his successful transatlantic flight from New York to Paris in the *Spirit of Saint Louis,* Charles Lindbergh returned to New York City, to "the greatest welcome any man in history has ever received in terms of numbers."[1] An estimated 3 to 4 and a half million people lined the streets from the Battery to Central Park. 25,000 extra tons of newsprint were required to publicize the affair; the same year 10,000 poems were submitted to a national contest in commemoration of the feat: "Never in history did an event so brief provoke so many poems in so short a time."[2] Throngs of people came to see the person who had flown alone. The pilot himself had seen almost nothing, flying blind over a body of water through fog, sleet, and nocturnal darkness.

When Lindbergh arrived at City Hall, Mayor Walker delivered a speech not about, but addressed to the hero:

> Everybody all over the world, in every language, has been telling you and the world about yourself. You have been told time after time where you were born, where you went to school, and that you have done the supernatural thing of an air flight from New York to Paris. I am satisfied that you have been convinced of it by this time.
>
> And it is not my purpose to reiterate any of the wonderful things that have been so beautifully spoken and written about you and your triumphal

> ride across the ocean. But while it has become almost axiomatic, it sometimes seems prosaic to refer to you as a great diplomat, because after your superhuman adventure, by your modesty, by your grace, by your gentlemanly American conduct, you have left no doubt of that. But the one thing that occurs to me that has been overlooked in all the observations that have been made of you is that you are a great grammarian, and that you have given added significance and a deeper definition to the word "we."
>
> We have heard, and we are familiar with, the editorial "we," but not until you arrived in Paris did we learn of the aeronautical "we." Now you have given to the world a flying pronoun.[3]

The "flying pronoun" Lindbergh bestows on the world will serve as the title of a memoir he writes under the auspices of the publisher George Palmer Putnam, who understands that the book must reach its public before the story of the flight fades as front page news. Lindbergh agrees to convey his tale to a journalist who would then retell it in the third person. When the final story is written in the first person under Lindbergh's name, Lindbergh rejects the ghost-written manuscript, but agrees to write another book. *"WE,"* completed within three weeks, sells over half a million copies, breaking another record, that of a first-time author.

Lindbergh is unable to complete the story. While providing a narrative that will become the aviator's standard life history: flying student, barnstormer/wing-walker, flying cadet, airmail pilot, record long-distance flier, etc., he refuses to provide a description of what happened after the flight, claiming lack of skill as an amateur author. As late as 1953 he will receive the Pulitzer prize for his second autobiography, a rewriting of the first, *The Spirit of Saint Louis.* "I am not an author by profession, and my pen could never express the gratitude which I feel towards the American people," he writes. "The voyage up the Potomac and to the Monument Grounds in Washington; up the Hudson River and along Broadway; over the Mississippi and to St. Louis—to do justice to these occasions would require a far greater writer than myself."[4] The hero's return journey, this time marked by identifiable landmarks and scores of first-hand witnesses, is no longer tellable by the solo pilot whose heroism requires, above all, modesty. Fitzhugh Green, a staff writer of Putnam's, is commissioned to complete the memoir. Entitled "A Little of What the World Thought of Lindbergh," it largely consists of quotations from politicians' speeches.

Two intermediary texts facilitate the transition from one author to another. George Putnam writes a "Publisher's Note" that agrees that "Somehow it wasn't a story for him to tell"[5] and thus allows the second part of the record to be written in the third person by someone of Lindbergh's choosing. An "Author's Note," followed by Lindbergh's actual signature, appoints

Green, nowhere mentioned on the title page, as additional author, as someone who "has caught the spirit of what I have tried to do for aviation."[6]

The hyperbolic rhetoric of the politicians' discourses underscores the modesty of the long-distance flier whose symbolic function is to provide the focus of a mass spectacle, while at the same time relinquishing any credit that rightfully belongs to the "American science and genius" that designed and constructed the plane. Green's role is to interpret the event in world-historical terms by naming it historically unprecedented and thereby inaugurating a new age. This age will be characterized by "airmindedness," a moment between the two world wars when flying evolves from an aristocratic sport into a commercial industry. This requires repressing both its military origins (the flying ace whose heroism was marked by the number of enemy planes he shot down) and its origins in popular amusement (the flying circuses that developed when discarded military planes were reclaimed by those seeking to earn a living flying). By physically transcending the site of social arrangements through flight, the aviator will assist others in ideologically transcending the symptoms of social disorder: the unprecedented human destruction wrought by aerial bombings of urban populations during World War I, the unchecked industrialization of monopoly capitalism as evidenced by the railroad companies, and the disregard for a Constitutional Amendment mandating Prohibition.

While Lindbergh insisted that the title *"WE"* referred to himself and his backers (the eight men from Saint Louis who financed the flight that enabled him to collect the $25,000 prize money), reviewers preferred the meaning given by the ghost-writer who had originally coined the title. The first person plural was the pronoun Lindbergh used to refer to himself and his plane. The "aeronautical 'we'" can additionally be read in terms of a joint authorship necessitated by this particular form of the modernist memoir. On the one hand, the memoir relies on syndicated accounts of the flight that have been paid for before take-off by a newspaper editor to increase circulation; on the other hand, the first person pronoun lends an air of authenticity to the accomplishment of an individual being publicized for mass consumption. The solo flier was the only one there and thus remains the only one able to tell the tale. At the same time, the hero who tells his own story must stay clear of the self-promotion made possible by publicity available through the mass media. Promotion and publicity, necessary to the financing of flights and thus to fueling the profits of an emergent industry, must always be left to someone other than the pilot, thereby creating an "authorial we" that replaces the plane of the aeronautical "we" with the function of the publisher/manager.

The phenomenon of Lindbergh is not just about the relation of pilot to public in the arena of the mass spectacle. It is also, as suggested by another passage in the Mayor's speech, about the reinvention of a notion of nationhood as it was being reconfigured in the 1920s and 1930s through the figure of the flier:

> That "we" that you used was perhaps the only word that would have suited the occasion and the great accomplishment that was yours. That all-inclusive word "we" was quite right, because you were not all alone in the solitude of the sky and the sea, because every American heart, from the Atlantic to the Pacific, was beating for you. Every American, every soul throughout the world, was riding with you in spirit, urging you on and cheering you on to the great accomplishment that is yours. That "we" was a vindication of the courage, of the intelligence, of the confidence and the hopes of Nungesser and Coli, now only alive in the prayers and the hearts of the people of the entire world. That "we" that you coined was well used, because it gave an added significance and additional emphasis to the greatest of any and all ranks, the word of faith, and turned the hearts of all the people of the civilized world to your glorious mother, whose spirit was your spirit, whose confidence was your confidence, and whose pride was your pride; the "we" that includes all that has made the entire world stand and gasp at your great feat, and that "we" also sent out to the world another message and brought happiness to the people of America, and admiration and additional popularity for America and Americans by all the peoples of the European countries.[7]

The mayor of New York, "the world city," receives Lindbergh, the "world's greatest hero," as one son of an immigrant welcoming another. The status of son becomes equated with that of citizen, distinguishing the American from the foreign-born, those in teaming tenements surrounding Settlement houses in the industrial neighborhoods of large cities. President Coolidge, in his welcoming speech, will go so far as to portray Lindbergh as "inspired by the imagination and the spirit of his Viking ancestors,"[8] thereby seeking to remake the country by reinvoking the Northern European immigrant, or Nordic, who will come to represent an unmarked ethnicity and a new masculinity—blond, slim, silent, and, above all, young. By stating further that, "In less than a day and a half he had crossed the ocean over which Columbus had traveled for 69 days and the Pilgrim Fathers for 66 days on their way to the New World,"[9] Coolidge refigures the relationship between the Old World and the New by reversing the direction of the journey and by focusing on the difference in speed. Technological superiority on the part of the New World, spearheaded by the aircraft/aerospace and film industries, will manifest itself as a form of reverse colonization, making its appearance in the guise of goodwill.

Born in 1902, Lindbergh's age coincides with that of the twentieth century and of heavier-than-air flight, first accomplished by the Wright brothers in 1903. Politicians refer to Lindbergh as the son of his mother, thereby foregrounding a normative heterosexuality predicated on the asexuality suggested by his youth, and as a son of the people, a Minnesota farmboy educated at a large state university whose father served in Congress. He represents the new version of an old style national hero: "He was a plain citizen dressed in the garments of an everyday man."[10] An "ambassador without portfolio," he attends Swedish churches in European capitals and with heads of state visits cemeteries where the dead of World War I lie buried. If the diplomat has replaced the military general, it is because "airmindedness" is being imagined as a substitute for conflict between air forces in the relations between nations. Aviation from its inception will be organized as a national industry, irrefutable evidence of national superiority, while the aviator will serve as prototype for a super-race, beginning with the World War I flying ace and culminating in the *Luftwaffe* of the Nazis, to which Lindbergh will develop sympathetic leanings when he advocates for isolationism on the eve of World War II.

Lindbergh's relationship to the two French fliers, not the foreign-born but the foreign, Charles Nungesser and François Coli, who disappeared during their attempted flight across the Atlantic from East to West while Lindbergh was crossing from West to East, further complicates the meaning of the aeronautical "we." On the one hand, they represent the "we" of collaboration in contrast to the individualism of the solitary flier (even as every one person in the air requires nine on the ground); on the other hand, they embody the linguistic other that allows Lindbergh to become part of a "we" by speaking of them when others speak only of him. They signify the heroic as constituted through the danger of death, the ocean permanently claiming the "we" of pilot and plane, which in the case of aviation often takes the form of disappearance without a material trace. Without a body or a grave, the eulogy becomes even more of an imperative. Lindbergh insists repeatedly that what the two fallen heroes attempted was far greater than his own endeavor (headwinds make the flight from West to East longer and thus more hazardous), thereby undermining the reading of his own success as a form of national victory. While politicians invoke the achievement in terms of friendship between the United States and France, the aviator beckons to other aviators as a way of invoking the tightly knit community of fliers. The "we" of those who have taken to the skies transcends both the individual accomplishments of the solitary pilot and the arbitrariness of national boundaries, especially as seen from the air.

By effacing himself, Lindbergh leaves the meaning of the event, just as he does the meaning of "we," to others, to those who would profit from it, either ideologically, such as politicians, or financially, like newspaper editors and publishers. The aviator, whose historical origins lie with the military hero, will become the celebrity, whose cultural ties will be forged with Hollywood. Putnam eventually leaves the publishing house carrying his family's name to work for Paramount Studios and already in 1927 brings to their attention the book of a World War I pilot that leads to *Wings,* the first film to win the Academy Award for Best Picture. Keeping a plane in the air requires as much capital investment as making a movie, but unlike the movie star, the aviator can still claim that prize money and endorsements are necessary to keep flying and that publicity is good for the industry. As Lindbergh is being acclaimed in terms of idealism and authenticity, untempted by money or fame, nicotine or alcohol, the phenomenon of Lindbergh points to the artificiality of the construct of the celebrity that eventually exceeds the control of the individual.

When Lindbergh arrives at Le Bourget airport upon successful completion of his flight, he removes his flying helmet and places it on the head of a newspaper correspondent in order to escape the crowds that have lifted his body off the ground and dismantled his plane. If Lindbergh released the "greatest torrent of mass emotion ever witnessed in human history,"[11] this was partly due to the nature of the accomplishment, but also to the speed with which the news spread and his physical availability to incite a mass spectacle. What happened spontaneously in the case of Lindbergh will be harnessed with even greater efficiency in the case of Amelia Earhart, by none other than George Putnam, so that the same mayor of New York will be able to say five years later: "Five years ago we believed that the aeronautical 'We' had but one gender; now you've destroyed that. The Atlantic solo has gone co-ed."[12]

iii. "This coming conquest of the air offers an absolutely new element in progression; we enter, as it were, the third dimension. . . . The introduction of a new medium of communication which will throw all mankind together so much more freely carries with it the necesssity for a general rising of standards. When it becomes possible for rude or dangerous persons to flutter to our windows by night and day, we must simply see to it that there are no rude or dangerous persons." (Charlotte Perkins Gilman, "When We Fly: How the Accomplishment of Aerial Navigation will make Necessary a Revision of Human Laws and Customs," *Harper's,* 9 November 1907).

iv. "The woman at the wash-tub, the sewing-machine, the office-desk, and the typewriter can glance up from the window when she hears the rhythmic hum of a motor overhead, and say 'If it's a woman she is helping free

> me, too!' . . . In some strange way aviation is a door through which one may enter a new dimension." (Margery Brown, "Flying is Changing Women," *Pictorial Review,* June, 1930)

Amelia Earhart begins her career as aviatrix in the role of guest of the Honorable Mrs. Frederick Guest of London, formerly Miss Amy Phipps of Pittsburgh, wife of Right Honorable Frederick Guest, member of Parliament, international polo player and former British Air Minister. Mrs. Guest leases a tri-motored Fokker considered unsuitable by Commander Byrd for an expedition to the Antarctic in the hope of being the first of her sex to fly across the Atlantic. She names the plane the *Friendship* as a way of fostering Anglo-American relations, represented by her marriage between the British aristocracy and American industry. For personal reasons (her son phoned from Yale University saying he would leave college if she boarded the plane), she is unable to fly herself and, fearful that the first woman might be Miss Mabel "Mibs" Boll—a wealthy woman of questionable reputation known as the Diamond Queen—she commissions George Putnam, who has already made himself manager of the expedition, to search for a suitable substitute. She stipulates that the person be a woman and an American, and some speculate that she specifically suggests a resemblance to Lucky Lindy. According to one biographer: "She should be a pilot and well educated; preferably a college graduate. She should be physically attractive and have manners that would be acceptable to members of English society, who would undoubtedly welcome her on her arrival there."[13] Guest herself did not meet at least one of these criteria: she did not know how to fly; photographs show her to cut the figure of a "plump society matron." She nevertheless intends that the first of her sex will be a lady rather than a nightclub hostess, not an "ambassador without portfolio," but of "true womanhood." Putnam assigns Hilton H. Railey, *New York Times* correspondent, to place a call to a Settlement worker at Denison House in Boston, a "social worker who flies," named Amelia Earhart. The right kind of girl turns out to be "a tall, slender, boyish-looking young woman,"[14] in the words of Marion Perkins, Head Worker at Denison, where Earhart directed the evening school for foreign-born men and women. The resemblance to Lindbergh is unmistakable and Earhart acquires the nickname she will never be able to shed, Lady Lindy.

Railey claims: "Her resemblance to Colonel Lindbergh was extraordinary. Most of all I was impressed by the poise of her boyish figure. Mrs. Guest had stipulated the person to whom she would yield must be 'representative' of American women. In Amelia Earhart I saw not only their norm but their sublimation."[15] Other journalists are less generous. One even goes so far as to suggest that regardless of whatever natural resemblance there might have been, her image was intentionally exploited to simulate his: "By manipulation of pictures and publicity, Amelia Earhart, the Boston girl who is crossing the Atlantic with Wilmer Stultz, is to be made a feminine Lindbergh, unless plans go awry. The stunt is financed by George Palmer Putnam, publisher of *WE* who now plans a similar book, it is understood, called *She*. . . . Amelia Earhart has been in training, coached by the promoters, to emulate Lindbergh in every respect, in attitude, pictures and behavior."[16]

Unlike Lindbergh, who resists being positioned as lone pioneer by invoking a brotherhood of fliers, Earhart functions as the copy of an image already in circulation. While Lindbergh represents the American citizen as common man who has demonstrated national superiority vis à vis the French, Earhart represents the American Girl in contrast to the Diamond Queen, the society woman who fails to launder her self-procured millions by marrying into the British aristocracy. The regendering of the aviator requires that sporting adventures not be confused with sexual ones. If what they share is a modesty characterized by an unwillingness to engage in self-promotion, Lindbergh will attempt to retain that image by seeking the normalcy of private life and steady employment in the airline industry (temporarily interrupted by the kidnapping and slaying of his first child), while Earhart will displace that image onto the promotion of her sex, supplementing personal adventure with a sense of social obligation. Her eventual marriage to George Putnam will forge an even more powerful "we" than the aeronautical one inasmuch as the "marital we" will allow Putnam to devote himself full-time to her promotion. The solo flight across the Atlantic that Lindbergh accomplished at 25, Earhart will accomplish at 35, her boyishness not tied to her youth, but to her slacks and short hair. Whether accidental or intentional, Earhart managed to keep that image in the public eye for nine years, an extraordinary length of time for a celebrity image based on record-breaking events, yet no time at all given the longevity of her legend.

Where and how she received the famous phone call that launched her career as aviatrix will be retold in each of her memoirs, *20 Hrs. 40 Min.* (1928), *The Fun of It* (1932), and *The Last Flight* (1937), as well as in an article written for *American Magazine* entitled "Flying the Atlantic—and selling sausages have a lot of things in common" (1932). She was called to the phone one afternoon at work, surrounded by Chinese and Syrian neighborhood children. When asked whether "she would do something for aviation that might be hazardous," she first thought it was a joke and then asked for references. Ten days later she had an interview in New York with David T. Layman (New York attorney), John S. Phipps, and George P. Putnam, although in the final version she suggests that Railey, unimpressed with her, almost prevented her from appearing in front of this masculine jury. Faced with a positive verdict, she could of course not say no: "When one is offered such a tremendous adventure it would be too inartistic to refuse."[17]

How she assesses her position is worth quoting in all its variations. Initially she writes:

> It should have been slightly embarrassing, for if I were found wanting on too many counts I should be deprived of a trip. On the other hand, if I were just too fascinating the gallant gentleman might be loath to drown me. Anyone should see the meeting was a crisis.[18]

In "Flying the Atlantic" she writes:

> If they did not like me at all, or if they found me wanting in too many respects, I would be deprived of the trip. But if they liked me too well, they might be loath to drown me. It was therefore necessary for me to maintain an attitude of impenetrable mediocrity. Apparently I did, because I was chosen.[19]

Finally, in the third version, she begins: "The candidate, I gathered, should be a flyer herself, with social graces, education, charm and, perchance, pulchritude." She then adds:

> It should have been slightly embarrassing, for if I were found wanting in too many ways I would be counted out. On the other hand, if I were just too fascinating, the gallant gentleman might be loath to risk drowning me. Anyone could see the meeting was a crisis.[20]

The crisis requiring resolution has less to do with Earhart herself than with the gendering of the interview situation. A group of men appear to be deciding the fate of a particular woman when in fact they are reinforcing woman as marked category: a single individual represents the entire sex; a single casualty would produce its symbolic demise. The double-bind has an apocalyptic ring in that the two options Earhart presents are deprivation or drowning, and loss of opportunity or loss of life, the latter being the price of heroism denied women as a sex. Would she be deprived of a trip or the trip? Are they going to drown her or risk drowning her? Does being "found wanting" mean not being fascinating enough or not being liked? How will this dilemma be solved? Earhart seems to provide two solutions: either one has the qualities they are looking for—"social graces, education, charm, pulchritude"—or one has no qualities and remains "impenetrable." While each retelling is accompanied by greater insight into the stakes at hand, Earhart fails to make explicit the extent to which these represent two sides of the same image: by representing a type, no one will ever wonder who she is. To be the American Girl is to be mediocre in the sense of ordinary: middle-class, a girl not a woman, and above all, white.

Bessie Coleman, the best-known black aviator of the era, likewise befriended (rather than being befriended by) a newspaper editor, Robert Abbott of the *Chicago Defender,* who also promoted her image to increase circulation. Unlike Lindbergh, whose arrival in Paris promoted friendship between two nations, Coleman was forced to travel to France to obtain her pilot's license, since flying schools in the United States maintained a color bar. Unlike Earhart, whose husband doubled as her business partner, Coleman married an older man she never shared an address with and became known as difficult when she broke with a string of (male) managers. An impoverished migrant from the South, there was no place for a manicurist-turned-pilot in Chicago's black Society, just as there were no women in the pilot's union or black women in the first organization for women pilots. While her relationship to the public was almost exclusively mediated by the black press, promoting the first flying school for Negroes required a degree of self-promotion that crossed the fine line between publicity and falsification to become a marker of racial difference. Her need for self-promotion has led her biographer to characterize her seeming lack of modesty as a sign of self-dramatization, created by "her good looks, her sense of theater, and her eloquence."[21] These included performing impressions of other nationalities, handing out press releases about her accomplishments, and actual misinformation (particularly about her age). In a book dedicated to Coleman entitled *Black Wings* (1934), William J. Powell imagines aviation as an emergent industry where blacks could own businesses, like Jews, by hiring their own, and the air would offer a form of transportation that knew no color line, unlike railroad cars and busses segregated by Jim Crow laws. But unlike Earhart, who disappeared during her last flight, Coleman died at 34 by falling out of an exhibition plane piloted by a young, white, male flier. Memorialized by Powell's dedication, a marked grave on the South side of Chicago on which flowers are dropped annually (and a road recently renamed for her on the way to O'Hare Airport), Coleman left no memoir, having learned to speak French without having mastered the rules of English grammar. She was an aviatrix unable to forge a legitimizing "we" for reasons of racialized difference, and, one might suspect, sexual queerness.

v. "The girl in brown, who walks alone."

Unlike Lindbergh who refuses to finish his tale, Earhart retells the same story several times. It is not her tale that lacks completion but her identity that enacts a contradiction. The authorial "we" reverts back to the aeronautical "we," but this time regendered, not as pilot and plane, but as woman pilot and all other women. Earhart's memoirs resist a developmental model of autobiographical discourse by each time returning to the beginning. This reliance on repetition is partly due to their production status as "instant" books and partly the consequence of a topical rather than chronological sequence characteristic of the memoirs written by Progressive era social reformers. "Instant" or "fabricated books" was a genre invented by Putnam who thought of an idea for a book and then went in search of its author. The book needed to appear in bookstores before the author's name disappeared from the headlines in an attempt to diminish the time lag between newspaper and book publishing. Offering what the newspaper account could not, namely an adventure story written in the first person, the prototypes for such a system of authorship were Commander Richard E. Byrd's *Skyward* (1926), about the first flight over the North Pole, and Lindbergh's *WE.* For Earhart, who was expected to do this more than once in her lifetime, more and more material had to be written before or during the flight and/or recycled from previous writings. *20 Hrs. 40 Mins.* was finished 25 August 1928 and in the bookstores by 10 September, having been written at Putnam's home in Rye, New York, where he provided the space and necessary solitude. The last chapter of *The Fun of It* was added after Earhart's solo flight across the Atlantic in 1932 and *Last Flight* appeared posthumously and heavily edited by Putnam, based on the 30,000 words she wrote before her disappearance over the Pacific. Not only were first editions of *The Fun of It* sold with a record attached of a radio speech she delivered over transatlantic radio, but a year later she would write "Part of the Fun Of It" by Amelia Earhart for *Home and Garden* (April, 1933), a two-page advertisement which passed itself off as a first person narrative, endorsing Kodak cameras and film.

The autobiographies written by those engaged in Progressive era reform movements likewise resist the individual life history by including personal anecdotes only inasmuch as they explain the etiology and evolution of the exceptional woman. Topical headings replace historical chronology to allow for the embedding of intertextual documents into a genre that seeks to identify itself, at least partially, with the sociological report.[22] Jane Addams's *Twenty Years at Hull-House* (1910), the best known example, is more the story of Hull-House, the original Settlement House in the United States, than the story of its founder. With her own professional origins tied to the Settlement movement, Earhart expands the genre in order to construct her own role in aviation as a form of Settlement work and in order to provide a kind of advice book whose origins lie in women's magazines. She instructs women on how to become pilots as well as workers in the aviation industry, what shortcomings they need to overcome, what social barriers stand in their way. *The Fun of It* has chapter titles such as "Aviation as it Is," "Women and Aviation," "Some Feminine Flyers," and "The First Women Aeronauts," and includes diagrams of an instrument panel and flying maneuvers.

Contemporary biographers, such as Doris Rich and Susan Ware, have dismissed these texts with statements such as: "In spite of brisk sales and generally flattering reviews, the book [*20 Hrs. 40 Mins.*] was not very interesting. Other than entries from Amelia's diary, it was a dull summary of the problems of commercial aviation and a plea for more support from the government and the public."[23] Or, "In general Earhart's prose was pedestrian and lacking in drama. The books, already printed in very large type and illustrated by many photographs (often the best part), seemed padded with extraneous chapters and recycled material."[24] It is precisely their lack of conformity to the literary memoir that provides their cultural interest, offering a different relationship between writing and flying than that provided by the male homosocial *La Ligne* that produced the poetic prose of Saint-Exupéry in works such as *Night Flight* (1931), or the division of labor between flying and writing, husband and wife, that led to the lyrical musings of Anne Morrow Lindbergh: "Was I a modern woman? I flew a modern airplane and used a modern radio but not as a modern woman's career, only as wife of a modern man."[25] Earhart doesn't consider herself a writer and writes for a predominantly female audience. She writes books, magazine articles, syndicated newspaper columns, and answers to fan mail, the latter being her preferred activity. She is not writing for posterity, but for the future, when the plane will be as common as the automobile, itself a recent invention. She is not writing as representative of an age, but as role model for a new age, when women will be more like men, and men like women. The entrance into a profession not yet regulated requires, on the one hand, a reliance on personal experience that resists personal revelation and, on the other hand, a preoccupation with self-creation that foregrounds the image, and thus clothes. Earhart as a woman seeks to reproduce herself in other women, by disseminating information about aviation in a way that normalizes her identity as aviatrix in order to eventually make it obsolete.

vi. "A social worker on a bat."

Amelia Earhart is the first woman to fly across the Atlantic; three women have died in previous attempts. She is also the first "airwoman," meaning she knows how to fly although she never takes the controls due to poor weather conditions requiring blind or instrument flying, in which Earhart has no training. In 1932 she will become the first person to fly across the Atlantic twice. But in 1928, she flies as a replacement for Mrs. Guest. She flies as a look-alike of Lindbergh. And she flies as a passenger, not a pilot.

The only identity she is able to claim with any authenticity is that of social worker. Not only does she avoid self-promotion by insisting that her entrance into aviation occurred purely by chance, but she also attempts to direct publicity away from herself to where it is rightfully due, with pilot Wilmer ("Bill") Stultz and mechanic Lou ("Slim") Gordon. She begins by claiming that the flight was simply something she did during her vacation from Denison and that her purpose was to bring "a message of good-will and friendship from American to British Settlement Houses."[26] While Stultz and Gordon, "like old war buddies," drift about town and visit Croydon Airdome, Earhart remains the captive guest of Mrs. Frederick Guest, at whose dinners she meets, among others, Lady Astor, the first female member of Parliament and Lady Heath, the first woman to fly from Cape Town to London. Unlike other aviatrixes who either made the flying costume itself into a fashion statement (most notably, Harriet Quimby's purple satin bloomers) or immediately applied make-up upon arrival and packed an evening dress for the reception (Jacqueline Cochran, who developed her own cosmetics line), Earhart chose to take with her only what she had on. Mrs. Guest nevertheless greets her with a traveling case of Parisian gowns so that "donning a frock and other feminine attire for the first time in days," a reporter comments, she "was suddenly and miraculously transformed from a daring celebrated aviatrix to a typical, nice American girl having a celebration abroad with a party of friends from home."[27]

The first person narratives that appear on the front pages of the *New York Times* between 19 and 22 June 1928 begin as part of a public record that attempts to negotiate between a personal response and an international performance, by recreating the aviatrix as social worker. Although Earhart keeps a logbook and knows she is writing news, the nature of the adventure does not lend itself to the pure description characteristic of travel writing: it was uncomfortable, there was nothing to see, and she never took the controls. The value of the adventure lies not in what can be described, but in the fact that it took place at all: "It is all too recent, this flight, for me to compose my exact impressions or even to remember exactly what happened and when. But I know I would not have missed it for anything."[28] At the same time she resists the notion of "instant meaning" by refusing an identity that would follow from complete identification with the event: "I am sure I do not want to be known always merely as the first woman to fly the Atlantic. Aviation is a great thing, but it cannot fill one's life completely."[29] By making her what she calls a "public person," the event threatens to turn her into a static image: "Today I have been receiving offers to go on stage, appear in the movies, and to accept numerous gifts ranging from an automobile to a husband. The usual letters of criticism and threats which I have always read celebrities receive have also arrived. And I am caught in a situation where very little of me is free. I am being moved instead of moving."[30] In contrast to Lindbergh, who leaves the field to the newspaper correspondent and retreats from the public eye, Earhart appropriates public discourse by, on the one hand, making an extraordinary event ordinary (she, after all, did nothing), and on the other hand, by normalizing the female flier (she, after all, wore what she always wears). The first she does by promoting aviation as a form of social work; the second by insisting on the importance of the relationship between aviation and clothes.

On the second day, when she attempts to address "what this flight means," she begins with the observation that the mayor who greets her in Southampton, the first woman sheriff in England, is addressed as "Mister Mayor," pointing to the modern woman as oxymoron. She then considers the flight's meaning for aviation, for women, and for herself, always the order in which she will consider the importance of any aeronautical achievement. The meaning for aviation lies in the fact that future, i.e., regularly scheduled, transoceanic flights are best undertaken by multi-engined rather than single-engined planes, and by sea rather than land planes. For women, its importance lies in the fact that it should increase their interest in aviation and thus augment their influence on men. By convincing them that flying is safe, it should become more comfortable, comparable to the transportation provided by steamers or Pullman cars. And finally, the meaning for Earhart herself is not a personal one. She claims it decreases her isolation as aviatrix, and thus as celebrity, by giving her the opportunity to discuss flying as a sport and the fact that women in England have greater access to light planes through the proliferation of flying clubs. By making flying more ordinary, by making female fliers more normal, her ultimate and most personal goal is to make herself more the norm and thus increase the number of women like her: "I am lonesome for the companionship of women in aviation. . . . When I want to 'talk shop' in aviation at home there are only men to talk to. Bill, Slim and some other flying men I have met are wonderful, but once in a while one likes to talk about a common interest with a woman."[31]

One way in which she continues the conversation with other women is as aviation editor of *Cosmopolitan* magazine (after *McCall's* drops her when she endorses Lucky Strike cigarettes, even though she herself does not smoke and only agrees to the ad to raise funds for Stultz and Gordon when the endorser refuses to make the ad without her). She writes ten articles between November 1928 and November 1929, each one ending with a reminder to its readers that any questions received will be answered by the author. The editor of the magazine is chiefly concerned with keeping his readers informed, equating "airmindedness" with not becoming old-fashioned: "For flying is so much a part of life today that whether or not one wishes actually to fly one owes to oneself an intelligent well-informed interest in the subject."[32] For the aviatrix, having other women to talk to requires either educating them in the fundamentals of aviation or addressing their concerns as women, as defined by the woman's magazine. The first approach requires getting women into the air, thus the title of her first article, "Try flying yourself!" The second relies on maintaining feminine attributes but relegating them to a new social sphere, that of "aerial housekeeping."

Earhart encourages women to enter the air in two ways: by treating flying as a sport easily accessible through clubs (the European model) and by comparing the plane to the automobile, which began as a sport and then became a means of transportation (the American model). She not only offers tips on how to seek instruction, "Here is How Fannie Hurst Could Learn to Fly," but on how not to prevent others from seeking it, "Shall You Let Your Daughter Fly?" and by admonishing mothers, "Don't Say 'Don't!'" At the same time, she encourages women to become passengers, so air travel will increase in volume and comfort, thereby attracting more (female) passengers. Becoming either a pilot or a passenger involves overcoming a fear of flying that stems both from lack of personal experience (feminine knowledge) and lack of access to technical knowledge (male experience): "My point is that aviation is being sold to boys much more effectively than it is to girls."[33] Girls, for instance, are barred from participating in airplane model contests by stipulating that eligible contestants need to be members of manual training and shop classes. Here the attempt is to make girls more like boys. The alternative is to let girls be girls. Domesticating the airline industry means encouraging women to find employment in such a way that their domestic skills enhance the public arena: "I foresee that women will shortly become tea-room managers at airports, perhaps traffic managers, perhaps engineers in various branches, and I hope also as designers of the interiors of cabin planes—to mention only a few possibilities."[34] The aviatrix thus tries to have it both ways: women flying, which is what men do; women in aviation, doing what women have always done.

The double-bind that Earhart first articulates in the passage about how she was chosen for the *Friendship* flight can be recapitulated as follows. If a woman does something ordinary, like becoming a passenger, anyone can do it, i.e., flying is safe. If a woman does something extraordinary, like fly the Atlantic, it will become news, which still means it could either promote the industry or be written off as a publicity stunt. If a woman proves she can do it, i.e., breaks a flying record, she will be rewarded with a place in the industry, although even as a pilot she will most likely be relegated to public relations. If a woman fails to do it, i.e., crashes, the fact of her sex will make it even bigger news, so big that women might even be prevented from flying. This was the case in France when after the deaths of several female fliers women were barred from flying schools, such as the one that Bessie Coleman first sought to attend.

Joseph Corn in *The Winged Gospel* makes a plausible historical argument when he writes that by the 1940s, "the public's fear of flying was no longer economically significant. . . . the males who built the planes and ran the industry had no further business need to recruit women pilots as part of a strategy to sell flying to an airminded but timid public"[35] and women were out of a job, except as flight attendants. A narrative of progress might argue that because something does not require physical strength, like flying a plane, or because performance can be measured with mathematical precision, like speed, altitude and long-distance records, gender differences, and therefore gender bias, will be eliminated. Neither Corn's historical argument nor the narrative of historical progress succeeds in explaining how gender functions as double-bind within aviation history.

Aviation, in its short history between the first and second world wars, offers in miniature a pattern that recurs repeatedly in the history of women's emancipation as the narrative of their emergence into modernity. Earhart fought to instigate separate women's flying records because women, lacking training and experience, were not as good as men, and therefore there would be no record of them having flown at all. Once women's records were established, women caught up with and even surpassed men's performances. When the records were again combined, since they were now deemed unnecessary, women once more disappeared, partly because there were always fewer female fliers and partly because men now had access to higher performance aircraft. Women are regendered as masculine to promote an industry by regendering it as feminine so that in the end, all but the exceptional woman will find employment only at its margins. While Settlement work no longer required the regendering of the female subject, aviation still did. While the Settlement House distinguished itself from both the church and labor unions by "interpreting democracy in social terms,"[36] the contradiction between women flying and women in aviation was not one that could be resolved by invoking a humanitarian ideal.

Earhart's writing, in its repetition and topical organization, re-enacts this conundrum. When asked "to discuss aviation periodically in the magazine from my own experience and point of view,"[37] she is relying on an experience not only she has had. She writes that, "Tabloided my autobiography is simple": Her father's law work was connected with the railroads, which meant they moved alot; she became a nurse's aid to help the war effort, began studying medicine at Columbia, learned to fly, and turned to Settlement work. It is nevertheless a life history that can never be replicated. Unlike the predictable trajectory of an aviator such as Lindbergh, Earhart will work at making her exceptional position more normative.

vii. "But you don't look like an aviatrix. You have long hair."

Once Earhart has established the position of the aviatrix as social worker, she further normalizes the female flier through clothes. She does this, on the one hand, by insisting on the history of clothes within aviation, that "'flying clothes'—fleece or fur lined overalls of either leather or heavy cloth"[38] are obsolete given the fact that planes now have closed cockpits; on the other hand, by comparing flying to driving a car, which also once needed special clothes, but not anymore. The insistence on the suitability of ordinary clothes emphasizes that women neither have to look like men, that is, unsexed and thus unfashionable, nor do they need to belong to a particular social class, that is, engage in the extra expense of buying special sporting clothes. Most importantly, by wearing street clothes a woman does not have to look like an aviatrix and assume that identity in order to fly. But what is an aviatrix? What it means to look like a female aviator relies both on being taken seriously on the airfield and on posing as a modern woman. While Earhart insists on the normativeness of the female flier, she at the same time creates the most recognizable image of the aviatrix, one who continues to circulate in its postmodern appropriations, including Apple computer ads.

An anecdote recounted in Putnam's biography, *Soaring Wings* (1939), serves to illustrate Earhart's early investment in her look. In 1922 she buys a patent leather coat: "'But suddenly I saw that it looked *too* new. How were people to think I was a flier if I was wearing a flying coat that was brand-new. Wrinkles! That was it. There just had to be some wrinkles. So—I slept in it for three nights to give my coat a properly veteran appearance. When I decided not to go to bed in it any longer, I did give it a last going over—rubbing the sheen off here and there.'"[39] How can one be a flier if one doesn't look the part; how can one look the part if the coat doesn't look like it already belongs to someone who is a flier.

Responding to one of the two most frequently asked questions: "What did you wear?" (the other was "Were you afraid?") following the *Friendship* flight, she writes:

> Just my old flying clothes, comfortably, if not elegantly, battered and worn. High laced boots, brown broadcloth breeks, white silk blouse with a red necktie (rather antiquated!) and a companionably ancient leather coat, rather long, with plenty of pockets and a snug buttoning collar. A homely brown sweater accompanied it. A light leather flying helmet and goggles completed the picture, such as it was. A single elegance was a brown and white silk scarf.[40]

The necktie, its "antiquatedness" an allusion to those worn by turn-of-the-century reformers and suffragettes (as well as androgynes), will eventually be replaced by the silk scarf, transformed from a "single elegance" into a necessary sign. The leather coat, made to look "companionably ancient," will in 1932 be shortened to a jacket. "Breeks" or jodhpurs, reminiscent of flying's relationship to sports and sports clothes' origins in the riding habit, will give way to slacks. The flying helmet and goggles, the aviator's signature, will be discarded to display the short, unruly hair that marks Earhart as aviatrix.

Once again, like the relationship between books, syndicated columns, and endorsements, Earhart's look becomes a composite of body shape, public image, and queer identity. She not only considers comfort and safety by wearing slacks and sensible shoes, but she also designs and models a line of dresses that integrates techniques from airplane manufacturing.[41] She not only wears dresses to prove that female fliers are ordinary women, but she wears them at a certain length, so that, like slacks, they hide her too-thick thighs. She agrees to follow Putnam's advice that she smile with her mouth closed in order to hide the space between her two front teeth and complains of her complexion, the skin on her sunburned face often peeling. Most importantly, she agrees to discard the hats that Putnam calls "a public menace" and thereby reveals the tousled blonde hair that becomes her signature, even though the curls are not natural. Unlike Lindbergh, who escapes identification by placing his helmet onto another head, Earhart retains anonymity only by covering her hair with a cap. While Earhart herself prefers the studio photographs that combine the flier's helmet with a string of pearls or a velvet evening gown decorated with both pearls and wings, she will be remembered for the leather jacket, silk blouse, and tie.

viii. "I believe you've fallen in love,—yes, and his name's Airplane."

The boyish look that Earhart retains until her disappearance three weeks before her fortieth birthday produces a non-normative relationship to both masculine gender identity and lesbian sexual identity. This is in part caused by the confusion between the two categories, first established by nineteenth-century sexologists whose notion of the sexual invert equated homosexuality with gender inversion so that female same-sex object choice was the result of, for instance, "being a man trapped in a woman's body." This confusion seems to persist among contemporary feminist scholars. On the one hand, Doris Rich tries to imagine the expectations of Earhart's audiences, and in the process projects her own anxieties backwards: "If anyone came expecting a coarse or odd person, perhaps even a lesbian (what sort of a woman would challenge an ocean and suggest that other women become aviators?), they were disappointed."[42] On the other hand, the fact that Earhart shared certain fashion items with historical lesbians of the 1920s requires provisos such as Ware's:

> Amelia bore no resemblance to the stereotyped figure of the upper-class mannish lesbian, which was common in bohemian circles like Paris's Left Bank, New York's Greenwich Village, Harlem and occasionally in Hollywood. These lesbians dressed in tuxedoes and adopted such male affectations as top hats, cigarette holders, and monocles, a style which was foreign to A. E. Nor did she affect the style of working-class lesbians, with their exaggerated role divisions (and corresponding clothes vocabulary) of butch and femme.[43]

In both cases we have what Terry Castle, in *The Apparitional Lesbian,* calls "the ghosting of the lesbian," that is "an effort to derealize the threat of lesbianism by associating it with the apparitional."[44] In the first instance, she literally fails to appear, contrary to audience expectation. In the second, she appears as stereotype and in no way looks like Amelia. To invoke the lesbian only to dismiss her is, in itself, a queer gesture. What then is queer about Amelia?

Earhart was married, but unlike Eleanor Roosevelt, is not rumored to have been pursued by or interested in members of her own sex. At the same time, as Ware rightly suggests, "she was rarely, if ever, presented as a sex object or as exuding any kind of heterosexual attraction."[45] Rather than imagining the possibility of same-sex attraction, Ware solves this contradiction by resorting to the concept of "gender-blending" as one that reconciles both "a hint of manliness at the very heart of a feminine presence" and "an acceptance of sexual difference combined with a refusal of sexist inequalities," what other critics have written about Greta Garbo and Katherine Hepburn, respectively.[46] But in as much as the aviatrix and the cross-dressed movie actress have certain characteristics in common, a female pilot's only role is to play herself.

The aviatrix embodies neither married motherhood nor celibate, societal motherhood. Earhart is married but childless; as a former social worker and advocate of women in aviation, she nevertheless insists that most of her flying is "for the fun of it," not for social or scientific progress. As a married woman she retained her name, and agreed to marry George Putnam only under the conditions outlined in a pre-nuptial agreement.[47] While the companionate marriage has been both praised and blamed for her commodification, it nevertheless contradicted the normative model, which was that of "Mr. and Mrs. Pilot," true for female fliers who either married their flight instructors, or like Anne Morrow Lindbergh, learned to fly from their husbands. In contrast, Amelia and her husband managed their joint property, "Amelia Earhart," and Earhart agreed to this arrangement because it guaranteed regular solo flying. The marital "we" never compromises the aeronautical "we" of pilot and plane, even as Rich argues that the failure of the last flight can be attributed to a failing marriage.

She had short hair. She flew alone. She did it all for "the fun of it." Earhart represented an alternative to both the decadence of the heterosexualized flapper of the 1920s and biological motherhood as it was appropriated by the fascists in the 1930s. Ware positions her as a representative of post-Suffrage feminism, the missing link between the first and second wave of the twentieth-century women's movement, a generation marked by the liberal individualism and optimism of exceptional women who served as inspirational role models, but found it difficult to institutionalize their success. Earhart wears pants not just to fly, as required by the relationship to a machine such as the airplane that makes long skirts a safety issue, but also on the street: "It is possible that the advance of trousers for women is the most significant fashion change of the twentieth century."[48] She leaves the wearing of the suit to Putnam, her boyishness reinforced by the slacks' connotation of sport and leisure. Yet she continues to benefit from, and furthers, the single-sex organizations that characterized the same-sex environments of the Progressive era reformers: She insists on learning to fly from a female pilot, Neta Snook; the *Friendship* is organized and financed by a woman, Mrs. Guest; in 1930 Earhart founds and serves as president of the first organization for female pilots, the 99s; she becomes consultant in the department for the study of careers for women at Purdue University beginning in 1935.

Just as keeping her own name in a childless marriage signifies a nonreproductive sexuality, "for the fun of it" becomes emblematic of nonproductive work. By associating adventure with art, she divorces it from remuneration or social obligation, as required by the image of the American Girl: "What I am trying to work toward is this: that *beauty and adventure have a certain value of their own, which can be weighed only in spiritual scales.* I have the greatest respect for dollars and cents. They are quite important. They pay the rent and the grocer; they buy clothes and satisfy the tax collector. But they are not the final measure of the human spirit."[49] By advocating for women's right to physical adventure, she restates her commitment to women's right to endanger their own lives, not just to improve the lives of others. She also insists that what she does is something that does not require monetary compensation.

These traits have traditionally been associated with the figure of the dandy: "The role of the dandy implied an intense preoccupation with self and self presentation; image was everything, and the dandy a man who often had no family, no calling, apparently no sexual life, no visible means of financial support. He was the very archetype of the new urban man who came from nowhere and for whom appearance *was* reality."[50] Post-dating the dandy as historical subject, the aviatrix can be read as his successor in an American context inasmuch as she is constructed by her clothes and aestheticizes not *flânerie,* but flying.

The aviatrix is less preoccupied with creating her image than with selling it, and maintaining its marketability. On the one hand, this involves keeping grueling lecture schedules and making endless appearances for endorsements; on the other hand, it means reinvesting all profits into future flights that simply perpetuate the cycle. The aristocratic origins of the dandy have been replaced by the commercial demands of the flier. The aviatrix engages in the luxury of long-distance flying during the Depression and she flies alone, both of which contribute to her glamour. She enters the male dominated field of aviation yet insists on the company of her sex. A *flâneuse* of the air, she will never be confused with a streetwalker; a solo flier, she cannot be suspected of sexual desire. Neither tomboy nor butch, neither masculinized nor sexualized, the queer property of "A. E." is one that nobody owns, even as it continues to generate instant recognition.

ix. "Defense Secretary Les Aspin this week will order the military to drop most of its restrictions on women in aerial and naval combat, senior Pentagon officials said today. Mr. Aspin is expected to issue a directive on Thursday ordering the armed services to let women fly aircraft in combat. The administration will ask Congress to repeal a law barring women from serving on many warships. Finally each service will be directed to justify all remaining jobs that are off limits to women, including service in ground combat units." (*New York Times,* 28 April 1993)

x. "Flying a plane she calls 'Harmony' and accompanied by her flight instructor, a sixth-grader from Meadeville, Pa., believes she is the youngest girl to pilot a plane to Europe.

Twelve-year-old Vicki Van Meter completed her trans-Atlantic flight Tuesday after taking her single-engine plane above the clouds to rid it of ice on the wings." (*Ann Arbor News,* 7 June 1994)

Postmodern Postlude

To imagine Amelia as neither the solo flier nor the wife in a modern marriage, but to reimagine her as the lover of her navigator Fred Noonan, becomes a symptom of the postmodern desire to write beyond the modernist ending. Noonan was a known alcoholic, like Earhart's father, the only navigator Earhart could afford for her trip around the world, and the only person ever to accompany her on a long-distance flight.

In *Amelia Earhart: The Last Flight* (1994), a made-for-TNT movie with Diane Keaton, they go down together and vanish, Noonan in love with Earhart, not just her flying. In Jane Mendelsohn's novel *I Was Amelia Earhart* (1996), whose film rights have been sold to Fineline, they land on an island and become lovers in a life after death, even as Earhart hopes to escape their rescuers and Noonan begins to show signs of dementia. In Alison Anderson's *Hidden Latitudes* (1996) (with a sticker on the dustjacket marketing it as "A Novel of Amelia Earhart"), they become lovers while castaways on an island, perform a marriage ceremony, and anticipate a child. Noonan falls ill and is swept away by the ocean's current, all recounted from memory by an Amelia who has lived into old age.

The postmodern rewriting de-queers Amelia by imagining a heterosexual romance, the one she never had, perhaps the one the contemporary woman would like to have, or worse yet, fears she has renounced.

What if one were to land on a desert island, not preplanned and prepackaged as a tour? What if one had an affair with a male subordinate at work? What if one lived another 40 years in order to experience a postmarital relationship that involved neither adultery nor divorce, but potential motherhood, for the indecisive or the infertile?

In these postmodern fictions, Amelia either goes down because she's afraid of old age or she disappears and doubles her age. She's imagined as surreal survivor or as immortal. Are these the soft-porn fantasies of sexually liberated women or the symptoms of a feminist backlash?

The parallel narrative in *Hidden Latitudes* presents the anatomy of a contemporary marriage between Robin and Lucy, who escape modern life on a 35-foot yacht only to end up stranded on an island in the Gilberts. There a ghost (who may or may not be Amelia) makes herself known by stealing books and a jar of raspberry jam, leaving a coconut shell filled with potable water. Robin is a science teacher whose affair with a female student almost made him cancel the trip; Lucy is being pressured to get pregnant while wondering whether her marriage is worth preserving. When she does conceive, she decides to keep the child, to make up for the one that Amelia lost after Noonan's death.

Why does Anderson need to imagine Amelia differently in order to invent her own story? Why do we need Amelia, not as girls, but as adult readers, in order to reinvent our own lives?

What is it about the last flight that makes one want to rewrite it as the last fling? What is it about the modern heroine that makes one want to return her to the primitive, not as premodern but as the object of postmodern consumption: 30s retro, third world travelogue, desert island getaway? What makes Noonan the ideal lover, the sensitive man who has a weakness, but is strong enough to provide in the wild?

On the one hand, Earhart and Noonan are like a married couple, pilot and navigator; on the other hand, they are like lovers, because time and place have been suspended. Once the plane is grounded, the pilot loses her job; once the pilot has saved the navigator, all he has left is his sex.

If Amelia herself has been de-queered, these texts nevertheless have queer moments.

Mendelsohn's Amelia is in love with her plane, inasmuch as her desire is much stronger for "Electra" than for Noonan. She develops a homoeroticized connection to the plane's cockpit, just as Noonan seeks his narcissistic pleasure by getting high.

As Lucy feels more estranged in her marriage, she becomes increasingly drawn to the island, to the other woman, Amelia, who has been a mother and has lost her child, and who mothers Lucy so that she, in turn, will not make the mistake of aborting hers.

Finally, how can one not read Keaton's Amelia as a reincarnation of Annie Hall, who by wearing men's ties and failing to marry the hero, enables identifications one would have to call queer?

Beryl Markam, The Female Flyer as *Femme Fatale.* With permission from Brown Brothers.

Beryl Markham: The Female Flyer as *Femme Fatale*

i. "With every tool man is perfecting his own organs, whether motor or sensory, or is removing the limits to their functioning. Motor power places gigantic forces at his disposal, which, like his muscles, he can employ to any direction; thanks to ships and aircraft neither water nor air can hinder his movements; by means of spectacles he corrects defects in the lens of his own eye; by means of the telescope he sees into the far distance; and by means of the microscope he overcomes the limits of visibility set by the structure of his retina. In the photographic camera he has created an instrument which retains the fleeting visual impression, just as a gramophone disc retains the equally fleeting auditory ones; both are at bottom materializations of the power he possesses of recollection, his memory." (Sigmund Freud, *Civilization and Its Discontents* [1930], 37–8)

ii. "It was not until 1883, when the young Scotsman Joseph Thomson penetrated Massailand and returned to describe in some detail the country beyond, that the extent and fertility of the highlands was realised. Until his visit the discoveries of the German missionary Krapf, who first reported the existence of Kilimanjaro and Kenya mountains in 1848, had been very sceptically regarded. Scientists had written papers proving that the existence of snow-covered peaks on the equator was an impossibility." (Elspeth Huxley, *White Man's Country* [1935; 1953], 3)

Amelia Earhart and Beryl Markham never met, although they were asked to comment on each other's accomplishments: Earhart when Markham made her solo transatlantic crossing in 1936 and Markham when Earhart disappeared over the Pacific in 1937. They crossed paths, so to speak, by flying the same route between England and North America in opposite directions: Earhart from West to East in 1932 and Markham from East to West four years later. Headwinds require more fuel, which makes the plane heavier, and thus made Markham's flight a longer and more challenging one. Whereas Earhart's disappearance secured her status as a legend,

Markham lived until weeks before the fiftieth anniversary of her flight from England to Nova Scotia. Instead of disappearing or dying, like her fellow aviators, she aged, leaving a 40-year gap between her transatlantic flight and the publication of her memoir. Not the flight, but the record of her flying, not the publication, but the rediscovery of a previously published memoir, *West With the Night* (1942), generated enough publicity to warrant an editorial in the Sunday *New York Times* in 1993, entitled "Ghost Story": "'West With the Night' is, then a 'monkey'—which is what antique dealers call a piece that's been 'improved' or 'married' (highboy's top meets lowboy's bottom). Does that make it any less a triumph?"[1]

The representation of Markham's flight as both pioneering and belated refers to more than just the public's perception of record flights by the end of the 1930s: "We hope that she will never take off. The time for these 'pioneer' solo flights in overloaded radio-less machines has passed. The only Transatlantic flights which serve any purpose now are those which lay the foundations for a regular mail service."[2] It also points to her status as the offspring of one of the original white settlers in the highlands of British East Africa belatedly bringing European "civilization" to the African interior, proving that it was possible to rear European children on the equator at 7000 feet above sea level. Growing up in a corner of the empire that fought to retain an imperial ideology already outdated to those governing at its center, Markham became a pioneer in her own right: she was the first woman in Kenya to be granted a horse training license (not available to women in England until 1966), a "B" pilot's license (for passengers and transportation of goods), and the first person to offer aerial elephant scouting commercially. Inasmuch as the pioneer who settles in a colony is necessarily a home-maker, bringing his wife and children to work the land they will eventually inherit, there is little need to maintain gender distinctions, as long as women are willing and able to "muddle through" (Churchill) and/or "rough it" (Roosevelt). But inasmuch as East Africa also attracted sportsmen, and big-game hunting "is a craft, a pursuit of value in exercising and developing hardihood of body and the virile courage and resolution which necessarily lie at the base of every strong and manly character,"[3] it becomes unclear how to read the gendering of the aerial scouter as accessory to the White Hunter. Winston Guest, the son who prevented his mother from flying the Atlantic, enabling Earhart to be the first woman to do so, will become the guest of Markham and Bror Blixen on the safari she describes in detail in *West With the Night*.

Whose "top" was she, whose "bottom" (sexually)? Did she "monkey," that is, "meddle, trifle, fool" with other men, as a woman, or as another man? Did marriage "improve" her, that is, make her modern, or an antique?

> iii. "On being told that the animal was dead, I immediately suggested that I should be photographed standing upon it holding a gun—of course an unloaded one; I saw to that!
>
> Now, when I tell the story of that tiger, sometimes I say we did it, sometimes I say they did it; but in America, of course, I said *I* did it." (Honorable Mrs. Victor Bruce, *The Bluebird's Flight* [1931], 116–17)

The first successful solo flight around the world by a female pilot has been attributed to the vagaries of window-shopping. In 1930, the Honorable Mrs. Victor Bruce has an hour to spare on London's Regent Street and returns home not with a dress but with a Blackburn Bluebird, an airplane whose low price and advertised "readiness to go anywhere" allows for favorable comparison to the ease with which one purchases a car. Not yet knowing how to fly, but able to rely on the experience acquired as both a horsewoman and a racecar driver, Mrs. Bruce takes off two weeks after acquiring her license with only 40 hours of solo flying. She covers 20,000 miles in five months, 23 countries, and three continents, including the longest seacrossing since Lindbergh's transatlantic flight two years earlier.

The Atlantic and Pacific crossings are accomplished by folding up the wings of the plane and boarding a steamship, where she joins other members of an international elite in spite of her limited attire. The wardrobe she embarks with consists of "a sun helmet, two light cotton frocks, an evening dress and the clothes I stood up in,"[4] which include a leather helmet and coat for protection in the open cockpit. The return trip will involve being followed by an escort plane carrying trunks of clothes she acquired as gifts. One ostensible purpose of the flight is to return to New Albany, Indiana, to drop a flag from the air on the birthplace her mother had left 42 years earlier. Through this aerial display, the aviatrix appoints herself ambassador between the Old World and the New, between the American heartland and the British aristocracy.

In her memoir, *The Bluebird's Flight* (1931), based on the tapes she recorded for her husband by means of the dictaphone she chose over a parachute, the Honorable Mrs. Victor Bruce calls herself an "ordinary aviatrix," partly because she is able to code her accomplishment as simply the fulfillment of a daughter's promise to her mother, partly because she thinks nothing of leaving her husband and young child for several months to perform her role as adventurous aristocrat. However, a woman flying alone on a journey around the world offers a sight very much out of the ordinary every time she lands. On the one hand, she provides publicity for the airplane's peacetime function in promoting international relations, when, for instance, the governor of Arizona writes a letter to the King of England to document the first time in the history of the state that a British woman had arrived in an airplane. On the other hand, she contributes to the confusion of gender identities, enacted when the leader of the Baluchi tribespeople attempts to try on Mrs. Bruce's evening dress during her forced landing off of the Persian Gulf.

Twice the female flyer insists on identifying her gender by combing her hair—either because it remains hidden under her helmet or because its length, in the absence of a dress, seems to give her the appearance of a boy: "I tried to explain that I was a girl, and taking a comb out of my pocket I started to comb my hair, pointing at the same time to one of the female children."[5] Both times she is working under the assumption that, as a woman, she should enjoy immunity from state violence and, as a European woman, she can make herself exempt from sexual violence by insisting on her racial superiority. Although racial superiority is assumed, she is nevertheless willing to risk gender ambiguity for the promise of modernity in the form of "airmindedness." Unlike the dress she left in the shop, the plane offers a fashion statement that combines the ordinariness of the automobile as a modern machine with the class distinction of a club sport. Even when adventure doesn't result in misadventure, Bruce's one regret is having to spend several hours at the end of each day attending to the engine.

iv. "For Kilindini (or Mombasa, as I may be permitted to call it) is the starting point of one of the most romantic and most wonderful railways in the world. The two iron streaks of rail that wind away among the hills and foliage of Mombasa Island do not break their smooth monotony until, after piercing Equatorial forests, stretching across immense prairies, and climbing almost to the level of the European snow-line, they pause—and that only for a time—upon the edges of the Great Lake. And thus is made a sure, swift road along which the white man and all that he brings with him, for good or ill, may penetrate into the heart of Africa as easily and sagely as he may travel from London to Vienna. . . . And here is presented the wonderful and unique spectacle which the Uganda Railway offers to the European. *The plains are crowded with wild animals.* From the windows of the carriage the whole zoological gardens can be seen disporting itself. Herds of antelope and gazelle, troops of zebras—sometimes four or five hundred together—watch the train pass with placid assurance, or scamper a hundred yards farther away, and turn again. Many are quite close to the line. With field-glasses one can see that it is the same everywhere, and can distinguish long files of black wildebeeste and herds of red kongoni—the hartebeeste of South Africa—and wild ostriches walking sedately in twos and threes, and every kind of small deer and gazelle. The zebras come slow enough for their stripes to be admired with the naked eye . . . the scenery about Kenya far surpasses anything I have ever seen in India or South Africa, and challenges comparison with the fairest countries of Europe. Indeed, looking at it with an eye fresh from Italy, I was most powerfully reminded of the upper valleys of the Po." (Winston Churchill, *My African Journey* [1908], 2; 6; 22)

Earhart herself contrasted the British to the American model of women's introduction and access to flying by distinguishing between flying as a sport, i.e., making available lightweight airplanes through flying clubs, and flying as a form of transportation—learning to fly as analogous to learning to drive a car. She considered the British model a superior one, inasmuch as it neutralized gender differences by making planes readily available to either sex, thereby overlooking the fact that club membership relies on class privilege. She contrasts this to the American model where a woman had to hang out at the local airplane hangar hoping some male pilot would notice her and be generous enough to teach her how to fly. For those women who didn't reside on either side of the Atlantic, like Amy Johnson, the first woman to fly from England to Australia (1930), and Jean Batten, the first woman to fly from Australia to England (1935) and from England to New Zealand (1936), taking to the air meant undertaking solo long-distance flights that would bring together not the Old World and the New, but the farthest reaches of the British Empire. In such cases flying was neither a sport nor analogous to driving an automobile, but rather a form of transportation that served to unite geographically, and thus symbolically, disparate colonies with the metropole.

At the time of Beryl's arrival in the East African Protectorate, the main form of transportation, the Uganda Railway, built in 1901, was considered pioneering both because of the terrain it traversed—reducing a march of many weeks to a 48-hour train-ride—and because of the capital investment involved—10,000 pounds a mile. Originally planned as a way to secure British dominance over the Upper Nile, by the time of Churchill's journey in 1908, the Lunatic Express or "iron snake," as it was called by the natives, had already become commercially viable, due to sufficient settlement. From its origins Kenya was a settlement colony, like South Africa, where the next generation of colonizers was raised to stay, rather than a colony of planters, like in the Caribbean, where wealth was amassed while living elsewhere. It was to remain in the hands of individual farmers, rather than large financial interests, from the time it became a crown colony in 1920 until the country's independence in 1963. Markham's father's main source of income would come through government contracts for posho (ground maize) for the railway workers. Roads were scarce and cars difficult to maintain; airways were built before highways.

Flying also maintained ties with visitors from the colonial center, including royalty, by facilitating big-game hunting through aerial elephant scouting. This involved searching for herds of elephant, estimating the size of their tusks, and reporting back to camp so that hunters could track the elephant spoor on foot. This eliminated time wasted, either losing track of herds, or following bulls the size of whose tusks weren't worth the effort. Although valued by tradespeople from the coasts for their ivory long before the arrival of Europeans, elephants, considered among the most intelligent animals, but also the most dangerous to pursue, were not systematically hunted by native tribes. Theodore Roosevelt publicized such safaris as sport, when in 1909, he set out for the Smithsonian to collect specimens of big game for the National Museum in Washington, accompanied by gun-bearers and trackers, in addition to 500 porters, each carrying 60 pounds.[6] While much of the load involved supplies necessary to preserve animal skins for the exhibition hall, it also included Roosevelt's "Pigskin Library," a collection of "good books" bound in pigskin as a form of protection from soiled hands in the absence of water for washing, a load sufficient for one porter. Before the days of aerial scouting, this allowed the big-game hunter to steal a few moments of reading "while resting under a tree at noon, perhaps beside the carcass of a beast I had killed, or else while waiting for camp to be pitched."[7] Even before World War I, Newland, Tarlton & Co., in Nairobi, the company that organized such expeditions commercially, was the largest employer in the Protectorate.

The main club sport, as well as regular form of entertainment in the colony, remained horse-racing. Markham's father was among the first settlers to import horses from England in order to improve the blood lines. Beryl spent almost 20 years, both before and after she learned to fly, as the colony and country's most renowned horse trainer, including the first trainer to work for black owners after Kenya's independence. Thus, from the very beginning, flying in the colony involved a form of transportation without competition from the automobile and promoted a form of sport that largely involved hunting on foot. In both cases, the airplane furthered a different relationship to sight.

v. "This railroad, the embodiment of the eager, masterful, materialistic civilization of to-day, was pushed through a region in which nature, both as regards wild man and wild beast, did not and does not differ materially from what it was in Europe in the late Pleistocene. The comparison is not fanciful. The teeming multitudes of wild creatures, the stupendous size of some of them, the terrible nature of others, and the low cultures of many of the savage tribes, especially of the hunting tribes, substantially reproduces the conditions of life in Europe as it was led by our ancestors ages before the dawn of anything that could be called civilization. The great beasts that now live in East Africa were in that by-gone age represented by close kinsfolk in Europe; and in many places, up to the present moment, African man, absolutely naked, and armed as our early paleolithic ancestors were armed,

> lives among, and on, and in constant dread of, these beasts, just as was true of the men to whom the cave lion was a nightmare of terror, and the mammoth and the woolly rhinoceros possible but most formidable prey. . . . In many ways it reminds one rather curiously of the great plains of the West, where they slope upward to the foot-hills of the Rockies. It is a white man's country. Although under the equator, the altitude is so high that the nights are cool, and the region as a whole is very healthy. . . . There is no more danger to health incident to an ordinary trip to East Africa than there is to an ordinary trip to the Riviera." (Theodore Roosevelt, *African Game Trails* [1910], 2; 38; 148)

What then, were the available subject positions in the modernist period for the female offspring of the colonial settler, a member of the upper class who had become a pioneer? Beryl arrived in Kenya in 1905, at the age of three, ten years after it became the Protectorate of East Africa. Both of her parents had grown up in England's premier fox-hunting country and were accomplished horseback riders. Her father, Charles Clutterbuck, a youngest son whose military income proved insufficient without a forthcoming inheritance, migrated first to South and then to East Africa. There he purchased 1,000 acres from Lord Delamere, one of the "old Etonians" who became known as "the Rhodes of East Africa," whose original 100,000 acres brought into existence the settlement that came to be called the "White Highlands."

European women who followed their husbands and were expected to become farmer's wives either didn't last long, like Beryl's mother, who returned to England a year later, (where she stayed until 1918 when she reappeared in Kenya with two additional children by a second husband who had left her a widow), or Lady Delamere, who came to serve as a surrogate maternal figure, but died at the age of 36. Ada Orchardson was first the mistress and then the wife of a European settler, before becoming Beryl's governess and then her stepmother. Other women, like Karen Blixen, provided havens for White Hunters who sought the regular, if sporadic, shelter of a European interior: "I had been on the farm longing to get away, and they came back to it longing for books and linen sheets and the cool atmosphere in a big shuttered room."[8]

European children either didn't survive, like Beryl's sickly brother, who likewise returned to England (and died at 21), or like Arthur Orchardson (the only other settler offspring with whom Beryl had extended contact), spent many more years in school in Nairobi than the two and a half she managed before being dismissed due to disciplinary action. Thus Beryl grew up with no maternal influence and minimal paternal supervision, except that by age 11, her father had taught her to be an accomplished horsewoman. When not seeking refuge in the stables, she lived in her own mud rondoval, away from her father's house, speaking Swahili, and learning to handle a spear.

Her closest childhood friend beside Arthur (who is never mentioned in her memoir), was Kibii, a member of the Kipsigis tribe, allied to the Nandi, the child of Maina, assigned to her by her father as a personal servant, and who, once circumcised, as *arap* Ruta, was to groom horses for her, then go on to maintain her plane. In her 50s, having referred to him in her memoir as servant, friend, even "animate household god," Beryl fired him. At 16—although her father claimed she was 17 and the legal age for marriage in the Protectorate was 18—Beryl became engaged to and then married Jock Purves, a Scottish rugby player, rumored to have been bartered by her father either for the forgiveness of debts, or in exchange for educating her.

Raised by Africans, who taught her to jump higher than her own height and walk on the balls of her feet, Beryl nevertheless considered them her servants, whom she simply ordered to take her hunting. Treated more as a son than a daughter by her father, Beryl was nevertheless married off to a European as a minor. Consequently, when drought and the reevaluation of the rupee brought farmers to the verge of bankruptcy overnight, he was able to sell the farm and leave without her to accept a position as horse trainer in Peru. By the age of 18, she was earning an income as horse trainer as well, which in Kenya was remarkable more because of age than gender, and in England would stigmatize her among the aristocracy as a woman who earned her own living. Brought up in neither the Edwardian society of the expatriates, nor as a Kipsigis girl, in her memoir it is nevertheless the moment of the male warrior Kibii's circumcision that marks the difference of her gender:

> "When I am circumcised and become a Murani," Kibii said, 'and drink blood and curdled milk like a man, instead of ugali and nettles, like a woman, I will find whoever it was that killed my father and put my spear in his heart.'
>
> "You are selfish, Kibii," I said. 'I can jump just as high as you can, and play all our games just as well. I can throw a spear almost as far. We will find him together and put both our spears in his heart.'[9]

Markham attempts to resist the difference gender makes by continuing to disavow the racial differences mandated by the colonial project. Her reinscription into European culture prescribed for her by race will regender her as feminine, even as it will highlight the ambiguity of her social class. For her second marriage, she marries into the aristocracy by becoming the wife of Mansfield Markham. But when she becomes the paramour of Edward, Duke of Gloucester, third in line to the British throne, her husband petitions for divorce. In order to prevent Edward from being named in the petition, thereby releasing Mansfield from all future financial claims, the royal family pays Beryl an annuity from 1929 until her death in 1986. The child she has while married to Markham, rumored to be Edward's although recognized by Markham as his own, is left in England to be raised by his paternal grandmother. For her final husband, she chooses an American, even as she retains her aristocratic name.

vi. "Are you married, or do you live in Kenya?"

All three of Beryl's marriages ended in divorce, at a time when divorced women were not accepted for presentation at the British court, although an exception was made for her in 1928. It was not just her multiple marriages that marked a life of scandal, but what has come to be known as her sexual promiscuity, beginning with the story about the six-inch nail Jock Purves knocked into a post each time she took a lover, and continuing with her sexual liaisons with both Edward and his brother, Henry, Prince of Wales, whom she met when they came to Kenya on safari. Then there were the men she wasn't married to, like Denys Finch Hatton, who wouldn't leave Karen Blixen for Beryl and wouldn't teach her to fly, yet whose supposedly "last great love" she was, before losing his life in an airplane crash; and Tom Black, for whom she supposedly flew the Atlantic in an attempt to retrieve him from the actress he was about to marry, who did teach her to fly and whose lover she did become, but who died shortly after her transatlantic flight.

Between multiple marriages and named and unnamed lovers, it becomes difficult for either of her biographers to unconditionally reclaim her as modernist heroine. Mary Lovell, who completed *Straight on Till Morning* (1987) shortly before Markham's death and includes a preface by her that testifies to their friendship, ends her prologue with: "She is the most remarkable person I have ever met, and perhaps even greater than her great adventure with life was her ability to inspire others. For myself, I love her still, with a passion which often takes me by surprise."[10] Lovell prefers to tone down Markham's love life in order to preserve her as a source of feminist inspiration, based on a model of infatuation for the female role model. Errol Trzebinski, in *The Lives of Beryl Markham* (1993), in part to distinguish her biography from Lovell's, sensationalizes Markham's sex life by simply listing the names of known lovers during a several month period in the early 1930s. A list of ten names, some of them titled, is followed by the statement: "Each was hopping into bed with Beryl whenever it suited her."[11] Listing the names of notable men is constitutive of the madame, although in this case she does it for free; sex with men without names or remuneration characterizes not women, in dominant cultural narratives, but queer men.

If her sexual exploits fail to make her heroic as modernist heroine, then her disloyalty toward men and her dislike of women begs the question of what a female biographer is to do with her as female subject. Lovell adheres closely to the family romance, identifying the origins of Markham's lack of gender solidarity in maternal abandonment and a father fixation. Women become insignificant because she never knew her mother and thus becomes incapable of being maternal herself, while each new encounter with a male figure becomes a futile attempt to find a father substitute. Trzebinski, in contrast, traces the carelessness of her relationship to men to the so-called African side of her: "The way in which she was to take lovers as lightly as she discarded them, is also ample proof of how Kipsigis attitudes robbed her of inhibition, a loss that perpetuated her legendary promiscuity. Africans attach no shame to losing virginity; . . . Females were taught to drop whatever they were doing in favour of sex."[12] Africa replaces the failed family romance as explanatory fiction for her nonexemplary femininity.

In an attempt to normalize Markham's gender identity, each biographer positions her as romantic heroine within a central romance plot. Here the hero plays the surrogate father, even as he ultimately fails to take on the role of husband. For Lovell this figure is Tom Black, her flying instructor:

> Some friends say that Tom was the one man in her life who came anywhere near her father in her estimation, even superseding her feelings for Denys Finch Hatton. Certainly when I interviewed her in 1986 she spoke of both men with great respect and obvious affection, but it was Tom's photograph she kept over her chair. . . . His firm, almost paternal control of her behaviour was probably the essential recipe for Beryl's happiness. . . . [13]

For Trzebinski, the role is played by Denys Finch Hatton, the man Beryl tried to wrest from Karen Blixen, another woman who didn't like women: "It was the essential 'child' in Beryl's make up that made her endlessly appealing, earning the forgiveness of others, as well as a need to protect her; many agree that in spite of the veneer of sophistication Beryl was to cultivate so as to impress Denys, beneath she remained a straightforward child of Africa."[14] Beryl remains the child who doesn't grow up, either because every man is really a father or because Africa produces only eternal children.

In each case the father takes on the role of Professor Higgins, teaching her how to dress or educating her in the classics, as a way of making her non-African, i.e., a lady. But the child who won't grow up is really a boy, that is, Peter Pan, who captured the British imagination from 1904, when J. M. Barrie's play was first produced on stage and revived in London every Christmas, until 1911, when it was published in novel form. "Straight on till morning" are, after all, the flight directions Peter Pan gives to his fellow children. In other words, these queer romances take place between a man and a boy, even as, in the Walt Disney film, the girl is dressed as a boy. Each man takes on the role of the absent father, while Beryl plays the role of the boy, the colonial settler who can only be made into a lady through marriage to a man from the metropole.

Finch Hatton made Beryl want to fly, and Black taught her how. This leaves Bror Blixen, with whom she scouted elephants, and John Carberry, who gave up his title to become a coffee planter in Kenya, who dared her to fly the Atlantic from West to East, and offered to lend her his plane. He nevertheless insisted on repossessing it at the end of the flight, thereby depriving Beryl of the financial rewards of an American tour. Beryl involved herself with too many men to conform to the marital "we" of the aviatrix. The authorial "we," consisting of the female flyer and her ghost writer, produced additional scandal, this time around the authenticity of the authorship of her only piece of writing. *West With the Night* was published in 1942, republished in 1983, and made the bestseller list in 1986, having sold over a million copies.

> vii. "She is tall, slender and has long golden hair which I've never seen covered except by a flying helmet. Her legs are very long and she is one of the few women who really look good in slacks which she wears most of the time." (Molly Castle, *Daily Mirror,* 16 January 1940)

By the time Molly Castle, a British journalist, suggests to Markham that she write a book about her adventures, Beryl is in Hollywood, where she has been lured, like many aviators before her, by the film industry in the hope of cashing in on her name. But she has failed her screen test and Paramount Studios hires her to serve as technical advisor to a film entitled *Safari,* at which point Castle concludes, "though full of thrills, [it] is by no means as exciting as some of her own adventures."[15]

Two years later her adventures will appear in print under the title *West With the Night,* with the following acknowledgment: "I wish to express my gratitude to Raoul Schumacher for his constant encouragement and his assistance in the preparations for this book." Schumacher was both her third husband, with whom she was living in California, and a known ghost-writer for Hollywood scripts. Whether Markham produced the manuscript in the Bahamas before she even met Schumacher, encouraged and influenced by Saint-Exupéry; whether she wrote it after Pearl Harbor when Schumacher joined the army and she was alone and bored; or whether Schumacher, who had never set foot in Kenya, actually wrote the book based on lists of facts Beryl provided because she, many would argue, was illiterate, we will never know. What we do know is what Hemingway wrote to the publisher Maxwell Perkins in 1942, reprinted on the back of the North Point Press edition:

> Did you read Beryl Markham's book, *West With the Night?* I knew her fairly well in Africa and never would have suspected that she could and would put pen to paper except to write in her flyer's log book. As it is, she has written so well, and marvelously well, that I was completely ashamed of myself as a writer. I felt that I was simply a carpenter with words, picking up whatever was furnished on the job and nailing them together and sometimes making an okay pig pen. But [she] can write rings around all of us who consider ourselves as writers. The only parts of it that I know about personally, on account of having been there at the time and heard the other people's stories, are absolutely true. . . . I wish you would get it and read it because it is really a bloody wonderful book.

Although Hemingway claims to have been there, what he knows is based on facts already circulating as stories.

Like the unknowability surrounding Earhart's disappearance, which has produced a small industry of hypotheses clamoring for truth status, contested claims to truth can only sell more books. The controversy surrounding the authenticity of Markham's authorship was reopened when Scott O'Dell waited until her death to release a letter to *Vanity Fair* in 1987 claiming that Schumacher had confessed to him: "Suddenly out of nowhere he said, 'You are my best friend. I want to make a confession. I want you to know that Beryl did not write *West With the Night* or any of the short stories. Not one damned word of anything!'"[16] Trzebinski not only shares but adopts O'Dell's point of view by constructing a biographical narrative that downplays Markham's accomplishments. Lovell, in conformity with her intense admiration, argues that Markham is indeed the author: "My subsequent researches resolved all my personal doubts. Beryl wrote her book and the autobiographical short stories that came later. There are still a few rumoured incidents in her life which I have not been able to verify to my personal satisfaction and so they are not included here. Her ability to have written the book was not one of them."[17] Lovell will go on to write a biography of Amelia Earhart (half of which will be devoted to the life of Putnam), while Trzebinski comes from completing a biography of Denys Finch Hatton and serving as advisor to the film *Out of Africa* (1985), partly based on Markham's biography, thus its subtitle, "*Out of Africa*'s Hidden Free Spirit and Denys Finch Hatton's Last Great Love." The fact that Beryl and Raoul's parties where known to regularly include members of Santa Barbara's gay community and that Schumacher was rumored to have had sexual encounters with men bears on the potential relationship between Schumacher and O'Dell in ways too queer for either biographer to imagine.

Scott O'Dell's letter is written in response to a story that appeared in *Vanity Fair* three years earlier, James Fox's "The Beryl Markham Mystery," which in turn relies on the introduction to the Virago edition of *West With the Night,* also published in 1984, by Martha Gellhorn, once married to Hemingway, and in the 1970s a neighbor of Beryl's in Kenya. While Fox ostensibly sets out to solve the Markham mystery, he manages to perpetuate the mystique of the Hollywood star by reminding us of Beryl's resemblance to Greta Garbo: "She was . . . extremely good-looking: tall, broad-shouldered, with a mixture of tomboyishness and grace" and "at the age of eighty-two she still had the glamour that men had always found irresistible—the blue eyes, the coltish manner, and the wit."[18] Failing to solve her mystery, he becomes distracted by a different one: "But who was Shumacher?" which is likewise left unanswered. When asked whether she had had an affair with Dennis, Markham answers: "He wasn't the sort of chap who wanted to have affairs," and about the Duke of Gloucester: "Somebody thought he was having an affair with me. He was very *kali* [angry] about it."[19] The colony as a site for queer women, those in search of physical adventure, has displaced the queer men who escaped to the colonies as a way to avoid both a suitable marriage and suspicions about sexual non-normativity.

If Fox sets out to solve and thus sustains a mystery steeped in the nostalgia of the silver screen, Gellhorn refers to Markham's memoir as "a freak event in her career" and refigures Beryl not as Garbo, but as Circe: "Imagine Circe casting a spell on Ulysses so she could go along on the journey, learn navigation, see the world. In passing, she bewitched his company of men so that they did not resent her intrusion in their macho society, but welcomed her. It was easy to entrance the whole lot, that being her nature, and she knew what she wanted: knowledge and adventure."[20] While Fox asks who Schumacher is, Gellhorn never wonders who the real Ulysses might be. Inasmuch as Markham was "a woman of action, the way men are," like Gellhorn herself, she was able to be like a man by "bewitching" other men into treating her like one. What is missing is her seduction of men, those very men able to assimilate tomboys who wouldn't grow up into the male homosociality of the ship or the settlement colony.

viii. "Now, being in Africa, I was hungry for more of it, the changes of the seasons, the rains with no need to travel, the discomforts that you paid to make it real, the names of the trees, of the small animals, and all the birds, to know the language and have time to be in it and to move slowly. I had loved country all my life; the country was always better than the people. I could only care about people a very few at a time." (Ernest Hemingway, *Green Hills of Africa* [1935], 73)

If the authorial "we" of *West With the Night* remains a contested one, it nevertheless continues to be so in relation to the aeronautical "we." Lindbergh's *"WE"* was first ghost-written and then cowritten without mentioning the second author's name on the title page. Putnam put pressure on Earhart to produce "instant books" based on notes taken while flying or by compiling pieces previously issued to the popular press. Whether Schumacher edited what Beryl wrote or Beryl dictated and he wrote, his responsibility for her story nevertheless enabled him to bring his name into print for the first time, signed to a magazine story, two years after the appearance of Markham's memoir. Apart from several short stories published between 1944 and 1946, mostly in *Collier's* and *Ladies Home Journal,* and now collected in an edition by Mary Lovell entitled *The Splendid Outcast* (1987), Markham was never to write again. And yet, of all the memoirs by female aviators, hers is considered the most literary and became the only bestseller.

Markham's text has most often been discussed in the company of two other memoirs written by what one critic has called "Kenya's literary ladies," Isak Dinesen, the author of *Out of Africa* (1937) and Elspeth Huxley, the author of *The Flame Trees of Thika* (1959). These three texts can be said to constitute a minor literary tradition, which on the one hand, includes only women, and on the other hand, stands in sharp contrast to the travel narratives written by big-game hunters in Kenya such as Churchill, Roosevelt and Hemingway. While the first generation of college-educated women are living in Settlement Houses in the "urban jungle-slums" of England and North America, men of their class are traveling to the African jungle to hunt for big game. The texts written by white women are narratives of settlement even as only one of the protagonists permanently settles in Kenya. The travel narratives by white men, while focused on the tracking and bagging of game, nevertheless linger on the setting up of and conversations at camp. What these masculine narratives share is a notion that, because of the African setting, simply to present what happened in a true way will necessarily rival a work of imagination, and thus there is no need to offer the true stuff of fiction, a love interest. As Hemingway writes in his foreword to *Green Hills of Africa:* "Unlike many novels, none of the characters or incidents in this book is imaginary. Any one not finding sufficient love interest is at liberty, while reading it, to insert whatever love interest he or she may have at the time." For Hemingway the true and the imaginary blur in such a way as to enable a novel not focused on men's relationships to women. For Dinesen and Markham, leaving out the love interests insisted on by their biographers enables them to imagine roles characterized not by desire for, but identification with, the masculine.

In "Kenya's Literary Ladies and the Mythologizing of the White Highlands," Thomas Knipp has correctly identified the mood of these autobiographical texts as "elegiac," evoking a mood of "collective cultural nostalgia," that allows contemporary readers to engage in a kind of "triple nostalgia," for an imperial Europe, an empty Africa, and a younger Europe, both feudal and Edenic.[21] This stands in sharp contrast to Earhart's memoirs, which were written for the future, for a new age transformed by the technology and industry of aviation, in which the role of women likewise would undergo radical transformation. By reading these memoirs as romances, Knipp also rightly suggests that "the three women construct not past lives but romantic roles based on past lives"[22] that involve representing Africans as other by figuring them in feudal terms and as part of the fauna. But because the authors are all women, members of a separate literary tradition, he considers their roles only in relationship to race and class, and not as variations on the construction of a gendered identity. Markham's romantic role, "knight-errant," seems less gender-biased than Dinesen as "sorceress-queen" or Huxley as "white princess," only inasmuch as it hints at a contradiction in her gender role by suggesting a form of cross-gender identification, or female masculinity.[23]

At the beginning of the third section of *West With the Night,* when at the age of 18 her father has left for Peru and she is about to embark as a horse trainer (having omitted any mention of her marriage to Purves), Markham writes: "But I am no knight," with the entire passage as follows:

> I ride my father's gift, my horse with wings, my Pegasus with the dark bold eyes, the brown coat that shines, the long mane that flows like a black silk banner on the lance of a knight.
>
> But I am no knight. I am no knight that would earn the greeting of any other save perhaps of that fabulous and pathetic one who quested the bypaths of a distant and more ancient Spain. I am clothed in work slacks, a coloured shirt, leather moccasins, and an old felt hat, broad-brimmed and weather-weary. I ride long-stirruped, my idle hand deep in a pocket.[24]

Pegasus, the horse with wings, will serve as a transitional figure between her life as horsewoman and her life as pilot, an actual horse functioning as convenient literary device. A paternal legacy, he represents a masculine ideal that can only draw attention to her own lack, a lack that is nevertheless, through literary allusion, rendered quixotic. (This is one of those passages proving to some that Markham could never have authored her own text, since she would have been incapable of acquiring and/or utilizing this much literary knowledge.) She fails to be recognized for her "knightliness" because of her clothes, which declass and ungender her by placing her nowhere, having lost her place on the farm (which has been sold), her father (who has left for Peru), and her dog, a constant companion (who has died). Unrecognizable except by that belated and outdated figure of chivalry, Don Quixote, she is nevertheless a girl, and can't be a knight, except cross-dressed, although one who looks and rides like a boy, since women in England still rode side-saddle. The horse, in contrast and through contiguity, remains the signifier of privilege whereby select breeding guarantees a natural aristocracy. He is a sign of what she owns in terms of identification, the masculine as an inheritance from her father that will enable her to survive without him. The masculine is something she has to be, but also something she desires, possible only through her relationship to a thoroughbred.

There are two moments in the memoir when the first person narrative takes on the point of view of an animal. In the first case, the narrative switches to a third person narration that neutralizes the difference between horse and girl by representing the thoughts and emotions of the horse, as well as giving attributes of the horse to the girl. Not only does Markham adhere to the tradition of equating Africans with fauna (particularly pronounced in Dinesen), but unlike the other "literary ladies," she includes herself among the fauna as a way of negotiating an unstable gender identity produced at the intersection of race and class.

When Camciscan, a horse brought from England for breeding purposes, arrives in the fifth chapter of Book II, she writes, "I was a straw-haired girl with lanky legs and he was a stallion bred out of a stud book thick as a tome—and partly out of fire."[25] The horse represents lineage recorded in a book in contrast to the girl who resembles the stuff of his stable, while at the same time signifying an eroticized energy. "A white man came up to him now and walked around him. Other men, all of them very black, as black as his own mane, stood in a circle and watched the first man. . . . The white man said, 'So you are Camciscan,' and the black men repeated, more slowly, 'Camciscan,' one after another. And a girl, who was white too, with straw-coloured hair and legs like a colt's, said 'Camciscan' several times."[26] Through the naming of possible subject positions according to race and gender, Markham constructs a non-normative family whereby the white man (her father) remains the source of ownership and therefore knowledge of the name, with both the black men and the white girl subordinate to him. Their difference (signified by a relationship to language, i.e., they speak slowly, she repeatedly) will establish itself in relationship to the horse: The black men will groom him (in the role of servants) while the white girl will ride him (like a lover). Yet both the black men and the white girl are also compared to the horse: their blackness like his mane, her legs like a colt's. Ultimately the horse's position exceeds even that of the father, who is after all an expatriate, a settler, and a farmer, by equating it with that of the British aristocrat.

The depiction of the girl, whose legs are twice compared to those of a colt, is several times described as being "too familiar," as "trying to break through the loneliness that he lived by," as attending to him "with a kind of intimate knowledge of his needs and with a scarcely hidden sense of possession which he felt—and resented."[27] One time he throws her; another time he flings her against the wall of his box. Eventually she strikes him with a whip, thereby demonstrating her dominance, even as the erotic component remains intact when she makes her bed in his stall. Thus between the white man (her father) and the black men (maternal surrogates), the horse becomes an object of desire, but from the point of view of mastery.

In the episodes with her as flier, Markham will be joined by other "knights" in the form of fellow pilots, but once again it is she who will take on the masculine role, the one who flies, the one who comes to the rescue: She flies Bror to England, even though no woman is allowed by international law to fly over the Sudd, a 12,000 mile swamp; she rescues Woody (Tom Black) from dying of thirst in the desert, bonding with him when he concludes that the cause of his predicament is that his plane "is a bitch." Unlike her relationship to the horse, her relationships to European men are represented as de-eroticized, while planes are gendered feminine: "frail and feminine," "frivolous and inconstant," "an aerial Jezebel." She herself denies the feminine, disavowing it as a possible source of identification in an environment where her desire can only be for racial inferiors, unreliable adventurers, or distant aristocrats.

Two minor scenes in the memoir, the only ones that feature other women, rely on native women to represent the female embodiment Markham herself imagines escaping. When describing a Nandi girl she writes, "They were shy and they were feminine and they did the things that women are meant to do, and they never hunted."[28] And when she and Bror spend the night in a brothel in Benghazi, she writes of their hostess, "Put her in an apron and soak the mask of paint from her face and she could be used as a fit subject for any artist wanting to depict the misery and the despair and the loneliness of all women driven to drudgery."[29] In both cases, a femininity marked by racial and class differences is disavowed in order to identify with the masculine, either black or white. When landing in Sardinia, she, like the Honorable Mrs. Victor Bruce, will be mistaken for a man in disguise, once again suggesting the female masculinity of the female boy.

> ix. "To Denys Finch Hatton I owe what was, I think, the greatest, the most transporting pleasure of my life on the farm: I flew with him over Africa. There, where there are few or no roads and where you can land on the plains, flying becomes a thing of real and vital importance in your life, it opens up a world. . . .
>
> Every time that I have gone up in an aeroplane and looking down have realised that I was free of the ground, I have had the consciousness of a great new discovery. 'I see:' I have thought, 'This was the idea. And now I understand everything." (Isak Dinesen, *Out of Africa* [1937], 237–239)

Unlike Karen Blixen, who equates seeing with knowing, Tom Black, Beryl's flight instructor, equates seeing with owning:

> "When you fly . . . you get a feeling of possession that you couldn't have if you owned all of Africa. You feel that everything you see belongs to you—all the pieces are put together, and the whole is yours; not that you want it, but because, when you're alone in a plane, there's no one to share it. It's there and it's yours."[30]

Once again, Markham's ambiguous subject position as female flyer places her in a different position vis à vis both seeing (the female passenger) and owning (the male pilot). Markham as aerial elephant scouter mediates between the White Hunter, whose job it is to find the game desired and make it visible to his employer, and his employer, who shoots the game in order to own a piece of Africa by taking home as trophy the head, or in this case, just the ivory tusks, of one of its non-human inhabitants. But without the White Hunter, who employs the native tracker who follows the animal spoor (in addition to the native gun-bearer who carries the gun large enough to kill an elephant and the porters who carry the tents, the canvas bathtub, the beer, and the books) until the elephant is visible, there would be nothing to see worth owning.

Scouting by plane makes this process more efficient by reducing the time it takes to follow elephant spoor from six months to several days. Once again, the gendering of Markham's position is marked by her willingness to imagine the elephant's point of view:

> A: The thing that flew over us was no bird, since no bird would have to work so hard to stay in the air—and, anyway, we know all the birds. B: If it was no

> bird, it was very likely just another trick of those two-legged dwarfs against whom there ought to be a law. C: The two-legged dwarfs (both black and white) have, as long as our long memories go back, killed our bulls for their tusks. We know this because, in the case of the white dwarfs, at least, the tusks are the only part taken away.[31]

The initial reaction of a herd of elephants to the sound of her plane is to take cover, with one or two of the bulls preparing for attack, a response they nevertheless abandon after the first encounter. Thus, the very purpose of the aerial view, i.e., to see better, is defeated through the noise that sends the elephants to the bush, their heads buried in the thicket so that their tusks become invisible. Once the hunter encounters the animal on the ground, the elephant, who is nearly blind, is driven by scent. In order to see the size of the tusk one needs to get within eyesight of the elephant, at which point the hunter's life (like the pilot's when she begins to see too well) is already endangered.

Markham rejects a view of femininity that protests against "the brutality of elephant hunting" by suggesting that it is no "more brutal than ninety percent of all other human activities" and that from the animal's point of view, "there is nothing more tragic about the death of an elephant than there is about the death of a Hereford steer,"[32] except that the elephant can outwit, if not destroy, the hunter. But Markham would never shoot one herself, unlike Dinesen, who arrives an avid markswoman, an identity she eventually abandons.

Instead, Markham evokes an even rarer sight, a white woman and a plane, "the Lady from the Skies," and describes what it is that she sees from a point of view held by no other member of her sex, yet not by means of identification with her sex. On the one hand, the elephant is hardly conspicuous, since from the air it blends in almost completely with its surroundings, and is thus difficult to see. On the other hand, when it is seen, it seems inauthentic, in that in contrast to the "tidy and svelte stainless steel" of the plane, signifier of the modern age, it looks like a prehistoric monster: "Even in Africa, the elephant is as anomalous as the Cro-Magnon Man might be shooting a round of golf at Saint Andrews in Scotland."[33] Rather than seeing better, one sees less well:

> A herd of elephant, as seen from a plane, has a quality of an hallucination. The proportions are wrong—they are like those of a child's drawing of a field mouse in which the whole landscape, complete with barns and windmills, is dwarfed beneath the whiskers of the mighty rodent who looks both able and willing to devour everything, including the thumb-tack that holds the work against the schoolroom wall.[34]

Thus, rather than making the point of view more scientific, an aerial view makes it more like the drawing by a child who has not yet learned perspective. Making the aerial view visible to the reader involves analogies to European sights, a child's schoolroom drawing, or a golf course in Scotland. And, once again, the contrast between the modernity of the airplane and the prehistoric quality of the mammoth creates a place that can't really be seen, only imagined: Africa as "both Mecca and mirage," "the last vestige of a dead world or the cradle of a shiny new one,"[35] what Anne McClintock in *Imperial Leather* calls the "anachronistic space" of the colonial journey, "figured as a journey forward in space but backward in time."[36]

While it is possible for Markham to imagine and adopt the animal's point of view, it is nevertheless not possible to imagine the point of view of the laborer, the African tribesmen forced into a wage economy as porters, trackers, and gun-bearers, in exchange for the money and clothes they had no use for, as a way of counteracting the idleness that Europeans found so intolerable: "The safari represents a great advantage to the porter; who in his turn alone makes the safari possible."[37] The inscription of the African into a visual economy takes the form of a refusal to look. When Makula, a respected tracker, is given a ride in Markham's plane, "[h]e waited until the plane moved and then he snatched from somewhere about his waist a thin blanket and bound his head with it, around and around, until he was blind as night and shapeless as fear. And then I took off."[38] When they land and he is asked about his first flight, his response is: "I have done many things—and so this was no great thing to me. To a Kikuyu, or a Wandorobo, or Kavirondo, it might be a great thing to fly through the air. But I have seen much of the world."[39] When he begins to list exactly what he saw, his audience replies that those places couldn't possibly have been visible to him, since a) he didn't fly over them and b) he was blindfolded. To have seen is the same as to remember, while to be blinded is not the same as having nothing to see. When asked, by another African, "Can men see, then, through darkness?," he answers: "Not *all* men, Farah. Who could expect so much of God?"[40]

Markham begins her memoir by saying: "I was my own employer, my own pilot, and as often as not my own ground engineer as well,"[41] thus the equivalent in the air of the self-sufficient settler of the Highlands. By the time she is airborne over the Atlantic, at the very end of the memoir, she will fly blind (which is not the same as flying blind-folded), for 19 hours out of the 21 hours 25 minutes and thus have nothing to see, in sharp contrast to what she sees over East Africa. The self-sufficiency of the settler in the wilderness will be rewritten as the solitariness of the solo flier, where immobility, in spite of speed, leads to an encounter with the self:

> Being alone in an aeroplane for even so short a time as a night and a day, irrevocably alone, with nothing to observe but your instruments and your own hands in semi-darkness, nothing to contemplate but the size of your small courage, nothing to wonder about but the beliefs, the faces, and the hopes rooted in your mind—such an experience can be as startling as the first awareness of a stranger walking by your side at night. You are the stranger.[42]

The stranger remains ambiguously gendered, vacillating between the (masculine) stranger who appears at the side of a woman, a menacing presence, or at the side of another man, in the form of an invitation. In either case, to be that stranger means to be gender neutral, or masculine.

Sidonie Smith in "The Other Woman and the Racial Politics of Gender: Isak Dinesen and Beryl Markham in Kenya" would position Markham as imperial subject between the privileged status offered by her race and the marginal position imposed by her gender:

> Life in colonial Kenya offered her the freedom to cross-dress as a young boy and consequently to assume the identity of the boy-child. As a result she could take from native Africans, all men, the education they could provide; and she used the power of that education to claim the spoils of male adventure and the pleasures of male bonding at the exclusion of identification with both white and native women.[43]

Laura Doan, in contrast, in "Passing Fashions: Reading Female Masculinities in the 1920s," offers a language for a historicized female masculinity performed by straight and Sapphic women alike:

> The pervasive phenomenon of masculine fashion for women, with its concomitant openness and fluidity, allowed some women, primarily of the upper middle and upper classes, to exploit the ambiguity that tolerated, even encouraged, the crossing over of fixed labels and assigning categories, such as female boy, women of fashion in the masculine mode, lesbian boy, mannnish lesbian, and female cross-dresser.[44]

Doane argues that before the boyish female, who wore boyish clothes and rivaled effeminate men, became the mannish lesbian via the Radclyffe Hall trial in 1928, no one knew for sure what her sexual proclivities were. In addition, within the colonial context, the boy-child is also the subject position of the unmarried man, inscribed neither in heteronormativity by choosing a native woman, nor in homosexuality by choosing another man. If Markham did embrace the "spoils of male adventure and the pleasures of male bonding," these involved neither another woman, nor could she do so as a man. Instead the tomboy who never grows up is figured as *femme fatale,* the object of every man's desire, including male homoerotic desire, "a bad garçonne," whose own desires are too fluid and too fleeting to be anything other than queer.

As aerial elephant scouter, Markham was able to participate in the safari that was closed to her as White Hunter because of gender and closed to her as traveling big-game hunter because of class. As tracker in the air, she was positioned between the African tracker on foot and the white male scout who made sure the employer hit his target and bagged the game for which he had paid. While the lover of virtually every man she mentions in her memoir, she nevertheless chose not to represent herself as royal paramour or as hunter's mistress, thereby producing a persona outside the romance plot. She worked hard at making a living, both as horse trainer and as flier, since unlike other "literary ladies," she permanently settled in the colony. As imperial subject, she was expected to keep up the lifestyle of those of her race, even as the royal family's annuity by no means enabled her to do so. Her cross-gender identification makes her the exceptional woman attractive to liberal feminism, while her lack of sisterhood makes her the impossible subject of feminist discourse.

If nonproductive work positions the American aviatrix as dandy, then the female flier as boy-child of Africa becomes the tomboy. The sexual promiscuity of the *femme fatale* serves not to detract from the category of the tomboy, but to queer it further, by making it reverberate with both the anonymous sexual encounters of the queer man and his infatuation with the diva.

x. "Denys Finch-Hatton and I went with Mr. Bulpett for a picnic to the top of the Ngong Hills on his seventy-seventh birthday. As we sat up there we came to discuss the question of whether, if we were offered a pair of real wings, which could not be laid off, we would accept or decline the offer.

Old Mr. Bulpett sat and looked out over the tremendous big country below us, the green land of Ngong, and the Rift Valley to the West, as if ready to fly off over it at any moment. 'I would accept,' he said, 'I would certainly accept. There is nothing I should like better.' After a little time of thought he added: 'I suppose that I should think it over, though, if I were a lady.'" (Isak Dinesen, *Out of Africa* [1937], 211)

xi. "It was those very inventions that to us appeared so obvious and simple, like lamps and matches and wheels, and putting water into pipes, that struck these people with the force of wonder and amazement. Later, when Europeans displayed the inventions in which they themselves took so much pride, like aeroplanes and radios, they were often disappointed at the Africans' attitude of indifferent acceptance. But if you had lived for many centuries without control over the elements, quite at their mercy, it would be the realization that fire and water, your daily companions, could be mastered, that would come as a revelation to you, not the ingenuity of some more refined device for enabling you to do something you had never thought of doing, like travelling through the air." (Elspeth Huxley, *The Flames Tree of Thika* [1959], 29)

The Auto/biographer

"We were at a party at Edith Sitwell's last night, where a good deal of misery was endured. Jews swarmed. It was in honour of Miss Gertrude Stein who was throned on a broken settee (all Ediths furniture is derelict, to make up for which she is stuck about with jewels like a drowned mermaiden.) This resolute old lady inflicted great damage on all the youth. According to Dadie, she contradicts all you say; insists that she is not only the most intelligible, but also the most popular of living writers; and in particular despises all of English birth. Leonard, being a Jew himself, got on very well with her."

—Virginia Woolf, "Letter to Vanessa Bell," 2 June 1926

"Roger Fry, who had visited the rue de Fleurus, asked me to spend a day with him in the country. He was a Quaker and a descendent of chocolate manufacturers and had inherited considerable wealth. He could afford to buy pictures and establish an art center in London. He had discovered Picasso for himself.

It was Roger Fry who had brought Clive Bell and Mrs. Bell to see Gertrude in Paris. Mrs. Bell was the very plain sister of the very beautiful Virginia Woolf. They were daughters of Sir Leslie Stephen. The two sisters, impersonating Indian princesses, had once been received by an admiral on a man-of-war and cannon had been fired in their honour. A typical English prank."

—Alice B. Toklas, What is Remembered *(1961)*

Vita Sackville-West photographed in London Studio as Sir Peter Lely (1618–80), portrait painter. Public domain.

Orlando as "Imaginary Portrait"

i. "The description of the lover's discourse has been replaced by its simulation, and to that discourse has been restored its fundamental person, the *I,* in order to stage an utterance, not an analysis. What is proposed, then, is a portrait—but not a psychological portrait; instead, a structural one which offers the reader a discursive site: the site of someone speaking within himself, *amorously,* confronting the other (the loved object), who does not speak." (Roland Barthes, *A Lover's Discourse,* 3)

ii. "The Flying Princess, I forget her name, has been drowned in her purple leather breeches. I suppose so at least. Their petrol gave out about midnight on Thursday, when the aeroplane must have come gently down upon the long slow Atlantic waves. I suppose they burnt a light which showed streaky on the water for a time. There they rested a moment or two. The pilots, I think, looked back at the broad cheeked desperate eyed vulgar princess in her purple breeches & I suppose made some desperate dry statement—how the game was up: sorry; fortune against them; & she just glared; & then a wave broke over the wing; & the machine tipped. And she said something theatrical I daresay; nobody was sincere; all acted a part; nobody shrieked; Luck against us—something of that kind, they said & then So long, & first one man was washed off & went under & then a great wave came & the Princess threw up her arms & went down; & the third man sat saved for a second looking at the rolling waves, so patient so implacable & the moon gravely regarding; & then with a dry snorting sound he too was tumbled off & rolled over, & the aeroplane rocked & rolled—miles from anywhere, off Newfoundland, while I slept at Rodmell, & Leonard was dining with the Craniums in London." (Virginia Woolf, *Diary,* Sunday, 4 September 1927)

"Having solidified the visions of the flying Princess into words, I have, strangely enough, laid a phantom which has been very prominent before my eyes. Why should this be? Some dissatisfaction seems laid to rest. So, gradually, the urgency of the memory dies out too, as in one's own life; in about 48 or 96 hours all trace of the death of the Princess in her purple breeches is smoothed over." (Woolf, *Diary,* Monday, 5 September 1927)

Princess Löwenstein-Wertheim flew as a passenger on the first attempted westbound transatlantic flight (accomplished by a German crew in April 1928 and by Beryl Markham as the first woman in 1936) that took off from Salisbury for Ottawa in a Fokker monoplane, sighted the same evening 800 miles off the coast of Ireland, and then never again. Woolf imagines the final scene of an unsuccessful transatlantic flight as a theatrical one, in which each person plays a part—complete with costume—but no one hears the words. Woolf's role is that of author, who because she isn't there, imagines a sequence of events. Because there are no witnesses, she invents what people say. By putting into words the end of someone else's life, she lays to rest a phantom, a public rather than a private memory. For the author, it is not the life but the death of the aviator, that can only be made to "die out" by making it up as a scene. The problem is not that the airplane crash is a new form of death where the body leaves no trace, but that even when the body has disappeared, the mind cannot be laid to rest. What is shocking is not that it happens, but that while it happens one is asleep or dining with friends.

> iii. "I have just had the most awful shock: Virginia has killed herself. (Vita Sackville-West, "Letter to Harold Nicholson," 31 March 1941)
>
> "They have been dragging the river but are now giving up the search. As the river is tidal, she has probably been carried out to sea. I hope so. I hope they will never find her.
>
> She could swim; I know this because of a story she once told me about herself and Rupert Brooke at Cambridge, when they were both very young, and he took off all his clothes and plunged naked into a moonlit pool, and she thought she must do likewise, so did although very shy, and they swam about together. But it appears that when she went out to drown herself she was wearing big gun boots (which she seldom did because she hated them) and if those had filled with water they would have dragged her down. Also she may have weighted her pockets with stones. The river is banked with stones.
>
> The only thing that puzzles them is that they never found her hat floating. But Vanessa thinks it had an elastic to keep it on, so went down with her." (Vita Sackville-West, "Letter to Harold Nicholson," 8 April 1941)

Woolf walks into the River Ouse as fighter planes are flying over Rodmell on the eve of World War II. Although she never flew, as Hermione Lee, her most recent biographer, states: "She could swim, but she allowed herself to be drowned."[1] The scene that Vita remembers Virginia describing is one with Rupert Brooke—a poet known for his beauty—who died at 28, a casualty of World War I. The moonlit pool sets the stage for a classic male homoerotic scene and the site of an adolescent romance that was "more literary than libidinous,"[2] between a young woman and a gay man, both aspiring writers. The contrast between the naked body and the big gun boots exemplifies the difference between the adolescent boy and a militarized masculinity. The hat with an elastic evokes the middle-aged woman who, in her 40s, liked "to be slightly fallen in love with by younger men (best of all by witty, talented, attractive, and gossipy homosexual men)."[3] The ideal of masculine beauty Woolf desired physically was to be found only in another woman, the boyish, sometimes crossed-dressed, aristocratic Vita Sackville-West. What is shocking to Vita—married but a known Sapphist—is that she is faced with the sudden and premature closure to her most important friendship.

To begin with Virginia Woolf's death is to remember not only that she took her own life, but that the inability to narrate one's death provides the primary distinction between autobiography and biography as literary genres. While death supplies closure for the life of a biographical subject, an autobiographical life has so far managed to elude death. But inasmuch as autobiographical writing is the result of introspection, and thus associated with forms of morbidity (eventually we begin to contemplate our own death), and inasmuch as the completed vision of a life would itself be to aim for death (the book comes to an end even if the life continues), the difference between life and death has less to do with the auto/biographical subject than with changing conceptions of life-writing during the modernist period.

Virginia Woolf never flew, but the airplane appears as a recurring motif in several of her novels, including *Orlando.*[4] Between the plane that disappears (bringing death to the Princess in purple breeches) and the one that never leaves the ground (in Woolf's essay "Flying over London" the plane never takes off due to mechanical failure) is the plane that lands. For Lytton Strachey, this means the appearance of the pilot as a potential "divine Icarus," and the ensuing disappointment at a missed sexual adventure.[5] For Vita Sackville-West and Violet Trefusis, it means the arrival in 1920 of their husbands in France who, following their escapade, have come to restore them to their respective marriages. For Orlando, it means the reappearance of Shel, her husband, the ship-captain-turned pilot, who descends in an airplane while Orlando cries out for the wild goose, an image of lesbian elopement.[6]

Woolf rewrites Orlando, a Renaissance fiction—both Ariosto's and Shakespeare's—as the story of a character who lives through 300 years of British literary history—1586–1928—during which time he changes from a man into a woman. It is her only novel not to figure a death. As a woman, Orlando marries Marmaduke Bonthrop Shelmerdine, represented in *Orlando* by the detail from an anonymous portrait by an anonymous painter in Woolf's possession of an unidentified young man of the 1820s. The young man Orlando marries is the young man Orlando is when the novel opens. That these two figures are both masculine points not just to the exclusion of women from history, particularly literary history, but to Vita Sackville-West and Harold Nicholson's marriage as the marriage between a homosexual and a Sapphist, a Sapphist who renamed herself "Julien" in her relationship with Violet.

Orlando, subtitled "a biography," is the "imaginary portrait" of Vita, but it is also a fictional auto/biography in which Virginia plays the role of biographer: "In fact I sometimes think only autobiography is literature—novels are what we peel off, and come at last to the core, which is only you and me."[7] As biographer, Woolf fails to appear as a character in the reenactment of Vita's life, even as she constructs and thereby controls the text with which, in real life, Vita will fall in love. The biographer nevertheless appears as a character in the text in the form of a self-reflexive narrator. The biographer is the ungendered subject in search of a bi-gendered character as biographical subject. The fictional biographer poses this problem as a series of questions about writing: how to write the biography of someone who has lived so long that historical evidence becomes unreliable; how to write about someone who changes sexes when one knows that to be impossible; how to write the biography of someone who is not yet dead; and most importantly, how to write about same-sex desire, especially if the person is still living.

> iv. "It might be a way of writing the memoirs of one's own times during peoples lifetimes." (Virginia Woolf, *Diary,* 20 September 1927)
>
> v. "I rather like the idea of these Biographies of living people." (Virginia Woolf, *Diary,* 31 May 1928)

Woolf invents the term for a modernist form of life-writing, what she calls the "new biography," to describe the autobiographical nature of the biographies Harold Nicholson wrote of *Some People* (1927) and the psychosexual biographies Lytton Strachey wrote of *Eminent Victorians* (1918). Woolf's father, Leslie Stephen, the editor of the *Dictionary of National Biography,* had already sought to transform biographical writing by insisting on briefer entries and less pronounced eulogy, seeking to replace history as the biographies of great men with the many lesser-known men who constitute history.[8] But less eulogy and more facts come at the expense of character analysis, most successfully achieved by those who have known the biographical subject, not family members invested in historical reputation, but friends interested in the peculiarities of personality. To know the person means not having to wait until they die in order to tell their story. Thus the biographical begins to blur with the autobiographical as biographies of the living fail to distinguish between biographer and biographical subject (both are still living) as opposed to autobiographer and autobiographical subject (they share the same name).

In her review of *Some People* in an essay entitled "The New Biography" (1927), Woolf writes:

> Indeed, by the end of the book we realize that the figure which has been most completely and most subtly displayed is that of the author. Each of the supposed subjects holds up in his or her small bright diminishing mirror a different reflection of Harold Nicholson. And though the figure thus revealed is not noble or impressive or shown in a very heroic attitude, it is for these very reasons extremely like a real human being. It is thus, he would seem to say, in the mirrors of our friends, that we chiefly live.[9]

Inasmuch as "some people" refers to a random selection of nameless biographical subjects, these subjects, of little historical interest, refract in multiple ways the author to whom they are of interest as friends. Yet the author is less the producer of other people's biographies, than himself produced as autobiographical subject. The biographer expresses his interiority in the "mirrors" of others, performing an intimacy otherwise attainable only through representation in the first person. This "remaining aloof, enigmatic, and yet visible" is characteristic, in the modernist period, of what Maurizia Boscaglia and Enda Duffy in "Joyce's Face" identify as the celebrity photograph.[10]

Strachey, in *Eminent Victorians,* writes not about people he knows, but people he has read about, thereby eliminating the possibility of libel. But, if the biographical subject belongs to a different age, what then does it mean to know someone? What would it mean to write the biography not of the representative of an age, but of the age itself? Once again, the biographer is "signified without signifying in the first person,"[11] making transparent his own desires by focusing on the desires a previous historical age refuses to reveal. Historical detail, rather than uncovering the truth, can cover up the questions one has not yet learned to ask. To arrive at what might be hidden beneath the surface, Strachey as "new biographer," proposes the following method:

> He will attack his subject in unexpected places; he will fall upon the flank, or the rear; he will shoot a sudden, revealing searchlight into obscure recesses, hitherto undivined. He will row out over that great ocean of material, and lower down into it, here and there, a little bucket, which will bring up to the light of day characteristic specimen, for those far depths, to be examined with a careful curiosity.[12]

The initial metaphors are taken from the Great War, a war fought mostly in the trenches of "no man's land," in which Strachey as conscientious objector fights against the sexual hypocrisy of the Victorians rather than against German militarism. Published in 1919, it ushers England into the modern period by alluding to both asexual and same-sex intimacies that governed the public lives of a Victorian elite. "The great ocean" is neither like the moonlit pool nor like the Atlantic as graveyard, but like the stream into which Woolf drops her line at the beginning of *A Room of One's Own,* where a slight tug in the form of a fish means "the sudden conglomeration of an idea."[13] While Strachey at least knows there are places where no one has dared to look, he still imagines there is truth to be found, and dares not look too close to home.

In an essay on biography written over a decade later, "The Art of Biography," which takes as one of its examples Strachey's *Elizabeth and Essex* (1928), Woolf suggests that new forms of knowledge acquired by looking into "obscure recesses" might require new ways of storytelling:

> The accent on sex has changed within living memory. This leads to the destruction of a great deal of dead matter still obscuring the true features of the human face. Many of the old chapter headings—life at college, marriage, career—are shown to be very arbitrary and artificial distinctions. The real current of the hero's existence took, very likely, a different course.[14]

Faces are to be scrutinized for what they fail to reveal not because they are dead, but in order to remove "a great deal of dead matter." The bucket in the ocean that will bring up "characteristic specimen"—a surface-depth model of the subject—has now become the "current taking a different course"—the subject matter of biographical narrative. The truth about character, whether multiply refracted in the surface of a mirror or dredged up from the depths of the ocean, can only make a difference if not confined by conventional scripts. Sex, for Woolf, means both gender and sexuality, and thus refers equally to women denied entrance to the university and to both men and women who never marry. Biography, like a psychosexual history, is as invested in eliding as in laying-bare its subject. By rewriting the story an age has refused to tell about itself, the biographer both conceals and reveals his own.

> vi. "The age—it was that of Marlowe and Spenser, of the early Shakespeare and the Francis Bacon of the Essays—needs no description: everybody knows its outward appearances and the literary expressions of its heart. More valuable than descriptions, but what perhaps is unattainable, would be some means by which the modern mind might reach to an imaginative comprehension of those beings of three centuries ago—might move with ease

among their familiar essential feelings—might touch, or dream that it touches (for such dreams are the stuff of history) the very 'pulse of the machine.' But the path seems closed to us. By what art are we to worm our way into those strange spirits, those even stranger bodies? . . .

It is, above all, the contradictions of the age that baffle our imagination and perplex our intelligence. . . . How is it possible to give a coherent account of their subtlety and their *naiveté,* their delicacy and their brutality, their piety and their lust? Wherever we look, it is the same. . . . the flaunting man of fashion, whose codpiece proclaimed an astonishing virility, was he not also, with his flowing hair and his jewelled ears, effeminate?" (Strachey, *Elizabeth and Essex* [1928] 8–9)

vii. "The age was the Elizabethan; their morals were not ours; nor their poets; nor their climate; nor their vegetables even. Everything was different. The weather itself, the heat and cold of summer and winter, was, we may believe, of another temper altogether. The brilliant amorous day was divided as sheerly from the night as land from water. . . . Of our crepuscular half-lights and lingering twilights they knew nothing. . . . Translating this to the spiritual regions as their wont is, the poets sang beautifully how roses fade and petals fall. The moment is brief they sang; the moment is over; one long night is then to be slept by all. As for using the artifices of the greenhouse or conservatory to prolong or preserve these fresh pinks and roses, that was not their way. The withered intricacies and ambiguities of our more gradual and doubtful age were unknown to them. Violence was all." (Woolf, *Orlando* [1928], 26–7)

Inasmuch as for the moderns the biographical subject is no longer the representative of an age, the age itself becomes personified as biographical subject. If the Victorian age represents the one about which there is too much to know (the biographical subject as familial ancestor), the Renaissance is the age about which one can never know enough (like the friend who reflects the autobiographical subject back to him or herself). For Aesthetes such as Walter Pater and Oscar Wilde, the Renaissance represents the site of an aesthetic that both veils and reveals a Greek eroticism unavailable to the Christian moralism of their late Victorian contemporaries. Literary sources for a renewed understanding of same-sex relations as foundational to literary production range from Ficino's translation of Plato's *Symposium* to Shakespeare's sonnet sequence to the cross-dressed boy-actor of the Elizabethan stage. For Pater, the Renaissance represents "the love of the things of the intellect and the imagination for their own sake."[15] Aesthetic understanding relies on intimate knowledge of another person, putting into question the self-regulation of personality demanded by Victorian norms of manhood. For Wilde, it "sought to elevate friendship to the high dignity of the antique ideal, to make it a vital fact in the new culture, and a mode of self-conscious intellectual development,"[16] enabling a view of culture as a centuries-long tradition of male same-sex friendship.

While Pater focuses on the Italian and French Renaissance (as a way to achieve closer proximity with their Hellenic sources), and Wilde focuses on Shakespeare, both resort to the literary genre of the "imaginary portrait," a term coined by Pater that refers to fictional narratives of historical figures. The short prose pieces in Pater's *The Renaissance* (1873) and *Imaginary Portraits* (1887) take the form of non-narrative, non-dramatic and non-psychological portrayals of an artist: celibate, focused on the desire for companionship, and fascinated by death. In other words, "imaginary" because queer. As described by Pater: "Imaginary—and portraits: they present not an action, a story; but a character, [a] personality, revealed especially in outward detail."[17] Knowledge itself is predicated on the model of knowing a person, thus the generic undecidability of the portrait and the erotic appeal of the "outward detail" that offers a way to circumvent self-exposure. For Wilde, in "The Portrait of Mr. W. H." (1889), the ostensible addressee of Shakespeare's sonnets, the story begins with a forged portrait of W. H. and ends with the deaths of two friends who have martyred themselves to a literary theory, proving that W. H. is Willie Hughes, a boy-actor in Shakespeare's company. Shakespeare is the historical figure; W. H. the fictional character; and the "outward detail" is the sonnets whose sequence now only exists in service to historical knowledge. But Wilde transforms the "outward detail" into a sexual secret that has significance not just for the relationship between two men, actor and dramatist, but for the friendship between two men related, in life and death, through reading.

The figure of the boy-actor, who in the absence of women played women's parts on the Elizabethan stage, points not just to the secret of male homoerotic desire, but to the "contradictions of the age" as described by Strachey. For Strachey, it is no longer possible to give a coherent account of the Renaissance by tracing its Hellenic origins or solving its sexual secrets. It is not the age that has changed, but the "modern mind" that has intervened, unable to reach "imaginative comprehension" of a moment seemingly so unlike its own and yet, in its contradictoriness, seemingly so like itself. Instead of returning to old sources—"the path seems closed to us"—the modern mind sees itself reaching an impasse. Rather than alluding to an oblique desire, like Pater, or constructing a theoretical fiction, like Wilde, Strachey seeks to "worm his way" into not only the "spirits" but also the bodies of the Renaissance, bodies that wear codpieces as well as jewels in their ears. Homoerotic desire is not invoked by means of what can be suggested through aesthetic enjoyment of Hellenic forms, nor by what can be imagined about the love interest of England's most renowned writer, but is embodied by the effeminate man.

Strachey both distances himself from this figure by placing it in the distant past and imagines himself in relation to it as a form of sodomitic union. The biographer, for the first time, reveals his desire for the biographical subject by means of identification.

While Essex in many ways resembles Orlando, Strachey is less interested in his effeminacy than in the queerness of the asexual relationship between a virgin queen and a young earl. His biography explores the affective affinities between a queen of 53 and an earl not yet 20, between a woman whose father had her mother beheaded when she was three and who permanently postponed marriage, and a young man who is eventually beheaded by the queen for thinking that the sex of the sovereign is both an impediment to his political ambitions and one that can be disregarded. Strachey describes the queen in terms of an actor, particularly a boy-actor, "every part of her was permeated by the bewildering discordances of the real and the apparent,"[18] so that the "great Queen" of "posterity's imagination" "no more resembles the Queen of fact than the clothed Elizabeth, the naked one. But, after all, posterity is privileged. Let us draw nearer; we shall do no wrong now to that Majesty, if we look below the robes."[19]

Strachey assumes that the truth lies with the body—in Elizabeth's case a repulsion to sexual intercourse either as physical malformation or hysterical symptom—based on the model of the cross-dressed actor. Woolf refuses this truth for Orlando at the moment of his sex change: "He stood upright in complete nakedness before us, and while the trumpets pealed Truth! Truth! Truth! we have no choice left but confess—he was a woman."[20] In the first case, the female body is hidden by royal robes, while in the second, clothes play a primary role in regendering Orlando as a woman. On the one hand, Elizabeth turns to a model of Hercules, the strongest man on earth, and his uncontrollable grief at the death of his armor-bearer, Hylas: "She had read of Hercules and Hylas, and she might have fancied herself, in some half-conscious day-dream, possessed of something of that pagan masculinity. Hylas was a page—he stood before her . . . ,"[21] thereby exposing the insufficiency of Hellenic same-sex models for the female monarch. On the other hand, Orlando remains unperturbed by the sight of the loss of his manhood, i.e., his castration, suggesting that the body has little to do with fixing desire and even less with defining identity. The non-sexual relationship between a man and a woman and a man turning into a woman become the queer subjects of the "imaginary portraits" of the Bloomsberries.

Woolf positions herself in relationship to a male homosocial tradition by satirizing both the idealization of the Renaissance by the Aesthetes and the pessimism of Strachey, her fellow modern, by pronouncing, "everything was different." The way to approach another age is not to recover it or lament its irrecoverability, but to use it as a way of understanding the present. Rather than assume one can know another age, another age can at most point out the absurdities of one's own. For Woolf, the Renaissance is not the age of "artifices," "intricacies and ambiguities," but rather the age of violence. It is the age that both produced Orlando, first seen slicing at the head of a Moor, and in *A Room of One's Own,* murdered Judith Shakespeare. Like her brother, Judith runs away to London to appear at the stage door only to find herself impregnated by the actor-manager Nick Greene, who reappears in *Orlando* as literary critic. Judith subsequently kills herself and lies buried in an unmarked grave at the crossroads outside the Elephant and Castle.

Unlike Wilde, who is interested in Shakespeare's same-sex lover and Strachey, who focuses on the queerness of Elizabeth as female monarch, Woolf's "imaginary portrait" of Shakespeare's sister has no basis in historical fact. It is the biography of a woman who is already dead, even before she commits suicide, because she never existed. Woolf does not uncover a sexual secret or explain an asexual queerness, but imagines the female artist whose aesthetic and erotic desires must not be kept silent, but extinguished. The aesthetic does not veil the erotic; rather, the female body exposes the contradiction between them. Where the Renaissance had life and death, the moderns have doubt. Essex, the effeminate man, becomes Orlando, a man who wakes up one day to find himself a woman. W. H., the cross-dressed boy-actor, becomes Orlando, the transsexual. Doubt no longer pertains to sexual desires in their relationship to the sexual ambiguity of the body, but to the ambiguous relationship between the biographer and her biographical subject.

> viii. "It struck me, vaguely, that I might write a Defoe narrative for fun. Suddenly between twelve & one I conceived a whole fantasy to be called 'The Jessamy Brides'—why, I wonder? I have rayed around it several scenes. Two women, poor, solitary at the top of a house. One can see anything (for this is all fantasy) the Tower Bridge, clouds, aeroplanes. Also old men listening in the room over the way. Everything is to be tumbled in pall mall. It is to be written as I write letters at the top of my speed: on the ladies of Llangollen; on Mrs. Fladgate; on people passing. No attempt is to be made to realise the character. Sapphism is to be suggested. Satire is to be the main note—satire and wildness. The ladies are to have Constantinople in view. Dreams of golden domes. My own lyric vein is to be satirised. Everything mocked. And it is to end with three dots . . . so." (Virginia Woolf, *Diary,* 14 March 1927)

By naming the imagined narrative that would eventually become *Orlando,* "The Jessamy Brides," Woolf invokes an eighteenth-century usage of Jessamy as "a man who scents himself with perfume or who wears a sprig of

Jessamine in his buttonhole(?); a dandy, a fop" (Oxford English Dictionary).[22] Sapphism is suggested not only by the marriage between two effeminate men, but by invoking the Ladies of Llangollen who eloped in the eighteenth century from Ireland to Wales, where they shared the same roof for 30 years and were visited by European literary luminaries, including William Wordsworth. The two same-sex couples suggest an erotic fantasy, what Woolf called a "holiday book," that became a bestseller, in part because she chose to parody her own lyrical style. "Written as I write letters," Woolf began *Orlando* shortly after her sexual involvement with Vita.[23] While the fantasy begins with two same-sex couples in the eighteenth century, Virginia and Vita, themselves each part of a married couple in the twentieth, have very different views about the couple they might constitute together.

If Defoe, as the eighteenth-century novelist who usurps the first person narrative that until then had been the prerogative of non-fiction writing, begins the list of mock-acknowledgements of dead authors who appear at the beginning of *Orlando,* Pater brings that list to an end. Perry Meisel, in *The Absent Father: Virginia Woolf and Walter Pater,* claims that "*Orlando* is the consummate Paterien portrait,"[24] by making a Bloomian argument that the importance of Pater's influence lies in the fact that Woolf wrote not a single essay on him. Rather than acknowledge his influence and thus her historical belatedness, she sought, as a modern, to repress it. But rather than reading the relationship between a woman author and her male literary precursor as an oedipal one, implicated in the sexual politics of a daughter's relationship to her biological father, a literary father, and her husband as father substitute, one might instead read it as the intertextual relationship between a woman and a man who share a relationship, although not the same relationship, to queerness. On the one hand, Woolf uses Pater's text to negotiate between a celibate masculinity that can no longer escape the scandalous insinuations and punitive consequences of homosexual desire, and the sexually abusive forms of hetero-masculinity Woolf encounters with her half-brother George Duckworth. On the other hand, she uses Pater's life as a way to regender the male homoerotic tradition of the "imaginary portrait."

In a scene that appears as memory in an essay entitled "Old Bloomsbury," Woolf writes: "It was long past midnight that I got into bed and sat reading a page or two of *Marius the Epicurean*. There would be a tap at the door; the light would be turned out and George would fling himself on my bed, cuddling and kissing and otherwise embracing me in order, as he told Dr Savage later, to comfort me for the fatal illness of my father—who was dying three or four storeys lower down of cancer."[25] At a displaced deathbed scene (reminiscent of Victorian biography) that involves the loss of the father, Woolf turns to an alternative version of Victorian masculinity, the homosexual Aesthete in the form of Pater's longest "imaginary portrait," *Marius the Epicurean.* Neither the father nor the literary precursor is able to protect her against the sexual molestations of the half-brother who seeks to initiate her into Society via a quasi-incestuous form of heteronormativity. Once the familial father has died, he will be replaced by a representative of the medical profession, Dr. Savage, the proponent of the rest cure, prohibiting intellectual engagement during Woolf's bouts with mental illness. Unlike Judith Shakespeare, who, following in her brother's footsteps, never writes at all, Woolf writes herself into a male homoerotic tradition by writing about the death of the female artist at the hands of hetero-masculinity and rewriting the Hellenic student-teacher relationship as one between two women.

"Slater's Pins Have No Points," which Woolf mentions in a letter to Vita as the "little Sapphist story" (13 October 1927) she writes for the Americans while working on *Orlando,* can be read as a displaced *roman à clef* about Pater's sister, Clara. Clara Pater was instrumental in founding Oxford's Somerville College for Women, serving as both vice-principal and its first classics tutor, and began tutoring Virginia Stephen in Greek and Latin in 1898. Vanessa, Virginia, and Thoby, at the time, were three unmarried siblings sharing a household like Pater and his two sisters, Clara and Hester. While not excluded from the university, as women were, Pater was nevertheless prevented from receiving promotions within it due to alleged sexual contacts with students. After the publication in 1873 of *The Renaissance* scandalized Oxford because of its alleged immoralism, Pater was refused nomination for a proctorship that went to John Wordsworth, a former pupil. When, in 1885, he was passed up again as the successor to Ruskin's chair as Slade Professor of Fine Arts, he moved with his sisters to London.

In "Slater's Pins Have No Points," Woolf has rewritten the alleged accusation against Pater by killing off the brother in order to focus on one of his sisters, Miss Cray, a piano teacher, from the perspective of her favorite pupil, Fanny Wilt. Fanny Wilt "wanted to break the spell that had fallen on the house; to break the pane of glass which separated them from other people."[26] She imagines her teacher living in a "cool glassy world of Bach fugues" and tries to make sense of pieces of gossip about the brother who died, about whom she has "a feeling": "Needless to say, she had never spoken about it to anybody. Probably she scarcely knew what she meant by it. But whenever she spoke of Julius, or heard him mentioned, that was the first thing that came to mind; and it was a seductive thought; there was something odd about Julius Craye."[27] Fanny is obsessed by the fact that none of the Crayes have married. Wondering why, she makes up scenes for Julia who, as the sister of Julius, inherits his queerness.

When the pin attaching a rose to Fanny's dress falls to the ground, Miss Craye says to her pupil, "Slater's pins have no points, don't you find?" This leaves Fanny not caring about pins, but thinking about her teacher holding the rose. Seeing her not as a poor, lonely spinster (as her biographer surely would have), she instead becomes witness to a moment of ecstasy: "Julia blazed. Julia kindled. Out of the night she burnt like a dead white star. Julia opened her arms. Julia kissed her on the lips. Julia possessed it. 'Slater's pins have no points,' Miss Craye said, laughing queerly and relaxing her arms, as Fanny Wilmot pinned the flower to her breast with trembling fingers."[28] Woolf leaves unclear the referent of "it," even as she clearly alludes to the much-quoted lines from the conclusion of Pater's *The Renaissance:* "To burn always with this hard, gemlike flame, to maintain this ecstasy, is success in life."[29] Is Fanny imagining this or has it really happened? Has Julia kissed another woman, i.e., her pupil? Is she remembering a previous moment, triggered by the rose against which the pins offer a screen? Is Fanny trembling because she has been kissed or because she has witnessed a queer epiphany? Sapphism is suggested not by imagining a same-sex object choice but a moment of "ecstasy," both aesthetic and erotic, shared by two women obliquely inscribed in, but ultimately written out of, recorded history.

> ix. "The society of buggers has many advantages—if you are a woman. It is simple, it is honest, it makes one feel, as I noted, in some respects at one's ease. But it has this drawback—with buggers one cannot, as nurses say, show off. Something is always suppressed, held down. Yet this showing off, which is not copulating, necessarily, nor altogether being in love, is one of the great delights, one of the chief necessities of life. Only then does all effort cease; one ceases to be honest, one ceases to be clever. One fizzes up into some absurd delightful effervescence of soda water or champagne through which one sees the world tinged with all the colours of the rainbow. It is significant of what I had come to desire that I went straight—on almost the next page of my diary indeed—from the dim and discreet rooms of James Strachey at Cambridge to dine with Lady Ottoline Morell at Bedford Square. Her rooms, I noted without drawing any inferences, seemed to me instantly full of 'lustre and illusion.'" (Virginia Woolf, *Moments of Being,* 172–3)

> x. "I hesitate to write it here, but I must; shirking the truth here would be like cheating oneself playing patience. I dressed as a boy. It was easy, because I could put a khaki bandage round my head, which in those days was so common that it attracted no attention at all. I browned my face and hands. I must have been successful, because no one looked at me at all curiously or suspiciously—never once, out of the many times I did it. My height of course was my great advantage. I looked like a rather untidy young man, a sort of undergraduate, of about nineteen. It was marvellous fun, all the more

> so because there was always the risk of being found out. . . . I had wondered about my voice, but found I could sink it sufficiently. . . . The landlady was very benevolent and I said Violet was my wife. . . . Violet used to call me Julian." (Vita Sackville-West, *Portrait of a Marriage,* 109–10)

Virginia and Vita both produced autobiographical narratives in the early 1920s not published during their lifetimes, Virginia in the form of talks addressed to the Memoir Club, a postwar reincarnation of "Old Bloomsbury," collected in *Moments of Being,* and Vita in the form of a confessional diary she locked into a Gladstone bag discovered after her death in her study at Sissinghurst by her son Nigel Nicholson, published in *Portrait of a Marriage* (1973). While Vita's text is one she sought to keep secret, Virginia's is delivered to a small group of close friends. While Virginia has learned sexual explicitness from the very buggers whose company she shirks, including Rupert Brooke and Lytton, to whom she was very briefly engaged, Vita seeks to hide the affair with Violet that at the time widely circulated as public scandal.

In each case, there is an attempt to supplement the public record by revealing the desire to play a dramatic role. As the member of a male-dominated upper-class Bloomsbury, Woolf prefers the gatherings of an aristocracy where women are positioned at the social center. Rather than be grateful for a society of men who treat her as intellectual equal, she gravitates towards venues where she can "show off," a desire neither to desire nor be desired, but a desire for self-effacement that comes only at the moment when everyone is looking. Represented as a desire that is like sex, but not sexual, the performance enables Woolf to transcend the transparency of her own sexlessness in order to refashion herself as "incandescent," like the androgynous mind she associates with Shakespeare.

While Woolf compares rooms to a stage set allowing for specific kinds of performances, Vita performs the very role—the male undergraduate—whose rooms Virginia longs to escape. Vita desires to dress as a boy not in order to disappear into "delightful effervescence," but in order to be called "Julian." Male impersonation allows her to refashion her sexual identity by passing as the other gender. As an aristocrat, she rejects the role of salonnière and seeks instead the streets and second-class hotels she inhabits with her same-sex lover. By calling Violet her "wife," she borrows her sexual role from the structure of a marriage she renounces, but manages nevertheless to rescue.

One might conclude, then, that Virginia aspires to the role of diva in another woman's literary salon and that Vita desires to be the female husband in an adulterous affair. While, in both cases, desire crosses class boundaries, it is at the same time mediated by another woman, the woman (Lady Ottoline) who enables Virginia to forget the non-sexual nature of her femininity and the woman (Violet) who enables Vita to actively desire her. In spite of their shared sex and the significant relationships they each had to members of their own sex, it is their asymmetrical relationship to masculinity that finally governs their relationship to each other. Woolf desires to join, as equal, a male literary tradition that in its modernist rereading as homoerotic, becomes available to her, but only as disembodied author. Vita actively pursues her desire for women, but does so as sexual invert, by choosing to dress as a man. Whereas Virginia feels "altogether so queer in some ways"[30] in the presence of Vita, Vita's recurring interest in her own sex makes her not queer, but "promiscuous."

> xi. "Orlando: A biography. No sooner had I done this than my body was flooded with rapture and my brain with ideas. . . . But listen; suppose Orlando turns out to be Vita; and its all about you and the lusts of your flesh and the lure of your mind (heart you have none, who go gallivanting down the lanes with Campbell) . . ." (Virginia Woolf, *Letters,* 9 October 1927)

> xii. "I have never more wanted to see you than I do now—. . . . If you've given yourself to Campbell, I'll have no more to do with you, and so it shall be written, plainly, for all the world to read in Orlando." (Woolf, *Letters,* 13 [14] October 1927)

> xiii. "Should you say, if I rang you up to ask, that you are fond of me?
> If I saw you would you kiss me? If I were in bed would you—
> I'm rather excited about Orlando tonight: have been lying by the fire and making up the last chapter." (Woolf, *Letters,* 5 December 1927)

> xiv. "Directly you had gone, a faint smell, Orlando's, led me to look under a book and there they were: but not Vita. No. And where was Vita last night, and what did she do there? And is tickling a game for ladies or for housemaids? (This might be a passage from Orlando—so now you need have no doubt that it is the wittiest and most profound book in the world: the very spit and image of you into the Bargain.)" (Woolf, *Letters,* 21 December 1927)

> xv. "By the way, do you think I know you? Intimately? A question that I shall ask myself tomorrow morning—You are driving down to Knole [in *Orlando*], and as you go, you exhibit the most profound and secret side of your character." (Woolf, *Letters,* 6 March 1928)

> xvi. "ORLANDO IS FINISHED!!!
> Did you feel a sort of tug, as if your neck was being broken on Saturday last [17 March] at 5 minutes to one? That was when he died—or rather

stopped talking, with three little dots. . . .The question now is, will my feelings for you be changed? I've lived in you all these months—coming out, what are you really like? Do you exist? Have I made you up?" (Woolf, *Letters,* 20 March? 1928)

xvii. "For Promiscuous you are, and thats all there is to be said of you. Look in the Index to Orlando—after Pippin and see what comes next—Promiscuity *passim*. . . . (Woolf, *Letters,* 25 July 1928)

xviii. "And let me have your address so that I may write long impassioned letters: because 11th Oct. [publication date of *Orlando*] sees the end of our romance." (Woolf, *Letters,* 7 August? 1928)

To read Woolf's letters to Vita as she is writing *Orlando* is to foreground the epistle as a form of autobiographical discourse that enables both being with the other and being more intensely with oneself. It involves recognizing desire through an exchange of texts, but also confining it to an exchange of texts. In this case "epistolary desire" does not lead to elopement, as it did for the Ladies of Llangollen or for Vita and Violet, but to the publication of two texts, Vita's travelogue that begins with a treatise on letter writing, *Passage to Teheran* (1926), and Virginia's fictional biography. *Orlando* is dedicated to Vita and contains portraits of her, including the photograph taken when she won the Hawthornden Prize for her poem *The Land* (1926), the model for Orlando's "Oak Tree." These are public gestures. Privately, Virginia presents Vita with a bound copy of the original manuscript, now housed at Knole, and allows Orlando to inherit Knole, which Vita was prevented from doing because of her sex. Inasmuch as Woolf reads *Knole*—Vita's history of the Sackville's—and asks her to pose cross-dressed for the photograph entitled "Orlando as Ambassador," the novel could be considered a form of collaboration. Vita is not a sister, like Vanessa; she is a writer, like Virginia; and together Virginia and Vita are Hogarth Press' bestselling authors in the 1920s.

Virginia was 43 and Vita 33 when their friendship began in 1925. Finishing *Orlando* marks the end of a sexual relationship that had already ended before the writing began, and the beginning of a relationship to a reading public that for the first time proved financially lucrative: "We have sold over 6000 copies; & sales are still amazingly brisk—150 today for instance; most days between 50 & 60; always to my surprise. Will they stop or go on? Anyhow my room is secure. For the first time since I married 1912–1928—16 years—I have been spending money."[31] Woolf begins *Orlando* before she realizes that it is Vita. She writes about Vita when she can't be with her, because she can't be with her, since Vita is traveling with her husband Harold, a diplomat, first to Teheran and then to Berlin. Writing about her is like being with her, especially when writing in bed. It is like living "in her," not knowing how she will "come out." But when Orlando "dies," what will this mean for Vita? Orlando, in spite of all the changes he/she has gone through—living for several centuries, changing sex, getting married and giving birth, becoming a published author—has not changed. Vita is still the same; she is still promiscuous. The "most profound and secret side" of her character she exhibits only while driving. The writing between friends will continue, if not the romance, even after the lover has become a character in "the wittiest and most profound book in the world," subsequently referred to by Nigel Nicholson as "the longest and most charming love letter in literature" and by Angela Carter as "a slobbering valentine to an aristocrat."

How has this writing changed the writer? Does she know Vita better? Have her feelings for Vita changed? Does Vita even exist? These are the questions one might ask of any "imaginary portrait." And yet what difference does it make that the model has been a lover and that the relationship is between women? On the one hand, there is slippage between biographical and fictional subject, introduced by the "new biography" as the possibility of telling the life stories of those still living. On the other hand, there is need for negotiation between the mannish lesbian (Vita) and the married lesbian (Vita and Virginia) as available subject positions in the modernist period. The first becomes the target of an obscenity trial—Radclyffe Hall's *Well of Loneliness*—shortly after the appearance of *Orlando,* and the second enters the written record as open secret.

The similarity in the marriages of Virginia and Vita suggests a symmetry in their relationship to sexual difference, whereby the masculine is figured by the husband, even as Harold is gay and Leonard a Jew. As Suzanne Raitt has suggested in *Vita and Virginia:*

> In the case of Woolf and Sackville-West lesbianism was not disruptive of marriage. There was no simple way in which, for them, unconventional sexual behavior was inevitably either socially or politically subversive. . . . Lesbians similarly could derive some advantage from marriage (financial and emotional security, respectability, status), if they were able to negotiate an acceptable version of it, as Woolf and Sackville-West did. . . . For Woolf and Sackville-West lesbian possibility was one of the many things marriage was designed to allow.[32]

But this formulation elides the difference in their relationship to female masculinity. Given Vita's cross-dressing, it becomes unclear how to imagine Virginia in the role of Vita's "wife." On the one hand, Woolf appears nowhere in Vita's fictional biography, suggesting the invisibility of the femme, the femme as semiotically indistinguishable from the wife, i.e., she doesn't wear trousers. On the other hand, Woolf in the role of biographer takes on the role not of the sexually inverted, but the masculine as unmarked.

Woolf situates herself within the biography as autobiographical subject through the self-reflexivity of the biographer who narrates the difficulty of producing a biographical narrative. Unlike Orlando, who vacillates between two sexes, the biographer vacillates between two conceptions of biographical discourse. On the one hand, "Our simple duty is to state the facts as far as they are known, and so let the reader make of them what he may."[33] On the other hand, "We have done our best to piece out a meagre summary from the charred fragments that remain; but often it has been necessary to speculate, to surmise, and even to make use of the imagination."[34] On the one hand, the desire to tell the truth based on reliable sources; on the other hand, the unreliability of sources, given their material vulnerability—"a hole in the manuscript big enough to put your finger through"[35]—as well as their gendered instability—"the truth is that when we write of a woman, everything is out of place—culminations and perorations; the accent never falls where it does with a man."[36] On the one hand, masculine mastery; on the other hand, feminine fickleness, which together, one might say, produce a bigenderedness comparable to Orlando's.

Yet, at the very moment of both cross-class and cross-gender identification—the moment at which Orlando as a woman cross-dresses as a man in order to enjoy the all-female company of Nell and her fellow prostitutes—the problem of the biographer's gender as unmarked takes the form of a crisis in masculinity. On the one hand, he both represents and warns against "a man's step on the stair," knowing that "it cannot be denied that when women get together—but hist—they are always careful to see that the doors are shut and that not a word of it gets into print."[37] How can he know this, as a man? "All they desire, we were about to say when the gentleman took the very words out of our mouths,"[38] suggests that the "we" of the biographer both knows what women do when they are alone together and knows what men say about such women. "Women have no desires, says this gentleman, coming into Nell's parlour; only affectations. Without desires (she has served him and he is gone) their conversation cannot be of the slightest interest to anyone."[39] On the one hand, the biographer speaks like a man (another man took his words right out of his mouth); on the other hand, he is not the kind of man who seeks sexual services. So what kind of man is he?

The biographer continues: "As that is not a question that can engage the attention of a sensible man, let us, who enjoy the immunity of all biographers and historians from any sex whatever, pass it over, and merely state that Orlando professed great enjoyment in the society of her own sex, and leave it to the gentlemen to prove, as they are very fond of doing, that this is impossible."[40] As "a sensible man," he is seemingly not a "gentleman," since he takes the side of women, and at the same time no man at all, since, as biographer, he is immune "from any sex whatever." Inasmuch as he is not interested in sex (with women), he most resembles the buggers from whom Woolf both learns to speak about sex and make her feel sexless. Inasmuch as he has no sex, he embodies the "voice of anon," the anonymity that both protects the woman writer from violation and prohibits her from entering literary history. Sexlessness, as opposed to the vacillation between sexes, refers to both ventriloquism (he can speak like the man he isn't) and silence (he won't speak if the women ask him not to).

The sexless biographer is not a woman and the androgynous transsexual has the memory of a man and the ability to cross-dress as one, which makes this a queer lesbian couple. Unlike Judith Shakespeare, who has the mind of her brother and whose female body ends up dead by her own hands, Orlando lives for over 300 years in the body of both a man and a woman. Thus, the discussion shifts from the female body, whose truth lies with life and death, to a discussion of clothes, where the truth vacillates between two seemingly incompatible positions. On the one hand, "Vain trifles as they seem, clothes have, they say, more important offices than merely to keep us warm. They change our view of the world and the world's view of us."[41] On the other hand, "The difference between the sexes is happily, one of great profundity. Clothes are but a symbol of something hid deep beneath."[42] But what is "hid deep beneath" is nothing that can be seen, inasmuch as, "Different though the sexes are, they intermix. In every human being a vacillation from one sex to the other takes place, and often it is only the clothes that keep the male or female likeness, while underneath the sex is the very opposite of what it is above."[43] Inasmuch as clothes make the difference between the sexes, they are interchangeable (Orlando cross-dresses); inasmuch as there is sexual difference, desire is characterized by vacillation (Orlando still loves Sasha and is married to Shel).

The fictionality of Woolf's portrait (that which obscures) is undermined by the referentiality of eight photographs (that which exposes), still included in contemporary editions of *Orlando.* Three paintings are of Sackville's hanging at Knole and two involve dressing up in historical costume in the style of portraits by Julia Margaret Cameron, a Victorian photographer and Woolf's aunt. The remaining photographs of Vita—the publicity photo taken when she was awarded a literary prize and the photo taken by Leonard at Long Barn—expose her as Orlando. At the same time,

"Orlando as Ambassador" obscures the referent inasmuch as it is a studio portrait of Vita cross-dressed. Like Orlando vacillating between sexes, the photographs vacillate between "benign legibility and a mystifying obscurity."[44] By the time Vita sees herself in the mirror of her own image, the costume drama has moved from the artist's studio to the department store: "I feel like one of those wax figures in a shop window, on which you have hung a robe stitched with jewels. It is like being alone in a dark room with a treasure chest full of rubies and nuggets and brocades. Darling, I don't know and scarcely even like to write, so overwhelmed am I, how you could have hung so splendid a garment on so poor a peg."[45] The fictionality of the auto/biography has been supplanted by the referentiality of the photograph (Barthes's "the thing has been there"), even as the consumability of clothes, in turn, supplants the fictionality of the auto/biography. Clothes don't make the person; they are infinitely replaceable and the body simply a mannequin or "peg."

By the time Vita falls in love with Orlando, "you have invented a new form of Narcissism,—I confess,—I am in love with Orlando—that is a complication I had not foreseen,"[46] Virginia has fallen out of love with Vita. Vita has already "gone nutting in the woods with Mary Campbell, or Mary Carmichael, or Mary Seton, not me—damn you—,"[47] that, on the one hand, points to her promiscuity and the other hand, evokes the four Marys from an anonymous ballad who serve as historical fictions in *A Room of One's Own*. By the time Orlando is finished, Virginia has relinquished the role of sexless biographer to take on the role of Mary Hamilton (the lady in waiting who is made to hang on the gallows by the queen for having born a child to the king), a prototype for Judith Shakespeare. If Virginia pronounces the end of their friendship on 10 March 1935, "My friendship with Vita is over. Not with a quarrel, not with a bang, but as ripe fruit falls,"[48] Vita's friendship with Virginia ends with her death, even as Virginia's photograph continues to haunt Vita's study at Sissinghurst, the scene of her own writing.

xix. "Yes, the motor is turning out the joy of our lives, an additional life, free & mobile & airy to live alongside our usual stationary industry. . . . all as light & easy as a hawk in the air." (Viginia Woolf, *Diary,* 10 August 1927).

xx. "To be driven by Vita on a summer's afternoon at the height of the season through the London traffic—she was a very good, but rather flamboyant driver—and to hear her put an aggressive taxi driver in his place, even when she was in the wrong, made one recognize a note in her voice that Sackvilles and Buckhursts were using to serfs in Kent 600 years ago, or even in Normandy 300 years before that. She belonged to a world that was completely different from ours. . . ." (Leonard Woolf, *Downhill all the Way* [1967], 112)

By the time *Orlando* as familial history (Vita's biography as landed aristocrat based on *Knole*) and as literary history (Virginia's auto/biography as the intellectual heir of the *National Dictionary of Biography*) reach their end in the present moment, that is, the moment of modernism—1928, the country house has become the department store, not just a place of leisure, but also consumption, and Orlando has learned to drive. Unlike flying, which serves as a figure for death, motoring becomes a metaphor for multiple selves as the product of both mobility and middle-age. On the one hand, there is the instability of the single self of biography or of the conscious mind multiplied by memories: "'Time has passed over me,' she thought, trying to collect herself; 'this is the oncome of middle age. How strange it is! Nothing is any longer one thing.'"[49] On the other hand, there is the fragmented self that comes from motoring through London: "Nothing could be seen whole or read from start to finish. What was seen begun—like two friends starting to meet each other across the street—was never seen ended."[50] For Vita, as for Stein, the car allows for a new kind of mobility, whether as ambulance driver at the front or as fragmented self answering to itself in the London traffic. Driving avoids the public dangers of the railroad station and the dangerous intimacies of the railroad carriage. Easier to learn and more affordable than flying, it enables both solitude and same-sex sociability.

> xxi. "The motor-car has restored the romance of travel. Freeing us from all the compulsions and contacts of the railway, the bondage to fixed hours and the beaten track, the approach to each town through the area of ugliness and desolation created by the railway itself, it has given us back the wonder, the adventure and the novelty which enlivened the way of our posting grandparents." (Edith Wharton, *A Motor-Flight Through France* [1908], 1)

Modernist Interlude

Virginia Woolf and Gertrude Stein acquire their location in history in the form of an address: Bloomsbury, London and 27, rue de Fleurus, Paris. They are both living in exile: Woolf from the Victorian house and Stein from America. Before Stein arrives in France, she has already migrated from California to the East Coast; her family had already migrated as German Jews to America. Woolf removes the drapes, takes up the carpet, and lives in a house with unmarried men. She is surrounded by family members and friends of the family. Stein moves in with a brother who precedes her to Paris and is surrounded by pictures, some of which will end up in the Post-Impressionist exhibit curated by Roger Fry at the Grafton Gallery in London in 1910.

By the time they arrive at their respective addresses, they have lost both sets of parents. Their strongest affective ties are to a sibling, their feelings bordering on the incestuous. The brother, Leo Stein, and the sister, Vanessa Bell, are both painters. Virginia's marriage to Leonard, a Jew who has returned to England after seven years in Ceylon, never completely displaces her relationship to Vanessa. When Leo moves out so that Alice can move in, Gertrude bows to him on the boulevard St. Germain, but never speaks to him again.

Both women rely on private incomes, either inherited from an aunt who dies in India, or managed by the oldest brother, Michael Stein, who has moved to Paris and is also collecting paintings. They are not wealthy, but they are financially independent. Eventually they will make money. Their respective bestsellers will take the form of an auto/biography, a queer gesture towards a female lover who has already withdrawn, or is threatening to withdraw, her affection.

The urban address belies the existence of a country house, in the Rhone Valley, on the River Ouse. This is the setting for the conjugal couple, the one without sex (Virginia and Leonard), the other without marriage (Gertrude and Alice). This is where the writing takes place: the writing that for Woolf will be interrupted by bouts of mental illness, that for Stein will not find a readership until she is 60. This is where they wait out the second world war. Stein, a Jew, refuses to leave France. Woolf, married to a Jew, preempts a suicide pact with Leonard by staging a fatal encounter with the river.

Stein gloried in her fat and Woolf verged on being too thin. Leonard spent much of his time and most of their money on food, making sure that Virginia continued to eat. Alice collected recipes, gathered wild strawberries for Gertrude's breakfast, and eventually published a cookbook. Stein was likened to a monk, an emperor, a Buddha; Woolf was considered beautiful, like her mother, in the photographs of Julia Margaret Cameron. Both cut their hair, to make themselves look modern, by following the example of an aristocrat. Alice keeps on cutting for two days, never having done this before, inspired by the Duchess de Clermont-Tonnerre. Virginia is inspired by Vita Sackville-West, who is traveling in Persia and mourns the fact that Virginia will no longer look like her photograph. Picasso mourns the fact that Gertrude no longer looks like his painting.

The automobile facilitates the movement between the city and the country, the Ford that Stein learns to drive in the form of an ambulance during World War I, the motoring that Vita will add to her list of aristocratic attributes. The car will have a name, like the country house. When Stein arrives in America, she will find flying even more exciting than driving. Woolf never learns to drive, never flies, and never goes to America. Her adventure is her affair with Vita.

Woolf and Stein meet, but their antipathy is mutual.

In 1926, the Hogarth Press publishes Stein's "Composition as Explanation."

Alice remembers meeting Vanessa, but misremembers that only Virginia dressed as an Abyssinian prince when in 1910 she played a part in the "Dreadnought Hoax."

"Can we possibly, without apprehension, imagine two Ladies of Llangollen in this year of 1930? They would own a car, wear dungarees, smoke cigarettes, have short hair, and there would be a liquor bar in their apartment. Would Sarah Ponsonby still know how to remain silent? Perhaps, with the aid of crossword puzzles. Eleanor Butler would curse as she jacked up the car, and would have her breast amputated. No longer would there be a village blacksmith with whom she would have cordial relations; she would exchange familiar remarks with the garage man. And already, twenty years earlier, Marcel Proust had endowed her with shocking desires, customs, and language, thus showing how little he knew her."

—*Colette,* The Pure and the Impure *(1932)*

"Certain it is that two such ladies haven't made such a sensation in the literary world since William Wordsworth and Sir Walter Scott paid pious visit to Lady Eleanor Butler and Miss Sarah Ponsonby, 'the Ladies of Llangollen'. So please, Miss Stein and Miss Toklas, don't disappoint us: we do be expecting you!"

—*"The Editor's Uneasy Chair,"* Vanity Fair, *September, 1934*

Gertrude Stein and Alice B. Toklas, 1922 by Man Ray. With permission from Artists Rights Society.

The Autobiography of Alice B. Toklas as "Portrait Narration"

i. "By this time Gertrude Stein was in a sad state of indecision and worry. I sat next to her and she said to me early in the afternoon, What is the answer? I was silent. In that case, she said, what is the question? Then the whole afternoon was troubled, confused and very uncertain, and later in the afternoon they took her away on a wheeled stretcher to the operating room and I never saw her again." (Alice B. Toklas, *What Is Remembered* [1963], 173)

ii. "And in asking a question one is not answering but one is as one may say deciding about knowing. Knowing is what you know and in asking these questions although there is no one who answers these questions there is in them that there is knowledge. Knowledge is what you know." (Gertrude Stein, *Lectures in America* [1935], 102)

When Alice B. Toklas reaches the end of her memoir, *What Is Remembered* (1963), she ends by recounting the death of her lover. Anything that happens after that is not worth remembering. She ends not with a death scene, which takes place elsewhere, but with Gertrude Stein's last words: two questions, neither of which receive an answer. The confusion Alice feels at her impending loss is reminiscent of the confusion she felt when she met Gertrude and first laid eyes on a cubist painting. As long as Picasso's portrait of Gertrude hangs across from her in the apartment, Alice is able to live on in the company of her memory. Once it is removed (to the Metropolitan Museum of Art, to whom Gertrude has bequeathed it), she lives on, for another 20 years, in solitude, as the memory of her.

When Gertrude explains, in one of the lectures she delivers in America in 1934, that to ask a question is not to answer it, but to "decide about knowing," she insists on the process engaged in by the human mind. "Knowledge is what you know." If you already know the answer there is no point in asking the question, inasmuch as knowing has already been decided. If no one is there to answer, this does not mean that there is no answer. Knowledge continues to be decided in the process of talking and listening. When Gertrude dies, there is no one left to ask the questions. Knowledge is not what you remember, yet Alice has only her memories.

When Gertrude dies in 1945, she and Alice have been together for 38 years, having spent every single night under the same roof. They have lived their lives together in exile, not as elopers, like Eleanor Butler and Sarah Ponsonby, but as expatriates, mostly in Paris, eventually also in the Rhône valley. Their address, 27 rue de Fleurus, attracts visitors from all over the world, not because of its neo-gothic architecture, like Plas Newed, but because of its interior, which houses a renowned collection of modernist paintings. Their domestic life is minutely recorded, even as their domestic arrangement takes the form not of a romantic friendship, but of an open secret. And just as Colette predicts, Gertrude, the Eleanor of the couple, learns to drive a car and writes her first lecture, "Composition as Explanation," sitting in her Ford in the garage waiting for it to be repaired.

Both Virginia Woolf's *Orlando* and Gertrude Stein's *The Autobiography of Alice B. Toklas* (1933) begin as jokes—what Woolf calls a "holiday book" and Stein calls "audience-writing"—and end up bestsellers. At the time of publication, Woolf is 46 and Stein is 59, and in each case, they for the first time are making money, enough to spend money, which means buying, among other things, a car. Neither Virginia nor Alice learn to drive. To begin writing a book as a joke means in each case writing for "the fun of it." In Woolf's case this involves abandoning the stream of consciousness of the lyric novel that strives to represent character by means of "the mind's soliloquy in solitude." For Stein it requires abandoning the "continuous present" as a way of telling what happens without telling stories. Whereas Woolf's Orlando lives for 300 years, thereby avoiding death, Gertrude privileges the novelistic form of the detective story, because the hero starts out dead and thus the story has already come to an end.

Inasmuch as the hero is dead, the detective story eliminates both human nature, or fictional character, and the event, or novelistic plot. The interest of detective stories does not lie with the crime, that is with the answer to the question, who did it, which, if solved, will be reported by the newspaper, but with the process of detecting. When Gertrude arrives in America and is asked whom she would like to meet, she says in *Everybody's Autobiography* (1937), the sequel to *The Autobiography of Alice B. Toklas,* Dashiell Hammett. When they do meet, they talk about autobiography. During their conversation, they come to the conclusion that in the nineteenth century, male writers invented fictions and women wrote only about themselves, while in the twentieth it is reversed. By writing her own auto/biography, Gertrude comes dangerously close to resembling a nineteenth-century woman writer. So she writes, first someone else's and then "everybody's" auto/biography. Autobiography resembles the detective story in as much as it chronicles the death of a past self. Early twentieth-century women writers aspiring to join the avant-garde are no longer allowed to write about themselves, in contrast to the queer subject who cannot yet write about herself. And after 30 years together, the boundary between the one and the two within the lesbian marriage has become less clear.

> iii. "I said in England when I was talking to the Cambridge students that although it was the same language anybody could tell right away whether it was an American writer or an English writer who had written and that had a great deal to do with their making them alive and their making them dead, in England the dead are not dead because they are connected with other living, in America the dead are dead there is no connection with those left living. That had a great deal to do with deserts and religion." (Gertrude Stein, *Everybody's Autobiography* [1937], 113)

Thus in America, "the dead are dead." Neither the victim nor the killer is inscribed into a genealogy, in contrast to England where the dead are connected "with other living," which makes necessary and legitimates the role of the biographer. It also makes possible not a narrative with a dead hero, but a hero who never dies. Rather than creating a biographical subject Vita as part of an autobiographical project, Stein's autobiographical subject is not herself but Alice, the victim of a queer narrative death. When *The Autobiography of Alice B. Toklas* becomes a bestseller, Stein becomes a celebrity. Detection must be assigned to someone else, a lover, everybody, anybody. Detection will require writing autobiographically—*Everybody's Autobiography, Paris France* (1940), and *Wars I Have Seen* (1945)—for the rest of her life.

> iv. "In the room were Mr. and Mrs. Stein and Gertrude Stein. It was Gertrude Stein who held my complete attention, as she did for all the many years I knew her until her death, and all these empty ones since then. She was a golden brown presence, burned by the Tuscan sun and with a golden glint in her warm brown hair. She was dressed in a warm brown corduroy suit. She wore a large round coral brooch and when she talked, very little, or laughed, a good deal, I thought her voice came from this brooch. It was unlike anyone else's voice—deep, full, velvety like a great contralto's, like two voices. She was large and heavy with delicate small hands and a beautiful modeled and unique head. It was often compared to a Roman emperor's, but later Donald Sutherland said that her eyes made her a primitive Greek." (Alice B. Toklas, *What Is Remembered* [1963], 23)

The verbal portrait Alice paints of Gertrude at their first meeting suggests a physical presence that captures her attention, as it will those of many others.

Her hair is brown, her skin is brown and she wears a brown suit, an ecclesiastical brown that reminds some of a monk, while its corduroy reminds others of a military uniform. Her body, "large and heavy," remains shapeless, read by some as simply an excess of (feminine) fat, by others as a sign of (masculine) monumentality. This stands in contrast to the delicacy of the (feminine) hands and the beautifully modeled (masculine) head, the two features that seem most prominent in Picasso's portrait. What appears most striking to Alice is the brooch and the voice, the brooch as a source of the voice. As though the brooch were the entrance into the body, the way the mouth offers an entrance into the head, both openings serving also as erotic orifices. The voice sounds like two voices, coming not just from two sources, but from two bodies, the two octave range of the contralto, a woman's voice that comes closest to the depth of a man's. But what kind of man, a Roman emperor or a primitive Greek? Neither of these make a sound.

> v. "Within a year I also had gone and I had come to Paris. There I went to see Mrs. Stein who had in the meantime returned to Paris, and there at her house I met Gertrude Stein. I was impressed by the coral brooch she wore and by her voice. I may say that only three times in my life have I met a genius and each time a bell within me rang and I was not mistaken, and I may say in each case it was before there was any general recognition of the quality of genius in them. The three geniuses of whom I wish to speak are Gertrude Stein, Pablo Picasso and Alfred Whitehead. I have met many important people, I have met several great people, but I have only known three first class geniuses and in each case on sight within me something rang. In no one of the three cases have I been mistaken. In this way my new full life began." (Gertrude Stein, *The Autobiography of Alice B. Toklas* [1933], 5)

When the same scene appears in *The Autobiography,* Stein is not retelling the story based on Alice's telling, since Stein's text is chronologically prior to *What Is Remembered.* She is telling it as though Alice were telling it, imitating her voice, representing herself through her eyes. Like Alice, she privileges the coral brooch and the voice. But this time it is not the sound of the voice, but the sound of the bell that is most striking, not two voices, but three bells. The two of the couple, the conjugal dyad, has been replaced by the three of the trinity, the three geniuses. And yet, how is it that Gertrude belongs to the other two, since she is not a man, and in what way does she belong to the other man, Picasso, who paints her portrait? In both cases the voice of a woman, even if she has two voices, even if she speaks through the voice of another woman, is not sufficient. In either case she must be legitimized by a man. And yet, what makes Alice's role significant, is that "in each case it was before there was any general recognition of the quality of genius in them" that she recognized their genius. Without Alice, there would be no recognition of Gertrude's genius. It is not that Gertrude uses Alice to boast about her talents. It is that she needs Alice to have them recognized at all. By the time the genius has become a celebrity, it becomes unclear who Gertrude Stein is.

> vi. "Since the first announcement of the forthcoming publication of this book, innumerable questions have been asked about Alice B. Toklas. Who is this author? What is this extraordinary book she has written? Does she really exist?
>
> One newspaper critic, Harry Hansen to be exact, even went so far as to suggest that Alice B. Toklas did not exist. He was promptly rebuked by three correspondents. . . ." (back dustjacket of original edition of *The Autobiography of Alice B. Toklas*)

Gertrude becomes a celebrity because she has finally chosen to write in such a way that others can understand her, or so her audience thinks. The reasons she herself gives for writing *The Autobiography* are many and varied. Some explanations repeat themselves, sometimes within the same text, sometimes from one text to another. To begin again each time with a different explanation because "knowledge is what one knows," not what one remembers, is to adhere to the narrative structure Stein labeled the "continuous present." To tell it differently depending on whether it is a short piece for a small magazine, a lecture, the sequel to an autobiography, or an interview, is to be cognizant of an audience. The audience Stein acquires as a celebrity enables her, for the first time, to explain to herself what it is that she has been doing by writing the way she has. At the same time it makes her begin to doubt, for the first time, her identity, by inducing writer's block. She will explain herself to herself in front of an audience, as lecturer and as interviewee; she will wonder who she is in her autobiographies. She will shift from the portrait, telling "what each one is" without naming it and without telling stories, to "portrait narration," a narrative that "is not what is in your mind but what is in somebody else's."[1] And she begins with the portrait of Alice, Alice as memoirist whose auto/biography she will write at a moment when as she herself says, "I was getting older. . . ."[2]

Initially Stein is asked to write a biography, which she refuses to do. Then she admits to responding to a different request: " . . . indeed it was in telling Bertie Abdie [a wealthy British collector and dealer] in answer to questioning all there was to tell of Paris as it had been that I first put it together as it later was written in The Autobiography of Alice B. Toklas, he too is one to whom you tell what you have told to any one but telling it to him makes it be something that has come alive again."[3] If narrative is not exciting because it is about something that is just happening, then telling it to someone in answer to their question not only places Stein in a new role, that of respondent, but it also allows her to return to events of 25 years ago. What happened then "has come alive again" because it is as though it happened to someone else, i.e., a younger Gertrude Stein. If knowledge is not just what you know, but how you know what you know, then knowing becomes possible by answering someone else's question. In front of an audience at the University of Chicago, Stein is able to ask, "What is an audience and is it almost impossible or is it possible to make an audience of yourself and is it almost impossible or is it possible to rid yourself of yourself as an audience."[4] In other words, auto/biography makes the writer her own audience by recording perceptions of herself as though they were someone else's, because the self has become someone else, 25 years later.

The status of the self as audience, whether ontologically or linguistically, becomes a question at the moment when Stein's audience of one, namely Alice, becomes superceded by the literal audiences she encounters in the lecture halls during her American tour. The transition from one to the other, from having a reputation but no readership to having an audience, is not the effect, I would argue, of *The Autobiography,* but already anticipated and prepared for by that text. One might begin by considering the statement: "I write for myself and strangers," a statement that introduces one of the chapters in *The Making of Americans* and is reintroduced in *The Autobiography.*[5] Stein might be writing for herself and strangers, but the only reader she has had is Alice. Alice reads what Gertrude has written the night before because she types it every morning, in the role of secretary as well as editor. Stein writes knowing that she will be read by Alice. But this is the very thing she cannot write about. Earlier in *The Autobiography* she writes:

> One of the things that I have liked all these years is to be surrounded by people who know no english. It has left me more intensely alone with my eyes and my english. I do not know if it would have been possible to have english be so all in all to me otherwise. And they none of them could read a word I wrote, most of them did not even know that I did write. No, I like living with so very many people and being all alone with english and myself.[6]

Even if people wanted to read what she had written, they wouldn't be able to, inasmuch as they don't know the language. To be writing in English in France is as solitary as to be writing for an audience of only one. If there is to be a readership, one that extends beyond the apartment, it must be found elsewhere, since most of the visitors come for the collection of paintings.

By the end of *The Autobiography,* Stein has modified her pronouncement: "One writes for oneself and strangers but with no adventurous publishers how can one come in contact with those same strangers."[7] The problem now is not one of (foreign) language or (limited) readership, but of sales. The last task Alice accomplishes before writing her auto/biography is the publication of Gertrude's work, which she publishes herself under the imprint Plain Edition. But as with any task Alice undertakes, she has to begin at the beginning and can only get so far. At this point in the text, Madame de Clermont-Tonnerre (the model for Proust's Duchess de Guermantes and the inspiration for Gertrude's hair cut), arrives to say "the time has now come when you must be made known to a larger public."[8] In her estimation, this means translating the abridged version of *The Making of Americans* into French. But, as history will tell, the French audience for the story of three generations of an American immigrant family will in no way match the American audience for the story of Stein's expatriate years in France.

Stein provides two further explanations for how she came to write *The Autobiography,* both of which she delivers to an audience, first in the form of a lecture, "Portraits and Repetition," during her American tour, and second as "Transatlantic Interview" shortly before she dies. In the lecture she says:

> Beside that I had been going for the first time since my college days to lectures. I had been going to hear Bernard Fäy lecture about Franco-American things and I had become interested in the relation of a lecturer to his audience. I had never thought about an audience before not even when I wrote Composition as Explanation which was a lecture but now I suddenly began, to feel the outside inside and the inside outside and it was perhaps not so exciting but it was very interesting. Anyway it was quite exciting. And so I wrote the Autobiography of Alice B. Toklas and told what happened as it had happened.[9]

Although this is not the first time Stein delivers a lecture, having presented "Composition as Explanation" at Oxford and Cambridge in 1926, it is the first time she thinks about the relationship between lecturer and audience, in this case as a member of the audience. This can be attributed, at least in part, to the role of translation. Bernard Fäy is French, Professor of American history in France, and he is talking about Franco-American things. Eventually he will also undertake the translation of *The Making of Americans* into French. As a Frenchman teaching American history, he has learned a foreign language; he is observing another culture from the outside; he is translating one culture into another in the act of speaking to an audience. This is both analogous and not analogous to Stein's situation, who is an American writing in English for an American audience, even as she writes in France about the life she has lived in Paris. Speaking, then, like writing, is about being in the company of strangers, even as the problem of the inside to the outside shifts from being alone in a language, because surrounded by another language, to having a relationship to an audience that is enabled by translation.

In "Transatlantic Interview" she writes:

> And then as a joke I began to write the *Autobiography of Alice B. Toklas* and at that moment I had made a rather interesting discovery. A young French poet had begun to write and I was asked to translate his poems and there I made a rather startling discovery that other people's words are quite different from one's own and that they cannot be the result of your internal troubles as a writer. They have a totally different sense than when they are your own words. . . . Therefore narrative has a different concept than poetry or even exposition, because you see the narrative itself is not what is in your mind but what is in somebody else's. And so I did a tour de force with the *Autobiography of Alice B. Toklas* and when I sent the first half to the agent they sent back a telegram to see which one of us had written it![10]

In this case, Stein is involved in a literal act of translation, from French into English, where the relationship between inside and outside refers not to what one is speaking about, but to the position from which one is speaking. What Stein is suggesting is that narrative, as opposed to narration, like translation, is about what someone else has written. Woolf rewrites the history of English literature in *Orlando,* that is, a story that has already been written. For Stein, any story with a beginning, middle, and end is not about the process of narration, or what goes on in one's own mind, but what goes on in someone else's. But unlike a translation, where one rarely asks, "which one has written it," the relationship between Alice and Gertrude begs the question of authorship.

Stein, in the fourth lecture she delivers at the University of Chicago, suggests that to read a lecture is to account further the difference between what one has written and what is in someone else's mind: "Of course if you are reading what you are lecturing then you have a half in one of any two directions, you have been recognizing what you are writing when you were writing and now in reading you disassociate recognizing what you are reading from what you recognize as being written while you were writing. In short you are leading a double life."[11] By reading something one has written, one becomes aware of a splitting between the one who did the writing and the one who is doing the reading. This splitting finds its trope in that of the "double life." A double life generally refers to a public and a secret life, whether that takes the form of (legitimate) marriage and (transgressive) desire, like adultery, or whether it takes the form of passing as heterosexual while living a homosexual life in secret. A double life also involves the trope of translation inasmuch as a text has two lives, one in each language. Double life can also mean the same life lived by two different people, as in a lesbian marriage.

When *The Autobiography* was first published, Stein's name did not appear on the cover or on the title page, revealing her authorship only on the last page through oblique reference to Defoe and Robinson Crusoe. Thus the structure of *The Autobiography* relies not just on the translation of one language to another, but also on the translation of one medium to another, as Shirley Neuman reminds us in *Gertrude Stein: Autobiography and the Problem of Narration:* "Stein presents the entire narrative form as the 'fiction' of Alice's point of view, as what she would call a 'translation.' She simultaneously acknowledges the 'fact' of her composition, obliquely in the photograph which serves as frontispiece and in the absence of an author's name on the work's title page and directly at the end of the book."[12] The cover includes a photograph by Man Ray (ca. 1922) of Stein at her desk, writing, with Toklas standing in the doorway, about to enter the room. Like *Orlando, The Autobiography* is interspersed with photographs that are nevertheless missing in subsequent editions, making public the relationship between Gertrude and Alice as open secret. Thus, inasmuch as in a translation, the author cannot be confused with the translator, at least not on the title page, more needs to be said about the relationship between the two names, or for that matter, between the two women in the photograph. While Neuman focuses on the problem of narration in all of Stein's autobiographical writing, Charles Caramello in *Henry James, Gertrude Stein, and the Biographical Act,* considers the particular case of *The Autobiography* as "portrait narration." He suggests: "She melds the conventions of biographical memoir with those of autobiographical memoir. She relates the early histories of two individuals who became a couple so she then can recollect, systematically and comprehensively, the history of that *couple* as it moved on the cultural stage—a history that concludes with the couple's production of *The Autobiography* itself."[13] To meld the two genres (auto/biography) in order to create the (lesbian) couple means foregoing the process of translation, not just from one language to another, but from private mind to public audience. At the same time, by privileging translation as a trope, Stein is able to construct a double life not just as the product of expatriation, but also as queer.[14] The celebrity photograph as "interiority without intimacy" is signified by the image on the book's dustjacket that stages the intimacy of the same-sex couple in the interior of 27, rue de Fleurus.

> vii. "After all everybody, that is everybody who writes is interested in living inside themselves in order to tell what is inside themselves. That is why writers have to have two countries, the one where they belong and the one in which they live really. The second one is romantic, it is separate from themselves, it is not real but it is really there." (Gertrude Stein, *Paris France* [1940], 2)

What, then, is one to make of the explanation for how and why *The Autobiography* was written as it appears at the end of the *The Autobiography* itself? To begin, Stein writes that she was asked to write an autobiography, rather than a biography, as she claims later in the "Transatlantic Interview." Then she suggests that Alice should write her autobiography, thinking it would make money. But Alice is busy with other things, precisely because Gertrude as a writer has made so little money. Finally, Gertrude proposes writing the auto/biography herself. But whose auto/biography? Why not her own? Why not Alice's biography? Because (like Amelia Earhart, who doesn't smoke but needs to be in the cigarette advertisement to encourage name recognition and to raise money for her pilot and navigator, who, after all, did the flying, but that will in turn tarnish her name for use in future ads), "My Twenty-Five Years with Gertrude Stein" can only be told because of what Gertrude Stein has written, even if it remains unread. Since Stein hasn't yet been to America, the model for her enterprise originates in literary history: "About six weeks ago Gertrude Stein said, it does not look to me as if you were ever going to write that autobiography. You know what I am going to do. I am going to write it for you. I am going to write it as simply as Defoe did the autobiography of Robinson Crusoe. And she has and this is it."[15]

Why Defoe? The answers range from Gertrude and Alice live in Paris like Robinson Crusoe and Friday, to the notion that Defoe appropriated first person narrative for the novel the way Stein appropriates third person narrative for autobiography. Stein, as expatriate, clearly has two countries: "America is my country and Paris is my home town." It is because she is a writer that she has become an expatriate: "Writers have to have two countries, the one where they belong and the one in which they really live." The country she belongs to is America, the place of family origins, even if her German-Jewish family, as in *The Making of Americans,* originates elsewhere.[16] The genre associated with that place is biography. (Although, as Woolf discovers, biography can be about people who are still living and those people can be one's friends.) The place in which Stein really lives, namely Paris, is the place she has lived for 25 years with Alice. "It is romantic," but not in a way that can be narrated, either as Gertrude's autobiography or Alice's biography. "It is not real but it is really there." It is not real because she is writing in English and they are speaking French. She is really an American. But it is really there because it represents half of her life, "the half in which I made what I made," both her writing and her 25-year marriage with Alice. Thus, to write one's own autobiography would mean living in only one country. There would be no outside, no France, no Alice, no "really there." There would only be the "no there there" of Oakland, California, where Gertrude and Alice both lived but never met, and of Gertrude's birthplace, Allegheny, Pennsylvania, which, in addition to being misspelled on her tombstone in Père Lachaise cemetery, no longer exists, having been absorbed into Pittsburgh.

If the writer needs two countries, then the lesbian couple needs an auto/biography, not the biography that chronicles family history and not the autobiography that comes from living in one country. Rather, one woman writes the other woman's auto/biography as a way of documenting their double life. On the one hand, *The Autobiography* conceals its same-sex erotics; on the other hand, it publicizes the stability of its marriage, by opposing it to the myriad infidelities of opposite-sex couplings, such as Picasso's. Just as the public is to know of the marriage only in terms of an open secret, the marriage, in turn, contains its own secrets. What happens when a third party threatens the dyad?

Ulla Dydo has argued that in the spring before Stein began *The Autobiography,* she rediscovered her first work, an early, unpublished manuscript that told of her affair with May Bookstaver, eventually published under the title *Q. E. D.* The story takes the form of a triangulated desire between Stein and May and May's initial romantic attachment, Mabel Weeks. According to Dydo, Alice's jealousy stems less from the fact that the affair took place, than from the fact that Stein never confessed it, never completely broke off contact with May (who, in the interim, had become Mrs. Knoblauch and made attempts, some successful, to get Stein's worked published), and that she had memorialized the affair in a piece of writing. Alice made Gertrude destroy all of May's letters and "in the spring of 1932, Alice withdrew her validation—at least temporarily."[17] Stein's response was to write *The Autobiography,* which Alice claims, "was the only work Gertrude wrote for her,"[18] and the long poem *Stanzas in Meditation,* the "other autobiography," which is both about how writing in Alice's voice did violence to her own, and a symptom of the linguistic violence Gertrude directs at Alice's rage. This interpretation is reminiscent of how Gertrude met Alice, by reading all of the letters Alice wrote from San Francisco to Annette Rosenshine, who had arrived in Paris and met with Gertrude every afternoon. These sessions took the form of a kind of unorthodox psychotherapy that aided Gertrude in her character studies but left Annette, if not in love with, then extremely psychologically dependent on Gertrude, and Gertrude, if not in love with, then eager to meet Alice.[19]

The point here is not to engage in a character analysis of the author, but to consider the importance of other texts for the textual construction of a lesbian marriage in terms not just of what must be kept secret, but what must be forgotten. When this story gets told in *The Autobiography,* the novel under discussion, i.e., *Q. E. D.,* is repeatedly, almost obsessively, referred to as "completely forgotten."[20] The forgetting, of both the romantic attachment and the overtly lesbian story, is what makes possible the stability of the marriage and its public appearance as normative. It also anticipates *The Autobiography*'s sequel, which addresses identity not in terms of a relationship to a partner and its potential loss through the dissolution of marriage, but identity performed as celebrity through the mechanical forms of reproduction Stein encounters for the first time in America.

> viii. "In the first place she did not want it to be Alice B. Toklas, if it has to be at all it should be Alice Toklas and in the French translation it was Alice Toklas in French it just could not be Alice B. Toklas but in America and in England too Alice B. Toklas was more than Alice Toklas. Alice Toklas never thought so and always said so. (Gertrude Stein, *Everybody's Autobiography* [1937], 1)

Stein begins the introduction to *Everybody's Autobiography* with "Alice B. Toklas did hers and now anybody will do theirs."[21] The slippage between everybody and anybody, that suggests nobody, anticipates the effect on the couple of their trip to America. Alice does not prefer the name she was given by Gertrude as the fictional author of her auto/biography, her name in English, which includes her middle initial, her official name as it appears in print. She prefers the French version, the private version, the version of herself as part of a couple. While Gertrude tries to argue that Alice B. Toklas is more than Alice Toklas, i.e., it has more letters, it is more widely known, and the name has made more money, Alice considers it to be less. Alice B. Toklas is not her name, it is the name of her fiction, it is the name that Gertrude gave her and that has made her famous. With Gertrude's fame comes Alice's anonymity. In America she cannot be named anymore. The more Gertrude is lionized, the more Alice becomes anybody. Alice now lives "lost in translation."

> ix. "In the old days when they wrote novels they made up the personality of the things they had seen in people and the things that were the people as if they were a dream. But now well now how can you dream about personality when it is always being created for you by a publicity, how can you believe what you make up when publicity makes them up to be so much realer than you can dream. And so autobiography is written which is in a

way a way to say that publicity is right, they are as the public sees them." (Gertrude Stein, *Everybody's Autobiography* [1937], 71)

The distinction Stein makes between novels and autobiography is the difference between personality and publicity. Personality is how a writer sees another person; publicity is how the writer is seen by a public. For the moderns, what the public sees, mediated by the mass media, has become more powerful than the imagination, made analogous to a dream: the surrealism of the psychoanalytic unconscious represented by the dream, as opposed to the hyper-realism of technological reproduction. Now that Stein knows "these strangers" by having a public, now that "anybody can know anybody" because of publicity, novels are no longer possible, except in the form of detective stories, "where the only person of any importance is dead."[22] The only alternative to being known by everybody as a celebrity is to have died, at least in America.

x. "No, publicity in France is really not important, tradition and their private life and the soil which always produces something, that is what counts.

Mrs. Lindberg was in Paris and she I were talking. In America of course she had suffered they had suffered publicity. In England they had payed no attention to them but they the Lindbergs knew and England knew that they were there. In France they pay attention to you when you meet, but they do not bother you because in between they do not know that you are there." (Gertrude Stein, *Paris France* [1940], 10)

On the one hand, the difference between personality and publicity is the difference between "in the old days" and "now." On the other hand, it is the difference between America and France. Stein laments the fact that the American public is more interested in her than in her work, when it is her work that would make anyone interested in her at all. Being interested in her, they can only be too interested or not interested enough in Alice. In the case of the Lindbergs, the media is not interested in their flying, but in the kidnapping and subsequent death of their child. What gets lost between having no public and receiving enormous publicity is one's private life, in Stein's case, her marriage with Alice. Alice prefers her name without middle initial because that is where she really lives, in France, as Gertrude's "wife." Yet, as long as she writes in English, Gertrude's public will be in America, where Alice is known only as her "secretary."

If auto/biography becomes a form of publicity, and publicity precludes the possibility of a private life, what then marks the difference between the portrait painted by Picasso, which, after all, ends up in the Metropolitan, and the mass-produced images Stein encounters in America? If *Everybody's*

Autobiography is about being lionized as a celebrity, then *The Autobiography* is, as Caramello suggests, about both Stein's response to Henry James' *Portrait of a Lady* as literary precursor and her portrait by Picasso. Thus, the subtext of the history of Gertrude and Alice as couple is not just the couple of Gertrude and May as secret, but the story of Stein and Picasso as originators of a modernist avant-garde. But inasmuch as *The Autobiography* is about Toklas publishing Stein's work and Stein in turn publishing Toklas's persona, the portrait, as Caramello argues, is about Picasso's erasure of "Stein's importance as a *creative agent* in the initial formulation of Cubism by making her a *created icon* of that formulation."[23] How then does she reclaim her status as "creative icon"?

The first encounter between Alice and Picasso as told in *The Autobiography* is mediated by Gertrude's portrait: "After a little while I murmured to Picasso that I liked his portrait of Gertrude Stein. Yes, he said, everybody says that she does not look like it but that does not make any difference, she will, he said."[24] Just as Alice does not yet know how to look at modern art and/or does not yet know Gertrude, she will. At the same time, just as Gertrude will begin to look different, i.e., change over time, she will begin to resemble her portrait. The story of Gertrude's posing for Picasso ends not with the completion of the portrait, but with Gertrude cutting her hair:

> Only a few years ago when Gertrude Stein had had her hair cut short, she had always up to that time worn it as a crown on top of her head as Picasso has painted it, when she had had her hair cut, a day or so later she happened to come into a room and Picasso was several rooms away. She had a hat on but he caught sight of her through two doorways and approaching her quickly called out, Gertrude, what is it, what is it. What is what, Pablo, she said. Let me see, he said. She let him see. And my portrait, said he sternly. Then his face softening he added, mais, quand même tout y est, all the same it is all there.[25]

Gertrude changes, not to look more but to look less like her portrait, by cutting her hair, in order to look like, and thus reclaim, her status as modernist artist, even if her model, like Virginia Woolf's, is that of the female aristocrat. And it is Alice who cuts it for her, cutting it so short that she begins to resemble not her portrait, but its painter.

In between these two episodes there are two others, one in which, toward the end of the sittings, Picasso paints out the whole head, "because, as he says, "I can't see you any longer when I look" and the other, several months later, when he paints the head in, "without having seen Gertrude Stein again."[26] In the first instance, she has become so familiar that he can't see her anymore, while in the second, because he doesn't see her, he is able to invent her. Michael North, in *The Dialect of Modernism,* reminds us that on the first, "generally realistic portrait he [Picasso] superimposed a flat, expressionless mask with two eye slits cut against the angle of the rest of the face and body, a mask derived from ancient Iberian reliefs he had seen at the Louvre."[27] In other words, he covered a failed portrait with a mask of African origins used as a means of negotiating Picasso's discomfort with Stein's sexual ambiguity. Thus, on the one hand, the two countries, America and France, are mediated in a way particular to modernism, by African artifacts that confuse the mask with the African face. On the other hand, Picasso equates sexual indeterminacy not with the female avant-garde artist or with the lesbian couple, but with Americanness: "ils sont pas des hommes, ils sont pas des femmes, ils sont des américains. They are not men, they are not women, they are Americans."[28]

North argues further that Picasso's use of the visual mask can then be equated with the linguistic mask Stein uses in "Melanctha," where she resorts not just to a heterosexual retelling of the triangulated same-sex desire in *Q. E.D.*, but to a cross-racial dialect in her representation of the same story as enacted by African Americans. It was "Melanctha" that Stein was composing while she was posing for Picasso's portrait. One could argue further that the sittings are as much about posing, as they are about portraiture. After posing in Montmartre, Stein walks (she is known to walk eight to ten miles a day) the entire length of Paris back to the rue de Fleurus, alone or accompanied by her dog: "She had come to like posing, the long still hours followed by a long dark walk intensified the concentration with which she was creating her sentences. The sentences of which Marcel Brion, the french critic has written, by exactitude, austerity, absence of variety in light and shade, by refusal of the use of the subconscious Gertrude Stein achieves a symmetry which has a close analogy to the symmetry of the musical fugue of Bach."[29] Thus, while Picasso is painting his portrait to serve as the icon of cubism, Stein is composing prose described in terms of a painting, analogized to music, and resistant to the very idea that portraiture should in any way resemble its model. What she writes will be read, i.e., typed and edited by Alice. What is edited and typed will be favorably reviewed by a French critic and available to an American audience only by incorporating it into an auto/biography written by someone else.

xi. "Literature in the eyes of the human mind is like land seen from an airplane." (William Gass, introduction, *The Geographical History of America* [1936], 41)

When Gertrude and Alice arrive in America for a speaking tour in 1934, they are returning for the first time in 31 years. Four installments of *The Autobiography* have appeared in the *Atlantic Monthly* and the Literary Guild has chosen it as its book-of-the-month selection. *Four Saints in Three Acts* is premiering, with an all-black cast and to enormous acclaim, in Hartford, Connecticut. Stein writes seven articles for the *New York Herald Tribune* on various topics having to do with America, beginning with "I Came and Here I am," followed by six more articles for *The Saturday Evening Post* on money.

They stay for seven months, during which time the Lindbergh trial takes place, and visit almost 30 universities, during which time Stein delivers one of six prepared lectures. They spend the first month in New York and agree to return to Chicago where Stein delivers four additional lectures to a group of University of Chicago students. For the first time she and Alice fly in a plane, watch a film, and listen to the radio. For the first time in 25 years, Gertrude and Alice are traveling together, no longer, like the Ladies of Llangollen, waiting for visitors to come to them.

> xii. "Gertrude Stein returned to America yesterday after thirty-one years, a square-shouldered woman of 60 with a constant chuckle in her throat and a rollick in her gait.
>
> Dressed in rough tweeds and wearing the enigmatic countenance that has marked her literary adventures for the last score of years, she sat in the lounge of the French liner Champlain for more than an hour, crossing swords with a dozen baffled reporters.
>
> Her feet were in thick wooly stockings, and round-toed, flat-heeled oxfords. A brownish tweed suit covered a cerise vest of voluminous proportions and a mannish shirt of cream and black stripes. The hat was a Stein hat, a hat as persistent as the repetitions which are a feature of her abstruse writings.
>
> Peaked in front above her candid brown eyes, it roamed backward tightly about the close-cropped head to a fold at the rear; a gay hat which gave her the appearance of having just sprung from Robin Hood's forest to enunciate another word pattern of her own literature—." (*New York Times,* 25 October 1934, 25)

What the reporters want to see is a figure that will explain, by means of resemblance, the unreadable prose Stein produces as author. Her "enigmatic countenance" characterizes her prose, but is also characterized as something she wears, like the rough tweeds that make her look sexually anomalous. On the one hand, the "cerise vest of voluminous proportions" suggests feminine fat; on the other hand, it covers "a mannish shirt." On the one hand, the seriousness of her shoes, and their sensibleness, suggest not just a modern woman, but an asexual one. On the other hand, the "gayness" of the hat makes her look mythical and anachronistic, like Robin Hood, having come out of hiding, i.e., across the ocean, to spread not wealth but understanding. Every item of clothing is made to point to an element of her writing style. Somehow reading her clothing will undermine the illegibility of her writing. It is the focus on the shoes and the hat that most clearly reveals a discomfort with the subversion of femininity. The shoes that signify physical mobility and the hat that defies fashion together mark an independence from standard markers of gender. Like Amelia Earhart's hats that Putnum was so critical of and quickly censored, they hide the closely-cropped hair that, as with the aviatrix, will serve as visual signature.

Alice tells us it was she who had all the clothes prepared for Gertrude's voyage: "one to lecture in in the afternoon, one to lecture in on evenings, one to travel in, an odd dress or two."[30] It is Gertrude who tells us of the many shoes she has made: "I had many new shoes, I am very fond of new shoes, I do not care a great deal for new clothes, I have to let them hang a long time before I can wear them but I do like new shoes and at Chambery they made a great many of them."[31] As soon as they board the boat train, one of the buttons snaps off Gertrude's shoe. Trac, the Indo-Chinese cook whom they leave behind, disappears to find needle and thread and immediately sews it back on. "In this prosaic manner we went off on our great adventure," Alice rejoins. The manner may be prosaic but inasmuch as Alice and Gertrude both recall the episode, it is clearly significant. Their "great adventure" reminds one of Robinson Crusoe's, in reverse, where two elderly women are about to leave France, unaccompanied by their servant, i.e., Friday, originally from the colonies, where the loss of a button on a shoe signifies a kind of shipwreck. The very independence entailed by the "flat-heeled oxfords" has been impeded while the dependence on a racially other servant will potentially leave them stranded as repatriation requires going it alone.

The first thing that happens on the boat is that Gertrude fears losing her voice:

> . . . I had never thought about my throat but now I was going to lecture I at once was certain that my voice was failing me and meeting Doctor Wood [a throat specialist] was perfect because I could tell him all my symptoms and he could console me. He did but even so I knew it would happen and it did, and when I was to give my first lecture I had a cold and my throat was troubling me, he had said I might and we telephoned to him, hearing his voice was already soothing but having him come and feel my pulse was everything and he was there at the first lecture and so was my voice and we have never seen him again but we do not forget him.[32]

Stein reveals that first she fears losing her voice, which she talks to the doctor about, and then she actually loses her voice, which results in listening to his, thus enabling her own to come back. Losing one's voice at the moment when one has to speak publicly is clearly overdetermined as a hysteric symptom, in contrast to the button snapping off the shoe, which has to do with clothes rather than the body. Yet, in both instances, they impede the process of Gertrude's becoming a celebrity, and in neither case is Alice able to perform her role as wife. Instead, she is described as "her secretary and companion," who, "dark and small," sits at the periphery, gazing raptly at Miss Stein, "chuckling mellowly" at the discomfort of her interviewers.

> xiii. "Speaker's Dress, Almost Like a Nun's, Forms Contrast With Brilliance of Audience"
>
> "Promptly at 9 o'clock Miss Stein, in a simple brown dress, plain and voluminous, walked to the platform of the ballroom from a side entrance and began reading her lecture without the formality of an introduction.
>
> The simplicity of her garb, the only adornment of which was a brooch at her throat, was in marked contrast to the gowns of most of her hearers and of the crimson damask hangings of the white walled museum. A number of the museum's socially prominent directors and members were present in the audience." (*New York Times,* 2 November 1934, 25)

Alice takes over the management of the tour, by firing the official manager, making herself responsible for all the arrangements, and protecting Gertrude from the undesired and undesirable. She will no longer be the only one to interpret the meaning of the brooch, now no longer the source of the voice but clasping a "garb" inferior in quality to the fabric of both the auditorium's curtains and the audience's attire. She likewise enforces the three requirements that Stein has for each lecture: She is to have no introduction; she is to be alone on stage, with a table to lean on; the audience will not exceed 500, and will not be charged admission. With these rules, Stein hopes to make, not her person, but her work the center of the attraction: Why provide an introduction when everybody already knows her? Why not use each lecture as a means of introducing her work by reciting extended portions of it? Lecturing will fill the space between the writing block she experiences as an effect of fame and the sequel she will write to *The Autobiography.*

In "What Are Masterpieces and Why Are There so Few of Them?" Stein makes the distinction between identity and entity, between human nature and the human mind, between writing for oneself and writing for others, arguing that masterpieces are creations of the human mind, which has nothing to do with identity, with memory, or with being in relation: "It is extremely difficult not to have identity but it is extremely difficult the knowing not having identity. One might say it is impossible but that it is not impossible is proved by the existence of master-pieces which are just that. They are knowing that there is no identity and producing while identity is not."[33] Identity, or human nature, is only the clothing that holds the attention of the thing itself, or entity. Identity is knowing who you are because someone recognizes you, but recognition prohibits creation by making that knowing common knowledge. Entity is the loss of identity that enables the creation of a masterpiece, because one has ceased to remember oneself and one fails to be recognized by another. Talking is not about entity but identity.

What Stein discovers while she is lecturing is that "gradually one ceased to hear what one said one heard what the audience hears one say, that is the reason that oratory is practically never a master-piece very rarely and very rarely history, because history deals with people who are orators who hear not what they are not what they say but what their audience hears them say."[34] To not know who one is or what one is saying, but rather to hear what the audience hears, makes it impossible for the self to continue in the position of audience. On the one hand, one requires two countries (America and France) and two occupations (writing and painting)—the opposition of inside and outside necessary to creation. On the other hand, one needs to lose one's identity in the production of masterpieces—to overcome the splitting of one into two (of the couple, of the orator) that is detrimental to creation. If France is "the place where those who have to be left alone have to be," then America is the place where one is never long without being confronted by one's own image.

The first image Stein confronts of herself is a moving electric sign in Times Square with her name on it: "Gertrude Stein has arrived in New York." She continues: "Anybody saying how do you do to you and knowing your name may be upsetting but on the whole it is natural enough but to suddenly see your name is always upsetting. Of course it has happened to me pretty often and I like it to happen just as often but always it does give a little shock of recognition and nonrecognition. It is one of the things most worrying in the subject of identity."[35] Once again, the problem of inside and outside is made more complex when one is not only able, but required, to see oneself from the outside. And inasmuch as one likes to be known, who is being referred to by that name?

The film company Pathé films Stein reading "Pigeons on the Grass," which has been incorporated into a newsreel: "When I saw myself almost as large and moving around and talking I did not like it particularly the talking, it gave me a funny feeling and I did not like that funny feeling. I suppose if I had seen it often it would have been like anything you can get used to anything if it happens often but that time I certainly did not like it. . . ."[36] Here again, Stein is forced to encounter herself from the outside, not just in terms of her name, which may or may not lead to recognition, but in terms of her voice, the voice that has been the instrument of recognition by others, either as lover or as genius. If, in the first case, she likes to see her name, even if it is disconcerting, in the second case she doesn't like to see or hear herself speaking. Although she does like to know that everyone is listening, which is why she likes broadcasting.

For the broadcast, they first take a photograph of her as though she were on the radio: "There was nothing natural or unnatural about that."[37] Then she insists on writing out the answers to the questions they will ask. Then she and the interviewer sit down on opposite sides of the microphone and are on the air. "And then it is over and I never had liked anything as I had liked it."[38] In each case, Stein emphasizes the shock, of something happening for the first time, and thus of it not seeming natural. Or, as Bryce Conrad suggests in "Gertrude Stein in the Market Place": "Stein's American tour shocked her into recognition of the unrecognizable Stein that was the marketplace's commodification of her, yet she persisted in believing that she had exercised determining control over her public dissemination."[39] In the case of broadcasting, the unreal manages to become natural: "This then was the last completion, of what is, that is that the unreal is natural, so natural that it makes of unreality the most natural of anything natural. That is what America does, and that is what America is."[40] Thus the unreal of America is not, like in France, unreal because one does not belong, i.e., one is an American, that is, an expatriate. Rather the unreality of America is about the production of images, the reproduction of oneself, and the market value of that image. But if broadcasting is like lecturing, then one begins to listen from the position of the audience and, inasmuch as one can't be seen, except in a photograph that is not recording a real event, it feels more like being a writer. And because the format is one of question and answer, the text it will produce will explain, both to herself and others, why she writes the way she does.

What, then, is the difference between looking at one's own portrait and having one's name or one's image reproduced through technological means? As the sitter, portrait painting allows for one's own composing while one is posing; the painter uses the model to enable an aesthetic solution, while the model begs the question of resemblance by posing her own aesthetic problem. By the time Stein goes to America, she has been the object of several photographic series, by Alvin Cobra, Man Ray, and Carl Van Vechten. But in America, she encounters a new form of multiple photographs, the layout:

> A layout, I said yes he said what is that I said oh he said it is four or five pictures of you doing anything. All right I said what do you want me to do. Why he said there is your airplane bag suppose you unpack it, oh I said Miss

> Toklas always does that oh no I could not do that, well he said there is the telephone suppose you telephone well I said yes I never do Miss Toklas always does that, well he said what can you do, well I said I can put my hat on and take my hat off and I can put my coat on and I can take it off and I like water I can drink a glass of water all right he said do that so I did that and he photographed while I did that and the next morning there was the layout and I had done it.[41]

While encountering one's name or one's voice raises issues having to do with identity inasmuch as there are two, one looking at another version of itself, the layout introduces the question of the event, the same person doing different things in sequence. The layout reintroduces the question of the queer couple in as much as a portrait is about doing nothing, or at most composing, whereas a layout requires activity, which in this case is what Alice does. But Alice is not there to do it. The things that Alice does cannot be photographed, while the gestures that are photographed hardly signify a celebrity. Alice's collaboration becomes invisible at the moment when Gertrude refuses to impersonate her by insisting on a strict division of labor.

> iv. "One must not forget that the earth seen from an airplane is more splendid than the earth seen from an automobile. The automobile is the end of progress on the earth, it goes quicker but essentially the landscapes seen from an automobile are the same as the landscapes seen from a carriage, a train, a wagon, or in walking. But the earth seen from an airplane is something else. So the twentieth century is not the same as the nineteenth century and it is very interesting knowing that Picasso has never seen the earth from an airplane, that being of the twentieth century he inevitably knew that the earth is not the same as in the nineteenth century, he knew it, he made it, inevitably he made it different and what he made is a thing that now all the world can see. When I was in America I for the first time travelled pretty much all the time in an airplane and when I looked at the earth I saw all the lines of cubism made at a time when not any painter had even gone up in an airplane. I saw there on the earth the mingling line of Picasso, coming and going, developing and destroying themselves, I saw the simple solutions of Braque, I saw the wandering lines of Masson, yes I saw and once more I knew that a creator is contemporary, he understands what is contemporary when the contemporaries do not yet know it. . . . (Gertrude Stein, *Picasso* [1938; 1959], 49–50)

The activity involving technological advancement that nevertheless had an enormous positive impact on Stein was flying. She and Alice flew for the first time from New York to Chicago, insisting on the company of their friend Carl Van Vechten.[42] After that, they flew frequently on their own: "I love airplanes I like them even better than automobiles I like the peaceful hum and the unequal rocking and the way everything looks from them after all if you like and I do like miniature anything and things streets or houses or trees or foliage made of wood or metal for children you naturally do like airplaning, it is completely that thing, it is that itself and what you see when you are looking."[43] From the air, entity, "that thing itself," once again takes precedence over identity, looking at another version of oneself. What she sees from the plane is "a real America," divided into quarter sections, looking neat and clean like the map of the United States, where states are divided by straight lines. At the same time, what she sees reminds her of France, of cubism, of a painting by Picasso. And thus flying takes her back to knowing, to what it means to know something without having seen it, to create something before it can be seen, inasmuch as it allows her to understand how the earth from a plane looks like a cubist painting even though Picasso never flew. Like Beryl Markham, who flew over Africa and described what she saw in terms of a child's drawing, to see what has always been there, to see it differently, is to know something prematurely, as avant-garde artist.

By the time Stein returns to France, the view from the air has become a trope for the human mind in *The Geographical History of America,* and Wilbur Wright has his portrait rewritten as that of a painter in *Four in America.* Even "the question of identity" has been rerouted via her relationship to her dog, "I am I because my little dog knows me . . . he is my audience, but an audience never does prove to you that you are you."[44] The white poodle, Basket, when the first one dies, is replaced by an identical dog, who is given the same name. In other words, the double portraiture of *The Autobiography of Alice B. Toklas,* predicated on Alice's recognition of Stein's genius, has become a philosophical conundrum having to do with audience, where it is no longer Alice but the little dog that puts into question who Gertrude Stein is.

xv. "If a woman was living with another woman as a domestic precondition for writing, as Stein was, the risk of being labelled a pollutant might hamper the authentic revelation of experience. If a woman was living with a man, though often in complex ways, as Woolf was, the conflict between the desires of the mind and the demands of the body, be that conflict conscious or unconscious, might inhibit the transformation of physicality into any public speech other than letters or gossip." (Catherine Stimpson, "The Mind, the Body and Gertrude Stein")

The Auto-ethnographer

"A huge silver monoplane glided gracefully to the surface of Mines Field in Los Angeles and came to a pretty stop after a short run. A liveried footman stepped out of the forward compartment armed with a stool which he placed under the rear door. Simultaneously a high-powered foreign car swept up close to the airplane and waited. The rear door of the airplane opened, and to the apparent surprise of the nearby mechanics a tall, black, distinguished-looking Negro stepped out and down to the ground, assisted by the hand of the footman. Behind him came a pale young man and woman, evidently secretaries. The three entered the limousine which rapidly drove off.

'Who's that coon?' asked one of the mechanics, round-eyed and respectful, like all Americans, in the presence of great wealth.

'Don't you know who that is?' inquired another, pityingly. 'Why that's that Dr. Crookman. You know, the fellow what's turnin' niggers white. See that B N M on the side of his plane? That stands for Black-No-More. Gee, I wish I had just half the jack he's made in the last six months.'"

—*George Schuyler,* Black No More *(1931)*

"'Aviation is poetry, Tess,' he said gravely. In his boyish idiom he explained his meaning. 'It's the finest kind of moving around, you know, just as poetry is the finest way of using words.'"

—*Jessie Redmon Fauset,* Comedy: American Style *(1933)*

"I think 'Melanctha' is marvellous. What surprises me is that in it Gertrude Stein is the first (I believe I'm right) white writer to write a story of love between a Negro man and woman and deal with them as normal members of the human family. Her style, which on the surface seems so naive—some might say childish, is really consummate artistry."

—*James Weldon Johnson, "Letter to Carl Van Vechten," 15 October 1933*

"Mr. Van Vechten is the first white novelist of note to undertake a portrayal of modern American Negro life under metropolitan conditions. Mr. Van Vechten is also the only white novelist I can now think of who has not viewed the Negro as a type, who has not treated the race as a unit, either good or bad. In Nigger Heaven *the author has chosen as his scene Harlem, where Negro life is at its highest point of urbanity and sophistication. . . ."*

—*James Weldon Johnson, "Romance and Tragedy in Harlem: A Review of Carl Van Vechten's* Nigger Heaven*,"* Opportunity *(1926)*

James Weldon Johnson by Winold Reiss. With permission from the National Portrait Gallery, Smithsonian Institute.

The New Negro as "Ex-Coloured Man": A Fictional Autobiography

i. "There are, however, many other ways of avoidance of proscription and prejudice. Of these one of no small importance is that popularly known as 'passing,' that is, those whose skin is of such color that they can pass as white may do so. This is not difficult; there are so many swarthy races represented in New York's population that even colored people who could easily be distinguished by their own race as Negroes, pass as French or Spanish or Cuban with ease. Of these there are two classes. First are those who for various reasons disappear entirely and go over the line to become white in business, social and all other relationships. The number of these is very large—much larger than is commonly suspected. . . .

The other group is made up of the many others who 'pass' only occasionally. Some of these do so for business reasons, others when they go out to dine or to the theater.

If a personal reference may be forgiven, I have had the unique experience within the past seven years of investigating some thirty-seven lynchings and eight race riots by the simple method of *not* telling those whom I was investigating of the Negro blood within my veins." (Walter White, "The Paradox of Color," in Alain Locke, ed. *The New Negro* [1925], 364–5)

ii. Passing

On sunny summer Sunday afternoons of Harlem
when the air is one interminable ball game
and grandma cannot get her gospel hymns
from the Saints of God in Christ
on account of the Dodgers on the radio,
on sunny Sunday afternoons
when the kids look all new
and far too clean to stay that way,
and Harlem has its washed-and-ironed-and-cleaned-best out,
the ones who've crossed the line

to live downtown
miss you,
Harlem of the bitter dream,
since their dream has
come true.
(Langston Hughes, *Montage of a Dream Deferred,* [1951])

James Weldon Johnson's *The Autobiography of an Ex-Coloured Man* (1912), like *The Autobiography of Alice B. Toklas,* initially appears without the name of an author on the title page. In the first case, Alice is assumed to be her own autobiographer, even as the photograph of Stein and Toklas on the cover points to a queer collaboration. In the second case, the "ex-coloured man" is presumed to be Johnson himself. Rather than writing the autobiography of someone else, he is considered the first African American to write a novel in the first person. Whereas Stein reveals herself as the author on the last page, Johnson is compelled to authenticate the fictional story as not his own by writing his autobiography, *Along This Way* (1933).

To authenticate a fictional narrative as not one's own life story ironizes the historical need for authenticating documents to guarantee that a slave narrative was written by an ex-slave, given the legal prohibition against literacy. Authenticating documents were typically provided by white abolitionists who, on the one hand, facilitated the coming-into-writing in the first person of former slaves and, on the other hand, used their writing to advance their own political agenda. The transition from a text requiring authentication to one demanding authenticity suggests that the ex-coloured man is already a New Negro but does not yet have a name. On the one hand, there can be no such thing as an ex-coloured man, given that "one drop of Negro blood" makes "once a negro, always a negro." On the other hand, it is possible in post-Reconstruction America to be "too white to be black and too black to be white," so that to be an ex-coloured man means to have forfeited the color that would provide the identity of somebody. The absence of a visual marker necessitates the presence of a speech act, or, as Miss Delany suggests in Frances Harper's *Iola Leroy* (1892), someone could simply put "a label on himself, saying, 'I am a colored man,' to prevent annoyance."[1]

The ex-coloured man who is no longer an ex-slave but does not yet have a name, has a clearly marked gender. This is not an unmarked masculinity but rather a patrilineality that carries no patronym. The ex-coloured man, as the offspring of a white father and a black mother, fails to inherit the father's name but also to see himself in his mother's color. Thus, he compromises his status as New Negro or potential race man by eventually crossing the color line and passing for white. Marrying a white woman becomes doubly inscribed as the scene of violence. On the one hand, the race of the sexual object choice is not embodied by the mother. This makes the shift from a black to a white object choice similar to the girl's trajectory in the oedipal narrative that requires her to shift her desire from the same-sex mother to the father. On the other hand, it means marrying the white woman whose violation becomes the ostensible rationale for lynch mobs, in order not to remain a black man like the one whose lynching the ex-coloured man witnesses before he decides to permanently cross over.

What is missing is the relationship to the father—unmarked and absent—that would necessarily mediate the son's desire to become an ex-coloured man. As Hortense Spillers suggests in "Mama's Baby, Papa's Maybe," through the institution of slavery "a dual fatherhood is set in motion, comprised of the African father's *banished* name and body and the captor father's mocking presence."[2] The white father's "mocking presence" means that he exists as lover, even love object of the black mother, but fails to be named by her as father of her child. The impossible identification of the son with the father is thus rewritten as the heteronormative desire he has for a white woman and the homosocial desire a white man has for him. It is this doubleness that negotiates the ex-coloured man's relationship to queerness as both a disclosure of the secrets of racial passing and a disavowal of same-sex desire.[3]

> iii. "In the core of the heart of the American race problem the sex factor is rooted." (James Weldon Johnson, *Along this Way* [1933], 170)

When W. E. B. Du Bois in *The Souls of Black Folk* (1903) records exchanging visiting-cards with fellow students in primary school in Great Barrington, Massachusetts, one of the girls refuses his card, "peremptorily, with a glance. Then it dawned on me with a certain suddenness that I was different from the others, or like, mayhap, in heart and life and longing, but shut out from their world by a vast veil. I had therefore no desire to tear down that veil, to creep through; I held all beyond it in utter contempt, and lived above it in a region of blue sky and great wandering shadows."[4] The difference that makes all the difference is not sexual, which can be mediated by the purchase and exchange of expensive visiting-cards to facilitate cross-gender courtship, but racial, figured by a veil, translucent enough to see through, thin enough to tear, yet strong enough to make a person who looks white be seen as black. The glance that marks Du Bois as different is cast back, rather than down, by a white girl whose rejection is read as racialized even as it implies exclusion from heteronormativity. To live above the veil means embracing a form of male homosocial bonding among mulatto New Negroes who, during the Harlem Renaissance

(1919–1929), shared a commitment to racial uplift by consolidating themselves as members of the Talented Tenth.

When James Weldon Johnson is arrested in Riverside Park in Jacksonville, Florida in 1901 for conversing with a female journalist from New York who looks white, recorded in *Along this Way,* he responds to the charge: "'Major . . . I know there is no use in discussing law or my rights on any such basis as, 'Suppose she *is* white?' so I tell you at once that according to the customs and, possibly, the laws of Florida, she is *not* white.' In spite of appearances, he, of course, knew that I spoke the truth."[5] The ambiguity of racial identity is encoded in a scene of ambiguous sexual meaning: talking on a bench in a park at the end of the streetcar line at the end of the day, "the scene was one of perfect semi-tropical beauty."[6] On the one hand, a moment of misrecognition places Johnson and the journalist, members of the opposite sex, on opposite sides of the color line, policed by the prohibition against miscegenation that has already been violated inasmuch as the woman is black but looks white. On the other hand, the speech act required by Johnson for his legal defense relies on the very discourse that polices racial identity by reading this scene of heteronormativity as illegal. The professional encounter becomes violent because it blurs with the scene of romance. Racial passing results from a national disavowal of people of mixed-race based on the denial of a history of "transforming personality into property."[7] Whereas Du Bois confronts the ontological condition of the mulatto—predicated on the rejection of the Negro by the white girl—by joining other male mulattos who rename themselves New Negroes, Johnson addresses the oxymoron of the ex-coloured man—looking white, while legally being classified as black—as epistemological conundrum.

W. E. B. Du Bois develops his idea of a double-consciousness in the form of a gift of "second sight" that prevents "true self-consciousness" inasmuch as one is "always looking at one's self through the eyes of others":

> One ever feels his twoness,—an American, a Negro; two souls, two thoughts, two unreconciled strivings; two warring ideals in one dark body, whose dogged strength alone keeps it from being torn asunder.[8]

Du Bois imagines two Faustian souls—the American and the Negro—at odds with each other, although housed in one unmistakably "dark body." Inasmuch as the body's strength genders it masculine, manhood would mean merging two souls into one, not as amalgamation, but as the "true self-consciousness" of masculine identity that knows itself not through someone else. The stigma stems not from a marked body, but a marked soul, a soul not visibly marked, but divided by consciousness. This consciousness compromises the body's masculinity by internalizing the look of the other, characteristic of femininity.

Johnson recapitulates this tension in the figure of the "coloured man":

> He is forced to take his outlook on all things, not from the view-point of a citizen, or a man, or even a human being, but from the view-point of a *coloured* man. . . .
>
> This gives to every coloured man, in proportion to his intellectuality, a sort of dual personality; there is one phase of him which is disclosed only in the freemasonry of his own race. I have often watched with interest and sometimes with amazement even ignorant coloured men under cover of broad grins and minstrel antics maintain this dualism in the presence of white men.
>
> I believe it to be a fact that the coloured people of this country know and understand the white people better than the white people know and understand them.[9]

Rather than two warring souls in one black body—the American and the Negro—Johnson's protagonist represents a "dual personality"—the "man" and the "coloured man." The colored man is positioned not in relationship to nationality but to race, not to being American but to not being white. His personality is nevertheless an embodied one—in the "broad grins and minstrel antics" of black minstrelsy (where white men engaged in racial cross-dressing by painting their faces with black cork)[10]—that is now performed as authentic blackness in the presence of whites. Thus colored men reflect back a white imaginary in the form not of a divided idealism, but a set of historical contradictions. Rather than masculine and thus ungendered, these two positions are gendered masculine. Yet their reliance on masquerade, like the reliance on looking through the eyes of the other, positions them as feminine. Their relationship becomes one grounded, as it was for Stein, not in the question of identity, but in the question of audience.

If, for Stein, autobiography means turning the self into an audience and lecturing means leading a kind of double life, for Johnson the problem for the "Aframerican author" is the problem of the "double audience": "It is more than a double audience it is a divided audience, an audience made up of two elements with differing and often opposite and antagonistic points of view. His audience is always both white America and black America."[11] The white audience is limited by convention, by its investment in negative stereotypes, "broad grins and minstrel antics," while the black audience is constrained by taboo, defensive in its insistence on the dissemination of positive images. According to Johnson, "The situation, moreover, constantly subjects him to the temptation of posing and posturing for the one audience or the other; and the sincerity and soundness of his work are vitiated whether he poses for white or black."[12] Rather than absorbing the ontological category of race into the abstract category of citizenship, as Du Bois would wish to do, Johnson recognizes black and white as ontological categories that produce two different epistemologies. The problem is not the difference, but the asymmetry: " . . . coloured people of this country know and understand the white people better than the white people know and understand them." The problem is not a warring identity, but a divided addressee: It becomes impossible not to pose for either audience.

> iv. "If Joyce was *le maitre* of the ultra-moderns, Gertrude Stein was the *madame,* and her house was open to all without discrimination. Even Negroes. I cannot remember how often people said to me: 'Haven't you been to Gertrude Stein's?' . . . 'Everybody goes to Gertrude Stein's.' . . . 'I'll take you to Gertrude Stein's.' . . . 'Gertrude Stein does not mind Negroes.' . . . 'Gertrude Stein has written the best story about Negroes, and if you mean to be a modern Negro writer, you should meet her. . . . 'I never went because of my aversion to cults and disciples. I liked meeting people as persons, not as divinities in temples. And when I came to examine 'Melanctha,' Gertrude Stein's Negro story, I could not see wherein intrinsically it was what it was cracked up to be.' (Claude McKay, *A Long Way From Home* [1937], 248)

From William Wells Brown's *Clotel* (1850) to Nella Larsen's *Passing* (1929), most tragic mulattos in literary texts have been women. For Barbara Christian, this can be explained by the appeal to a readership of romance fiction, whereby white female readers could identify with an octoroon heroine, someone who was equally white but failed to marry the wealthy lover because of the tragic "drop of black blood," from which they themselves were exempt.[13] For Hazel Carby, the mulatto serves as a mediating device at a particular moment in history, enabling the exploration of social relations during the entrenchment of Jim Crow laws after Reconstruction, as well as sexual relations between white masters and female slaves that remain the legacy of slavery and thus fall outside the narratives of romantic love.[14]

The image of the tragic mulatto as both beautiful and destined to die is both the offspring and agent of an illicit sexual union, suggesting that there is something feminizing about racial passing. Gertrude Stein, in making the heroine of her story "Melanctha" (1909) a mulatto, participates in a narrative tradition of cross-race romance by inflecting it with same-sex desire: "Melanctha Herbert was a graceful, pale yellow, intelligent, attractive negress. She had not been raised like Rose by white folks but then she had been half made with real white blood."[15] Not only is her mother a mulatto, like herself, but her father is not white, but black. But unlike Rose, "a real black negress," she is not about to be married. Melanctha is paired neither with the mulatto and pro-colored doctor, Jefferson Campbell, who acquires his knowledge from books, nor with Jane Harden, who can pass for white but drinks too much, and has a sexual knowledge that would allow her to act on her desire for Melanctha.

As varied as the potential trajectories of desire, the ontological status of mixed-race identity becomes variously described as "raised by white folks," "half white girl," and "so white hardly anyone could guess [Jane was a negress]."[16] Thus, Stein retells the triangulated same-sex desire of *Q. E. D.* as the heterosexual but racially other desire of "Melanctha," by constructing Melanctha as a sexual subject characterized by her "wandering," as both a desire for sex and for knowledge, that is, as a desire for sexual knowledge: "she wandered, always seeking but never more than very dimly seeing wisdom."[17] On the one hand, her wanderings take her to riding stables, railroad yards, and shipping docks, that is, the sites of promiscuity. On the other hand, she walks with Jeff Campbell on a Sunday in the country in the summer, a scene of romantic courtship. The phrases that recur to describe her relationship to sexual knowledge are clearly those that place knowing and narrating at odds with one another: "Melanctha's wanderings after wisdom she always had to do in secret and in snatches;" "She did not know what it was that she so badly wanted;" "Melanctha Herbert wanted very much to know and yet she feared the knowledge."[18] Inasmuch as cross-race sex is written on the body of the mulatto whose story is retold as tragedy, same-sex desire as not marked on the body remains untellable as a story, "Melanctha all her life did not know how to tell a story wholly."[19] Stein identifies with the tragic mulatto not as female reader but as queer writer, rewriting the trajectories of non-heteronormative romance as the multiple relations to whiteness on the part of black subjects ventriloquized by a white author.

v. "Harlem is today the Negro metropolis and as such is everywhere known. In the history of New York the name Harlem has changed from Dutch to Irish to Jewish to Negro; but it is through this last change that it has gained its most widespread fame. Throughout coloured America Harlem is the recognized Negro capital. Indeed, it is Mecca for the sightseer, the pleasure-seeker, the curious, the adventurous, the enterprising, the ambitious, and the talented of the entire Negro world; for the lure of it has reached down to every island of the Carib Sea and penetrated even into Africa. It is almost as well known to the white world, for it has been much talked and written about." (James Weldon Johnson, *Black Manhattan* [1930], 3)

vi. "'This here Harlem is a stinking sink of iniquity. Nigger Hell! That's what it is. Looka that theah ugly black nigger loving up a scrimpy brown gal right befoh mah eyes. Jes daring me to turn raw and loose lak them

> monkey-chasing womens thisanight. But that I wouldn't do. I ain't a woman abandoned to sich publicity stunts. Not even though mah craw was full to bursting. Lemme see'm tonight. . . . Yessam, this heah Harlem is sure nigger hell. Take me way away from it.'" (Claude McKay, *Home to Harlem* [1928], 99)

Harlem represents a place, the destination of a migration, this time not from slavery to freedom, but from an agricultural South to an industrialized North, another promise of a new geography of identity. Neither imperial colony nor immigrant ghetto, Harlem becomes, on the one hand, "the Mecca of the New Negro" as the "Culture Capital" of the Talented Tenth, and on the other hand, "Nigger Hell," "a stinking sink of iniquity," as farm laborers are transformed into an urban proletariat and Prohibition produces mob-owned nightclubs and working-class speakeasies. In between is "Nigger Heaven," the balcony in a theater reserved for Negroes who are prohibited seats in the orchestra, and the title of Carl Van Vechten's 1926 bestseller. Rather than looking at oneself through the eyes of others, one looks down on the white world, which occasionally looks up, but never beckons:

> It never seems to occur to them that Nigger Heaven is crowded, that there isn't another seat, that something has to be done. It doesn't seem to occur to them either . . . that we sit above them, that we can drop things down on them and crush them, that we can swoop down from this Nigger Heaven and take their seats.[20]

The new urban environment reproduces not just the difference between heaven and hell, which refers largely to class distinctions among Negroes, but also a color line that separates black from white, even as it enables crossing over the line or racial passing, for those of mixed-race able to circulate anonymously within a new public sphere. At the same time, a line divides Harlem from the rest of Manhattan, so that for Nordics like Van Vechten, moving above the line or beyond the Park, that is Central Park, enables a different kind of cross-racial identification, one that both relies on and disavows same-sex desire through slumming.[21]

For Van Vechten, the controversial patron of the Harlem Renaissance and the white person with whom Johnson has the longest and closest friendship, Harlem is less a place than "fresh, unused material" for the aspiring writer. The two protagonists of *Nigger Heaven,* Mary Love and Byron Kasson, are both New Negroes, in that they are light enough to pass but choose not to, and have never been South. Mary, the librarian, reads and attempts to promote expatriate avant-garde fiction: "She was reminded of a Negro story called Melanctha, in Gertrude Stein's Three Lives. A white assistant in the library had brought this book to her to read and she had been recommending it ever since, but it seemed that no other copies were available."[22] Byron, the would-be writer, is encouraged by a publisher to write about what he knows, which is assumed to be Harlem, but is actually an un-disguised version of Van Vechten's own novel: "Well, if you young Negro intellectuals don't get busy, a new crop of Nordics is going to spring up who will take the trouble to become better informed and will exploit this material before the Negro gets around to it."[23] Thus Mary and Byron, the failed romantic love interest, rewrite Stein and Van Vechten as queer couple, a woman in a lesbian marriage and a gay man married to the known lesbian Fania Marinoff, to whom the novel is dedicated. More importantly the novel generates publicity for two texts by white authors about black life. Thus Harlem becomes the source of ethnographic material for both whites and a black bourgeoisie, whereby whites rewrite their queer heteronormativity via the estrangement of the black middle class from its cultural origins in the South.

If Johnson's *The Autobiography* represents the first fictional first person narrative written by an African American, Bruce Nugent's story "Smoke, Lilies, and Jade" is considered the first piece of literature by an African American to treat the subject of homosexuality.[24] Published in 1926 under the pseudonym "Richard Bruce," in the first and only issue of the experimental magazine *FIRE!!*—conceived by Langston Hughes and Nugent, edited by Wallace Thurman, and financed by Van Vechten—the journal was meant to shock the older generation of "Niggerati" by declaring its independence from both established black periodicals like *Crisis* and *Opportunity* and white magazines such as *Harper's* and *Vanity Fair.* Considered the most experimental piece of writing to come out of the Harlem Renaissance in terms of its European modernist style, the story queers the subject of homosexuality by, on the one hand, making the protagonist, Alex, bisexual, and on the other hand, by making the object of his desire, Adrian—whom he names Beauty—neither white nor black, but Latin: "Alex was glad he had been addressed in Spanish . . . to have been asked for a match in English . . . or to have been addressed in English at all . . . would have been blasphemy just then. . . ."[25] Not only does Nugent seek to bypass the contradiction of racial difference by transcending it through a third term marked by linguistic differences, but Alex himself engages in a cross-racial identification with the European aesthete or dandy: " . . . was it Wilde who had said . . . a cigarette is the most perfect form of pleasure because it leaves one unsatisfied. . . ."[26] While sleeping next to Adrian, Alex has two identical dreams, first about Beauty, and then about Melva, his girlfriend: " . . . he was in love with Melva . . . and that explained that . . . he would like Beauty to know Melva . . . they were both so perfect . . . such compliments . . . yes he would like Beauty to know Melva because he loved them both . . . there . . . he had thought it . . . actually dared to think it. . . ."[27] While he dares to think that one can love two people of the opposite sex (together constituting a normative couple), he nevertheless dares to dream only about kissing Melva. The story ends with Alex thinking about Beauty, who has since departed on the train, as both embodying and transcending the mutual exclusivity of white and black, " . . . one *can* love two at the same time," even if one can never *be* two. Rather than queer whites disavowing same-sex desire by displacing it through racial difference, queer desire in Nugent's story is inflected by racial difference involving a bisexual subject who desires an object choice marked as neither white nor black.

Bruce Nugent reappears as Paul in Wallace Thurman's 1932 novel *Infants of the Spring,* one of the last novels to appear during the Harlem Renaissance and the one to deal most explicitly with homosexuality. Inasmuch as it provides a *roman à clef* to the major cast of characters frequenting "Niggerati Manor"—a rooming house at 267 W. 136th Street where rooms were provided rent-free to promote New Negro creativity by Iolanthe Sydney, the owner of a Harlem employment agency—it also functions as a summing up of the period in the form of a satire. It was those living at Niggerati Manor—Thurman, Hughes, Nugent—who organized, edited, and published *FIRE!!* Paul, who at one point is "amusing himself by conceiving a series of designs to illustrate Carl Van Vechten's *Nigger Heaven,*"[28] likewise has a dream: "I lay down. Then I became aware of a presence. An ivory body exuding some exotic perfume. Beauty dimmed my eyes. The physical nearness of that invisible presence called to me, lured me closer."[29] When asked by his audience whether the presence was male or female, he says he doesn't know. When asked whether he prefers affairs with women or men, he responds: "I really don't know. After all there are no sexes, only sex majorities, and the primary function of the sex act is enjoyment. Therefore I enjoyed one experience as much as the other."[30] Like Nugent's story, where it is possible to love two, in Thurman's novel, it is impossible to choose one, so that sexual queerness again takes the form of bisexuality as a way of constructing an already-stigmatized racial identity as less deviant. When Paul hears that his friend Aline is going to cross the line and pass for white, he responds:

> "I'm gonna quit being a nigger myself."
>
> "What are you going to do, Paul, be born again?"
>
> "No, Ray. I don't have to be born again. I can pass for Spanish. I have. Why, didn't I ever tell you about my trip to South America and how I was

> received at the Spanish Legation in Washington when I returned to this country?"[31]

Again the desire for the body that is both black and white, that is the mulatto, has been replaced with the desire for an identity that transcends black and white by passing for Spanish. The novel includes explicitly gay characters, like Eustace, a "swish" in a silk dressing gown. Yet the novel's protagonists, Stephen Jorgenson, a Nordic European who has never been to Harlem, and Raymond, a resident at Niggerati Manor who dreams of transcending race consciousness, form an interracial couple. Thurman's homoerotic subplot is neither redeemed by a third term, nor predicated on an emplotment of racial passing. The plot ends with the dissolution of the interracial couple and the death of the bisexual.

> vii. "There had been throughout the nation an announcement of a Negro Renaissance. The American Negro, it seemed, was entering a new phase in his development. He was about to become an important factor in the artistic life of the United States. As the middle westerner and the southerner had found indigenous expression, so was the Negro developing his own literary spokesmen." (Wallace Thurman, *Infants of the Spring* [1932], 61–2)

> viii. "For my part I was deeply stirred by the idea of a real Negro renaissance. The Arabian cultural renaissance and the great European Renaissance had provided some of my most fascinating reading. The Russian literary renaissance and also the Irish had absorbed my interest. My idea of a renaissance was one of talented persons of an ethnic or national group working individually or collectively in a common purpose and creating things that would be typical of their group.
>
> I was surprised when I discovered that many of the talented Negros regarded their renaissance more as an uplift organization and a vehicle to accelerate the pace of progress of smart Negro society." (Claude McKay, *A Long Way From Home* [1937], 321)

> viii. "The ordinary Negroes hadn't heard of the Negro Renaissance. And if they had, it hadn't raised their wages any. As for all those white folks in the speakeasies and night clubs of Harlem—well, maybe a colored man could find *some* place to have a drink that the tourists hadn't yet discovered." (Langston Hughes, *The Big Sea* [1940], 228)

Renaissance, understood not just as a relationship to the new, "a cultural blooming in a young nation,"[32] but as a return to a classical period, involves for the Talented Tenth, as it did for the Aesthetes, an indirect recovery. Like the Victorians who returned to the English Renaissance as a way to legitimate a same-sex desire that had initially been recovered in relationship to classical antiquity, the New Negro returns to an Africanism via the African primitivism of cubist painting influenced by artifacts found in the ethnographic museum in Paris. The Renaissance made same-sex desire legitimate for the European modernists by finding its origins with the Greeks; the Harlem Renaissance uses Africa, already appropriated by the Europeans, as a way of making themselves legitimately American.

Members of the Harlem Renaissance defined their project as two-pronged: writing against the old Negro as antebellum slave and against the "primitive" New Negro of the modernist avant-garde.[33] Yet the question remains where to locate the classical model from the perspective of Harlem, whether in Africa, as the origin of a culture that precedes slavery and offers the possibility of a pan-Africanism (Du Bois), or in the rural South, which relies on a nineteenth century understanding of nationhood in terms of a folk culture that is exclusively American (Johnson). If Renaissance likewise means "racial awakening in the form of arts and letters," then the Negro who has grown up in the North, like the ex-coloured man, becomes "new" by returning to the rural South, in order to revive the classical forms of an indigenous culture.

Rather than becoming a middle-class explorer in the urban slums of London's East End in the 1890s[34] or one of many "Anthropologists of Ourselves" who engaged in the "Mass Observation of British Life" on 12 May 1937,[35] the New Negro enters modernity as an ethnographer of his own race. For the ex-coloured man this means acquiring cultural capital not just by visiting the capitals of Europe—Paris, London, Berlin—but by recognizing Uncle Remus stories, Jubilee songs, the cake-walk, and rag time music as classical forms of American culture. Johnson's novel was first published in 1912, and then reissued by the publisher Alfred Knopf in 1927, with an introduction by Van Vechten. Passing into obscurity not just once but twice, the second time from "the Blue Jade Library"—the republication of a series of minor classics—Johnson's text serves as both a potential classical model for the Harlem Renaissance and the casualty of a cultural revival that begins to look more like a "vogue." Van Vechten's introduction authenticates that Johnson is not the subject of *The Autobiography,* while at the same time it confirms the text's status as "an invaluable source-book for the study of Negro psychology." Van Vechten himself relies on it for the writing of *Nigger Heaven* and recommends it for discussing "pretty nearly every phase of Negro life."

When Van Vechten reveals using Johnson's text as a sourcebook for his own novel, he authenticates it not as fiction, but as ethnographic material for his own fiction-making. Even though *The Autobiography* without autobiographical referent is fiction, it nevertheless "reads like a *real* autobiography," not because it depicts the author's own life story, but because "it reads like a composite autobiography of the Negro race in the United States in modern times."[36] A "composite autobiography" is only possible for a race to which one doesn't belong (otherwise one would negate one's own status as potential autobiographical subject), a race that in this case remains—as represented in the publishers' (Sherman, French and Co.) introduction to the first edition of the novel—"more or less a sphinx to the whites." The fiction, then, does not lie with the status of the text, but with the white reader who imagines being "initiated into the freemasonry, as it were, of the [black] race." The veil that Du Bois chose to transcend as a black man has been drawn aside for a white audience in order to offer "a glimpse behind the scenes of this race drama," "a bird's-eye view of the conflict which is being waged."[37] On the one hand, the text initiates white readers into the "freemasonry" of the black race; on the other hand, the text is about how blacks are successfully passing as white.

If the white reader imagines reading a composite autobiography, the New Negro writer produces a third kind of modernist memoir, the autoethnography. In *Imperial Eyes: Travel Writing and Transculturation,* Mary Louise Pratt describes "autoethnography" or "autoethnographic expression" as follows: "I use these terms to refer to instances in which colonized subjects undertake to represent themselves in ways that *engage with* the colonizer's own terms. If ethnographic texts are a means by which Europeans represent to themselves their (usually subjugated) others, autoethnographic texts are those the others construct in response to or in dialogue with those metropolitan representations."[38] But where is the metropole if, as Johnson argues, "the only things artistic in America that have sprung from American soil, permeated American life, and been universally acknowledged as distinctively American, [have] been the creations of the American Negro"?[39] And what does it mean for Harlem as Culture Capital if these "things artistic" are to be found in the South, as products of a former slave culture? What kinds of representations are available to the New Negro who has grown up in the North, migrates to Harlem, and eventually returns to the South, where the indigenous is already saturated by a history of literary authentication and a system of white patronage? What does it mean to investigate one's own culture as ethnographer in order to authenticate oneself autobiographically as New Negro?

The anonymity of authorship—the withholding of Johnson's name from the title-page—as well as the protagonist's anonymity—he is never given a name—reinforce the notion of the ex-coloured man as auto-ethnographer in search of a racial identity. Van Vechten's resistance to reading it as fiction comes not from knowing that it is true, based on interracial friendship, but from thinking that this is how he imagined it, as himself a Negro novelist.

Inasmuch as the story of an ex-slave belonged as much to the abolitionist as to the first person narrator, the story of the ex-coloured man becomes the story of anyone willing to claim authorship. Johnson remembers in his autobiography "being introduced to and talking with one man who tacitly admitted to those present that he was the author of the book."[40] Like the Aframerican author who, in his relationship to a double audience cannot escape posing for either whites or blacks, the ex-coloured man, who poses as both black and white, in the absence of a proper name, becomes the property of anybody. But unlike Alice, who becomes Alice B. in America and thus nobody by being lost in translation, the ex-coloured man lives only in the translation between white and black cultures. As "ex-" he is both erased and prior to his being named as somebody.

> x. "Tell them not to queer me, Ma, if they should ever run into me and the girl friend any place." (Langston Hughes, "Passing" in *The Ways of White Folks* [1934], 54)

When Johnson decides to maintain the anonymity of both the authorship and protagonist of his novel, he writes against the narratives of racial uplift, such as Booker T. Washington's *Up From Slavery* (1901), where the transformation of slave as private property into the ex-slave as freeman involves a process of renaming. Having had only one name, it was considered "far from proper" to supplement that name with the surname of the former slave-owner:

> If "John" or "Susan" belonged to a white man by the name of "Hatcher,'" sometimes he was called "John Hatcher," or as often "Hatcher's John." But there was a feeling that "John Hatcher" or "Hatcher's John" was not the proper title by which to denote a freeman; and so in many cases "John Hatcher" was changed to "John S. Lincoln" or "John S. Sherman," the initial "S" standing for no name, it being simply a part of what the coloured man proudly called his "entitles."[41]

On the one hand, paternity is literalized as property ownership, as in "Hatcher's John"; on the other hand, the middle initial serves as empty signifier. The surname refers to men who were neither known property owners, nor unknown biological fathers, but rather national emancipators, like Washington or Lincoln. Booker T. Washington himself had always been known simply as Booker, until the school roll-call made him realize that everyone else had two names. Thus, Washington comes to signify a process of self-naming. Later, he learns that his mother gave him the name Booker Taliaferro, the second name having been forgotten. Thus, the middle initial marks not a national promise in the form of legal "entitles," but engraves the memory of a black mother.

Although Johnson refrains from naming either himself or his protagonist, he nevertheless changes his own middle name from William to Weldon after the publication of *The Autobiography,* as he begins to think about embarking on a literary career. "'You can see,' he wrote George Towns [in 1913], 'that Jim Bill Johnson will not do for a man who pretends to write poetry or anything else.' James Weldon Johnson, he felt, gave him a distinctive literary 'trade mark.'"[42] Already a published author, Johnson nevertheless feels that his name fails to carry the authority that would allow him to pretend to authorship. The renaming also marks a reself-fashioning as Johnson abandons several previous careers, as schoolteacher, songwriter, lawyer, and journalist, to write his only novel while on assignment in Latin America as foreign diplomat.

The questions raised by naming, such as those having to do with paternity and maternity, citizenship and authorship, are questions that appear at the beginning of *The Autobiography* in the form of epistemological conundrums for the unnamed protagonist. As in the case of Washington and Du Bois, the moment of recognition, or misrecognition, takes place in the school room, a public institution that marks the transition from a private identity to its public performance. In the case of the ex-coloured man, this becomes the moment when he is told by his teacher to sit down while the white students are asked to stand up. Shocked by the knowledge that he is a different person from the one he thought he was, he runs home and confronts his mother with a series of questions:

> "Mother, mother, tell me, am I a nigger?. . . ."
>
> "No, my darling, you are not a nigger. . . ."
>
> "Well, mother, am I white? Are you white?. . . ."
>
> "No, I am not white, but you—your father is one of the greatest men in the country, the best blood of the South is in you—. . . ."
>
> "Who is my father? Where is he?. . . ."
>
> "I'll tell you about him someday. . . . No, not now. . . ."
>
> "This is your father."[43]

The first secret, then, is not that of racial passing, but that of paternity, the question that is both deferred and eventually addressed by the father's reappearance. The fact that the ex-coloured man's mother is not white but he is not a "nigger" requires the role of an intermediary that would enable the construction of an identity out of two negatives. The father can't be named, not because he doesn't have a proper name, but because it can't be known and thus appropriated, like that of Sherman or Washington. Even the father's racial identity can't be spoken, while his geographical location makes him unlocatable to a son who has been relocated from the South to Connecticut. When he does reappear, the "name 'father'" cannot be reconciled with the need for a father, which appears to be absent, since he is unlike any father the protagonist has encountered in his reading of literature.

The irresolution of the epistemological conundrum is preceded by an attempt at an ontological solution, in the form of an encounter with the mirror:

> I was accustomed to hear remarks about my beauty; but now, for the first time, I became conscious of it and recognized it. I noticed the ivory whiteness of my skin, the beauty of my mouth, the size and liquid darkness of my eyes, and how the long, black lashes that fringed and shaded them produced an effect that was strangely fascinating even to me. I noticed the softness and glossiness of my dark hair that fell in waves over my temples, making my forehead whiter than it really was. How long I stood there gazing at my image I do not know.[44]

The fascination with one's own reflection is clearly a rewriting of Ovid's Narcissus, as the encounter with an image that, in this case, makes present an absent white father at the very moment when the son has been identified as black. Feminized by both the secret of his mother's blackness and the fascination with his own image, the ex-coloured man encounters himself as male mulatto. Staged as both homoerotic and feminizing, the encounter with white masculinity is predicated on the Name of the Father that has no function and a father's name that cannot be mentioned. Paternity remains a fiction for the black son, whether legal (according to Freud) or literary (according to the protagonist). Thus, the ex-coloured man's relationship to white masculinity bypasses the heteronormativity of white master and former female slave (of which he is the illegitimate offspring) and ex-coloured man and white woman (whose offspring he will father), even as it never explicitly becomes sexual. Queerness does not refer to the sexual secrets of same-sex desire, but to racial secrets that must be maintained as fictions for a white audience.

> xi. "D— was, so far as I can remember, the only man I have known to 'pass'—and I have known numbers of them—without feeling it was necessary to 'pass up' his colored friends." (James Weldon Johnson, *Along This Way* [1933] 252)

Inasmuch as to queer means to straighten out a passing identity, the excoloured man, without name or autobiographical referent, represents not just anybody. Rather, he can be read as a composite compiled of a series of homosocial encounters recounted in *The Autobiography* and then reconstructed retrospectively in Johnson's autobiography. Johnson's close friend, referred to as "D—" in *Along This Way,* has been identified by Johnson's biographer, Eugene Levy, as J. Douglass Wetmore, a boyhood friend who joined him as roommate at Atlanta University and eventually became his law partner in Jacksonville. Wetmore moves to New York just as Johnson embarks for Venezuela as consul. Having begun to involuntarily pass as a law student at the University of Michigan, he opens a law practice in New York with an almost exclusively white clientele, marries a Jewish woman, makes and then loses money in the Florida real estate market, and in 1930, shoots himself through the heart, having pronounced as his last words that "he was just tired of life." Johnson learns of his death from reading the newspaper and writes in his autobiography: "Death has grieved me more deeply, but never has it more terribly shocked me."[45] Johnson acknowledges Wetmore as the model for his protagonist, but only in an unpublished note attached to the original manuscript. He writes the novel while in Venezuela, returns to New York to marry Grace Nail, and returns with her and the revised manuscript from Nicaragua, his second and last diplomatic post. Just as *The Autobiography* is not Johnson's autobiography, so the events of the life of the ex-coloured man are not those of J. Douglass Wetmore. Yet Johnson chose to keep secret the identity of his closest male friend in order not to queer his racial identity.

Inasmuch as Woolf and Stein as female auto/biographers produce the portraits of their lovers at the moment of the couple's pending dissolution, the male auto-ethnographer writes himself into public discourse by means of the legitimation provided by another man whose masculinity is unmarked. Rather than protecting a female friendship against the withdrawal of the sexual, male homosociality involves the protection of itself against the prohibition of homosexuality. Two moments in *Along This Way* produce a tension between racial and sexual identity that prohibit the homosocial from becoming sexualized in the relationship between Johnson and D—. One is constructed as a specular relationship that rewrites the scene in the mirror in the form of public spectatorship, while the other takes the form of a triangulated desire rewritten as narcissistic encounter. The first consists of a physical description of D— once he and Johnson both become college students:

> D— was a *rara avis* at Atlanta University; nothing like him had ever before been seen in that cage. Yet he was popular with the boys and girls, and strange to say, even with the teachers. His very rakishness had a definite charm. And underneath his somewhat ribald manner he was tender-hearted and generous. Moreover, he was extremely good-looking, having, in fact, a

> sort of Byronic beauty. He was short and inclined to stoutness. When he was a small boy, he was fat. His head, large out of proportion to his height, was covered with thick, dark brown hair that set off his pale face and fine hazel eyes. The only thing that marred his looks was the frequent raising of the drooping corners of his mouth in a cynical curl. But speaking of his face as pale does not convey the full truth; for neither in color, features, nor hair could one detect that he had a single drop of Negro blood.[46]

The autoerotic scene in front of the mirror in *The Autobiography* becomes a homoerotic scene in the autobiography. The childhood friend is represented in terms of his bisexual attractiveness and his biracial identity as a student who lacks any Negro features at an historically black university. His description as a "rare bird," as someone who had "never before been seen," lies in the fact that he can't be seen in any way as Negro. His whiteness becomes eroticized as both "rakishness" and "Byronic beauty," although "the full truth" to be disclosed is not sexual, but the illogic of a racial identity based on what is not visible. Thus, narcissistic attraction to one's own image becomes rewritten as the attraction of one male mulatto to another, where the one who fails to pass as white desires the one who does, as in Nella Larsen's *Passing.*

Looking at oneself through the eyes of others produces the position of the feminine as well as the racially other, and therefore fails to make of the Negro a man. The triangulation of desire, a desire "between men," is mediated by the presence of a woman who, in this case, is made present through the epistolary:

> Throughout our lives, D— in all his love affairs had sooner or later made me a sort of confessor. He frequently did something that I should rather have lost a finger than do, he would read me most ardent letters from his lady loves; I recall, in particular, letters he received for several years from a girl he met at the University of Michigan, letters too tender, too sincere, yes, too sacred to be seen by a third pair of eyes; yet he read them to me. It may have been an injustice to him, but I always suspected that the act was not purely confidential in its nature, but was more or less mixed with vainglory.[47]

Again Johnson positions himself as "a third pair of eyes," this time in relationship to a heteronormative couple. By making D— the recipient of a woman's amorous discourse, he is provided with a language to address another man. The anxiety produced by this exchange leads Johnson to confess that he would "rather lose a finger" than take another man into this sort of confidence. He defends himself against D—'s desire by reading the scene as narcissistic, "more or less mixed with vainglory." The fact that the letter originates from the moment when D— first begins to pass, makes the letter doubly charged with sexual exhibition and racial secrecy.

> xii. "One of the most promising of the young Negro poets said to me once, 'I want to be a poet—not a Negro poet,' meaning, I believe, 'I want to write like a white poet'; meaning subconsciously, 'I would like to be a white poet'; meaning behind that, 'I would like to be white.' And I was sorry the young man said that, for no great poet has ever been afraid of being himself." (Langston Hughes, "The Negro Artist and the Racial Mountain," *The Nation* [1926] in *Voices from the Harlem Renaissance,* 305)

The most eroticized scenes in *The Autobiography* are not those that involve the ex-coloured man's attraction to white women, like the beautiful "white thing" he will marry to ensure the "racial purity" of his biological offspring. Rather they focus on the relationship to his white male patron, his "millionaire friend," who hires and lends him out to play ragtime on the piano, takes him to Europe in place of his valet and tries to convince him to pass as the white man he has always been. The literary critical tradition has only recently begun to read this scene as also homoerotic.[48] Philip Brian Harper in *Are We Not Men?* recognizes the ex-coloured man as having a gender identity that "is anything but properly masculine," and "a sexual identity that is anything but hetero,"[49] and thus reads the millionaire's suicide as the tragic situation that "salvages for the protagonist the possibility of a feminine identification without the male-directed sexual orientation that it regularly implies."[50] Yet the significance of the suicide (which happens much later) lies not with its premature separation of the two men, but with its function as a sign of sexual queerness.

While the millionaire plays the part of a white man, historically the master and/or absent father, his attraction to the tragic mulatto takes the form of same-sex desire. Reminiscent of D—, a "curious, almost cynical, smile" grows on the millionaire's lips, as the ex-coloured man announces his desire to return to the United States after seeing his biological father with his legitimate sister at the opera in Paris. Unlike the father, who refuses to recognize him and prohibits recognition on the part of the son, the millionaire is the white man who recognizes him as the ex-coloured man he will become: "My boy, you are by blood, by appearance, by education, and by tastes a white man. . . . What kind of a Negro would you make now, especially in the South? . . . I can imagine no more dissatisfied human being than an educated, cultured, and refined coloured man in the United States."[51] In a world where the white father can neither be named nor recognized, white masculinity becomes both an impossible object of desire and a powerful object of identification. This leaves the homoerotic both unexpressed: "All this he did almost coldly; I often wondered whether he was in a hurry to get rid of what he considered a fool, or whether he was striving to hide deeper feelings," and unnarratable: "My affection for him was so strong, my recollections of him are so distinct, he was such a peculiar and striking character, that I could easily fill several chapters with reminiscences of him; but for fear of tiring the reader I shall go on with my narration."[52] The millionaire, by wanting to see in the protagonist a reflection of himself, stands in the place of the white father, between the black mother who allows her son to believe he is white and the white woman who will guarantee his racial passing. But he fails to function as the ex-coloured man's object of desire because he necessarily stands in as surrogate object of identification. By insisting on the ex-coloured man's whiteness, the millionaire desires the ex-coloured man like a son, that is, homosocially, rather than cross-racially, which would involve the additionally transgressive desire "between men."

Likewise modeled on a person who appears in Johnson's autobiography, the millionaire friend rewrites the aesthete not as queer but as cosmopolitan. Dr. Summers, a renowned surgeon in Florida who eventually takes his own life, hires Johnson as his receptionist and, in turn, Johnson shows him the poetry he is writing:

> Dr. Summers was an extraordinary man. Of course, he was educated; but I had by now known a number of educated people. What was unprecedented for me was that in him I came into close touch with a man of great culture. He was, moreover, a cosmopolite. He had traveled a good part of the world over, through Europe, to North Africa, to Greece and Turkey. He spoke French and German, the latter, because of his student days in Germany, as fluently as he did English. He had wide knowledge of literature, and was himself a poet. His local literary reputation was very high because of the poems he sometimes contributed to the *Times-Union*. He was an accomplished and brilliant talker. When alone, however, he was generally melancholy. He would sit for a long period inhaling from a small can of ether, seemingly lost in dreams.[53]

His library houses a collection of erotica and his travels take him to Richard Burton's Sotadic Zone, both code for the same-sex desires of the melancholy dandy who drowns his unmanly tastes in ether. Summers is the "man of culture," who speaks many languages and is at home in many places, thus escaping the conundrum of American as national identity that excludes the Negro (and the homosexual) as fully masculine. The cosmopolitan becomes a paternal substitute who enables Johnson to imagine transcending racial difference not by crossing over the color line, but by transcending it through the renunciation of a national identity.

A final figure completes the series of homosocial encounters rewritten as the character of the ex-coloured man, that of another childhood friend, this time the son of a friend of a friend from Cuba temporarily adopted by Johnson's parents: "The boy was Ricardo Rodriguez—later he added the name Ponce. He was about my age, very good-looking, with the light bronze complexion that so many colored Cubans have, and also with the proverbial Latin temperament."[54] From Ricardo, a surrogate sibling, Johnson learns to speak Spanish, which in more than one instance will enable him to pass, most significantly during his first train trip to Atlanta where speaking a foreign language allows him to remain in the first-class car. As in Thurman's novel, passing does not mean becoming, or reassigning oneself as white, but rather avoiding any assignment of color by re-fashioning oneself as cosmopolitan. As in Nugent's story, Latin refers not only to the foreign that escapes the illogic of a national understanding of race that constitutes "man" and "coloured man" as oxymoron, but also to the possibility of a same-sex desire not stigmatised as sexually queer.[55]

xiii. Lunch in a Jim Crow Car

> Get out the lunch-box of your dreams
> Bite into the sandwich of your heart,
> And ride the Jim Crow car until it screams
> Then—like an atom bomb—it bursts apart.
> (Langston Hughes, *Words Like Freedom* [1959]

The train, as means of transportation, connotes a pattern of flight, both to freedom via the underground railroad before emancipation, and from South to North during the Great Migration between the two world wars. It marks a liminal space, the place of a subject in transit, but also the site of racial policing. The Jim Crow car becomes a classic locus for both challenging and reinforcing the logic of the disavowal of people of mixed-race, whether in *Plessy vs. Ferguson* (1896) or *Up From Slavery.* Like the theater, where Johnson learns not to give his tickets to the usher who will exchange orchestra seats for those in Nigger Heaven, it is on the train that he invokes his knowledge of Spanish to confuse the racial distinction between white and black. Unlike the plane, which is imagined as transcending Jim Crow laws, the Jim Crow car becomes the site where racial differences are naturalized.

The ex-coloured man, by joining four other men riding between Nashville and Atlanta in the smoker, involuntarily passes. The conversation between a Jewish cigar manufacturer in Florida, a young man with spectacles from Ohio teaching at a state university in Alabama, an old Union soldier, and a cotton-planter from Texas, inevitably turns to the Negro question. The Jew empathizes with Negro oppression being himself a member of an oppressed group and the young professor guiltily confesses to having shifted his geopolitical allegiances after one year in the South. Thus the Jew and the professor, the men who are feminized by existing on both sides of the line, drop out of the conversation, leaving the union soldier and the cotton planter to discuss who should be held responsible for the Civil War. When the discussion turns to questions of racial inferiority, the Texan asks: "'Do you want to see a mulatto South? To bring it right home to you, would you let your daughter marry a nigger?'" It is a question to which the soldier responds: "'No, I wouldn't consent to my daughter's marrying a nigger, but that doesn't prevent my treating a black man fairly.'"[56] On the one hand, there is the racism of the Southerner; on the other hand, there is the duplicity of the Northerner. On the one hand, there is the fear of a "mulatto South" as a result of the marriage between a black man and a white woman; on the other hand, there is the presence of the ex-coloured man, the product of an unsanctioned love between a white man and a black woman. In the end, it is not his invisibility in the smoker that transforms his involuntary into voluntary passing. Rather it is witnessing the scene of violence that marks the difference between a black masculinity able to pass as foreigner and the black male body as legally lynchable.

> xiv. "In the first place, this passing business works both ways. All the passing is not passing for white. We have white folks among us passing for colored. They just happened to be born with a tinge of brown in the skin and took up being colored as a profession. Take James Weldon Johnson, for instance.
>
> There's a man white enough to suit Hitler, and he's been passing for colored for years. . . .
>
> So now you say 'Well, if you can't tell who my people are by skin color, how are you going to know?' There's more ways than one of telling, and I'm going to point them out right now." (Zora Neale Hurston, *Dust Tracks on the Road,* [1942], 215–16)

Although Johnson was born a Southerner, he says of himself he "was born to be a New Yorker."[57] When he contemplates a "magical change of race," as he imagines every intelligent Negro in the United States has done, he finds that "I do not want to be anyone but myself." Yet, were he at the mercy of a "jinnee" forcing him to choose a different race, he would respond: "Make me a Jew."[58] The Jew, like the white man, has unlimited economic potential. Unlike the white man, he is the member of an oppressed minority and thus potentially able to empathize with other oppressed groups. Able to pass for white, the Jew, like the dandy, becomes, at the turn of the century, a signifier of the potential threat of homosexuality to a homosocial masculinity.

Johnson never crosses the color line, although he imagines becoming a Jew, while D— engages in passing, although he meets his premature end as tragic mulatto. The ex-coloured man begins the story of his own passing as white by queering his racial identity in the language of a sexual secret: "I am divulging the great secret of my life, the secret which for some years I have guarded far more carefully than any of my earthly possessions."[59] The racial secret involves not just the relationship between black and white, but is saturated with encounters "between men." The conflation of illegitimacy (as the offspring of an unsanctioned love), miscegenation (as the union between a white man and a black woman), and lynching (as the retribution for the alleged rape of the white woman by the black man) inscribe the modernist narrative of passing within a racially inflected discourse that leaves repressed the predominantly same-sex desires of the almost uniform male mulatto identities of those who constituted the Harlem Renaissance. Most of these men attempt to divert the compromised manhood of a stigmatized racial identity into heteronormative marriage. For the sexually queer, homosexuality is rerouted through bisexuality and Spanish as a linguistic difference that serves to transcend the scopic illogic of the difference between white and black. For those who pass as white, to queer means to make known someone else's black identity to a white audience.

If D— is a Negro who passes for white and Summers a bachelor addicted to ether, both of whom commit suicide, and Ricardo, beautiful like D—, but neither black nor white, then the ex-coloured man becomes the signifier of an erotic, not just racial impossiblity, signified by the lack of a name. The ex-coloured man is predicated not on Johnson's own life story, but on the story of a queer desire, not to pass as white, but for another male mulatto whose passing Johnson refuses to queer. The relationship between Johnson's fictional autobiography of an ex-coloured man and his autobiography *Along This Way* confuses the distinction between identification and desire, just as mixed-race identities confuse the epistemological, given that seeing is a form of knowing.

xv. "The railway station is thus a concentration point for a number of dimensions in the homosexual form of existence, one of the spaces that collects, reflects and amplifies within it essential features of his life-world; on a par with the discotheque, the consulting room and the opera. The special thing about the station is that it is also a *travel space,* a place for departures and arrivals. Hence additional moods that vibrate with those of the homosexual; of breaking up, of something fluid, less complete and clear-cut, of chronic transit away, of experiences and adventures, of another country. We leave him there, absorbed in what is and with the dream that it might be different." (Henning Bech, *When Men Meet,* 159)

Sexological Prelude

"I found my way to Riverside Drive and the Soldiers and Sailors Monument." He still knew almost no one in the city, but his cruising quickly remedied that. "It was 1927, about two or three days before the big reception parade for Lindbergh after he came back from his flight to Paris, and the bleachers were already up there. I met a man there and we started talking. He was a Harvard man and taught ethical culture. And that was the best contact I made; he and I had a wonderful affair."

—*Quoted in George Chauncey,* Gay New York

"Vincent had on a white satin blouse and black breeches. Dear I'm master of ceremonies tonight and you should have come in drag you'd have gotten a prize. He had large eyes with a sex-life all their own and claimed to be the hardest boiled queen on Broadway. Frederick he said you look like something Lindbergh dropped on the way across. Dry yourself Bella!"

—*Charles Henry Ford and Parker Tyler,*
The Young and Evil *(1933)*

Cafe: 3 A.M.

Detectives from the vice squad
with weary sadistic eyes
spotting fairies.
Degenerates,
some folks say.

But God, Nature,
or somebody
made them that way.

Police lady or Lesbian
over there?
Where?

—*Langston Hughes,* Montage
of a Dream Deferred *(1951)*

E. M. Forster begins to write *Maurice* in 1913 after his second or third stay at Millthorpe in Sheffield where he visits Edward Carpenter and George Merrill. George, apparently, touched Forster's backside, "gently and just above the buttocks," in such a way that enables him to complete a novel in 1914 that won't be published until 1971. Lytton Strachey, an early reader, recognizes himself in the character Risley. Forster sends a copy of the manuscript to Carpenter, whose portrait Roger Fry painted in 1895.

Edward Carpenter, in turn, sends a copy of *Towards Democracy* (1892) to John Addington Symonds, who is residing in Davos, Switzerland, where he is being treated for tuberculosis. In 1889, Symonds begins to write his own memoirs, having just translated two from the Italian—Count Carlo Gozzi's and Benvenuto Cellini's. He thinks the work can't be published; he assumes there is nothing like it in print; he imagines it to be his most important piece of writing. He does not want the autobiography to be destroyed, but cautions against its publication. Symonds's literary executor, Horatio Brown—at his own death in 1926—leaves instructions that it not be published for 50 years. Brown nevertheless expurgates much of it in his own work, *John Addington Symonds: A Biography,* which appears a year after Symonds's death. In 1949, the green cloth box containing the manuscript is opened when Symonds's daughter requests permission to do so from the London Library. It is made available to scholars in 1954 and finally published—one fifth of the original—in 1984.

Symonds's "A Problem in Greek Ethics," written in 1873 and published in 1883—10 copies for private circulation—is considered the first historical study of homosexuality in English. Its focus: "Greek love" or *paiderastia.* Symonds also collaborates with Havelock Ellis, whom he never meets—although a nine-week trip to England would have allowed him to do so—on *Sexual Inversion.* "A Problem in Greek Ethics" originally appears as Chapter Three and then as Appendix A when *Sexual Inversion* is finally published in English. "A Problem in Modern Ethics," another treatise on homosexuality, is distributed in fragmented form throughout the book.

In 1886, the Labouchère Amendment to the Criminal Law Amendment Act makes the private and public "acts of gross indecency" between men a misdemeanor punishable with two years of hard labor and contact *per anum* a felony punishable with penal servitude for life.

Symonds dies suddenly in Rome in 1893.

Oscar Wilde is arrested in 1895.

Sexual Inversion is first published in German as *Das Konträre Geschlechtsgefühl* in 1896. When it finally appears in English in 1897, Horatio Brown, himself a homosexual, buys up the entire first run and has it destroyed. Brown asks Ellis to remove Symonds's name from the title page, to delete his essay on "Greek Ethics" altogether, and a bookseller, George Bedborough, is brought to trial on grounds of obscenity. Ellis, a medical man, is relieved that he will not have to share authorship with a sexual invert. Symonds composes the questionnaire and gathers the cases, although it remains unclear who actually writes them. Carpenter's case history (Case VI) is told "in the subject's own words," while Symonds's (Case XVIII)—"a very radical case of sexual inversion"—appears in the third person. Unlike Krafft-Ebing's *Psychopathia Sexualis* (1889), the first sexological bestseller, which contains 200 cases, Ellis claims that his work contains the first set of 33 cases unconnected to the asylum or prison. Ellis's *Studies in the Psychology of Sex,* of which *Sexual Inversion* is the first volume, has never been published in England to this day.

Symonds and Magnus Hirschfeld both make pilgrimages to Karl Ulrichs's grave in Aquila, Italy: Symonds in 1891 and Hirschfeld in 1909. Ulrichs, with whom Symonds engages in daily correspondence, coins the term "Urning" after the patron goddess of men who love men, Aphrodite Urania, in Plato's *Symposium.* Of the 12 pamphlets he authors—compiled and published by Hirschfeld in 1898—on "the riddle of man-manly love"—"Memnon" (1867) is the first not to appear under his pseudonym, Numa Numantius. The years in Aquila are spent publishing an international journal in Latin, the language of science and all things universal and enduring.

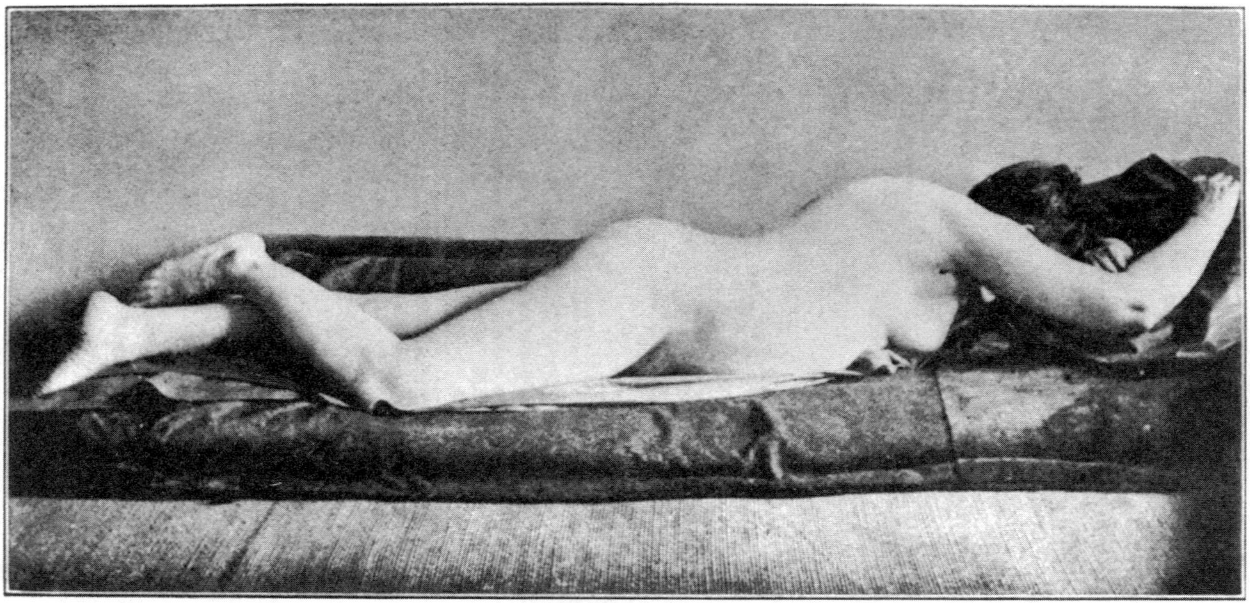

The author—a modern living replica of the ancient Greek statue "Hermaphroditos." Public domain.

The Androgyne as "Fairie": A Self-Authored Case History

> i. "To put it simply, the historical positing of the category of 'the homosexual' textualizes male identity as such, subjecting it to the alienating requirement that it be 'read,' and threatening, in consequence, to strip 'masculinity' of its privileged status as the self-authenticating paradigm of the natural or the self-evident itself. Now it must *perform* its self-evidence, must represent its own difference from the derivative and artificial 'masculinity' of the gay man. The homosexual, in such a social context, is made to bear the stigma of writing or textuality *as his identity,* as the very expression of his anatomy, by a masculinist culture eager to preserve the authority of its own self-identity through the institution of a homographesis whose logic of legibility, of graphic difference, would deny the common 'masculinity,' the common signifying relation to maleness, of gay men and straight men alike." (Lee Edelman, *Homographesis,* 12)

James Weldon Johnson's *The Autobiography of an Ex-Coloured Man* and *Autobiography of an Androgyne* both require introductions written by recognized authorities representative of an unmarked masculinity to enable the entrance of their autobiographical narratives into public discourse. In the first case, Johnson is not the ex-coloured man; in the second case, the text is authored by someone known only by his three pseudonyms—Earl Lind, author of *Autobiography of an Androgyne* (1918); Ralph Werther, author of *The Female-Impersonators* (1922); and the lesser used Jennie June. In the first case, authorship remains dependent on the white patron, Van Vechten, who testifies to the authenticity of black life in order to promote his own fictional narrative as much as to authenticate his friend's; in the second, on the medico-legal publisher, Alfred W. Herzog, who agrees to publish a text he considers of little scientific or literary value because it provides further evidence for the congenital, rather than criminal basis of sexual anomaly. If Johnson's text represents the first novel written in the first person by an African American, Earl Lind is one of the first users of the printed word "fairie," referring to "youthful androgyne" or "passive invert."

Each text requires a defense that makes claims for it as suitable material for a general reading public by defending it as "psychological study": the former on the grounds that whites finally will be able to enter the "freemasonry" of the black race, the latter on the grounds that knowledge about sexual inversion should not be limited to medico-legal professionals. The claim for psychological interest is made in order to justify inquiry into the life of a hybrid body, both as stigmatized individual and as deviant sociological type. The hybrid bodies of the racial passer and the passive invert require an ethnography inasmuch as they inhabit two cultures, one of them invisible to majority readers, and thus, in need of translation. The ethnography takes the form of an auto-ethnography, in this case not because the New Negro has to acculturate himself to the classical forms necessary to promote a Renaissance, but because the androgyne as autobiographical subject is native informant to the underworld of the fairy, an identity that likewise begins to emerge only in the modernist period.[1] Ethnographic inquiry relies on an urban geography that has as its focus New York City: not Harlem for European Americans who have never ventured that far uptown, but the sexual underworld of the Bowery for heterosexuals who have never ventured that far downtown in Manhattan. Whereas, in Johnson's novel the masculine subject who is feminized by passing is constructed in relationship to the failed homoeroticism of a male homosociality, the sexual subject in Lind's autobiography identifies himself as "a woman in a man's body" who seeks sexual encounters with other men marked by generational differences that are also inflected by class and ethnicity. Here, the issue is not the scopic illogic of the law, the "one drop of black blood" that produces black subjects who look white, but the anachronism of a legal code that continues to criminalize homosexuality in spite of its status as a victimless crime. The ex-coloured man is the offspring of miscegenation; the androgyne is accused of not producing any offspring at all.

Earl Lind proposes to write a "trilogy on sexology," or a three volume autobiography, consisting of *Autobiography of an Androgyne, The Female-Impersonators,* and *The Riddle of the Underworld*. Only the first two appear in print—*Autobiography of an Androgyne* 18 years after it was written—both with introductions by Werner Herzog, Ph.D., A.M., M.D., and Counselor-at-Law, the editor of the *Medico-Legal Journal,* "A Magazine for Physicians and Lawyers and the Thinking Public in General," devoted to medical jurisprudence and forensic medicine, published bimonthly in New York City. Both titles are eventually listed in the journal as books available for sale in the journal office, while the initial advertisement describes *Autobiography of an Androgyne* as follows: "Portraying the inner history and the life experience of a bisexual human. Something new in medical literature, 70,000 words, 5 full-page illustrations. Price $4.00. Sold only to physicians, lawyers, legislators, psychologists, and sociologists."[2] The journal contains original articles, book reviews and notices, society news and notices, items of interest, and recent decisions of medico-legal interest. The fact that the sale of medico-psychiatric literature is strictly limited to professionals and procurable for individuals only with a physician's permission confines the discussion of sexual inversion in the United States to medical literature. This stands in sharp contrast to England, where various kinds of texts circulate in more unanticipated ways—like calling cards, in the case of Oscar Wilde, or realist fiction, in the case of Radclyffe Hall. Often, it is bringing a bookseller to trial that unleashes a public discussion about the moral nature of the text and the morbid intentions of its author, requiring acts of interpretation limited by, but not to, legal discourse.

At the heart of the nexus between medical and legal discourse is the extent to which sexual reformers represented laws as not keeping in step with scientific knowledge, beginning with Karl Heinrich Ulrichs (1825–1895), who unsuccessfully sought to prevent paragraph 143 of the Prussian penal code criminalizing homosexuality from being extended to his native Hanover in 1869.[3] "Scientific knowledge," in the form of an emerging sexology or "anthropology of sex," demonstrates that homosexuality is congenital—even acquired inversion has a congenital basis—that predisposes one to being attracted to the same sex. For Ulrichs, sexual inversion meant the inversion of gender identity—"*animas muliebris in corpore virili inclusa*" [a female soul in a male body]—that produces the Urning: "Der Urning ist ein Naturrätsel. Sein Liebestrieb ist ein weiblicher. Nur körperlich ist er Mann"[4] [The Urning is a riddle of nature. His sexual instinct is feminine. Only his body is masculine]. For Havelock Ellis (1859–1939), it meant "sexual instinct turned by inborn constitutional abnormality towards persons of the same sex."[5] For Krafft-Ebing (1840–1902), whose *Psychopathia Sexualis* (1886) became the least reformist in its effect, same-sex attraction necessitated the distinction between perversion (perverse feelings for the same sex) and perversity (sexual acts with persons of the same sex).

What these sexologists all claimed, in spite of their varied discourses, is that science enables the distinction between a disease and a vice, thereby enabling changes in the law. For the sexologist as sexual reformer, the medicalization of sexual inversion facilitates the decriminalization of homosexuality enabling, according to Magnus Hirschfeld (1868–1935), "*per scientiam ad justitiam*" [through science to justice]. Science is able to recognize a sexual instinct or feeling and thereby create a taxonomy of sexual types that relies neither on a sexual act (sodomy), nor on a sexual object choice (homosexuality), but rather on a "sexual personality" that may or may not be written on the body, even as the body, often mediated by clothes (the military uniform, women's clothing) provides the site of sexual attraction.[6] In France and other countries that adopted the Code Napolean—Italy, Belgium, Holland, and Spain—the legal code distinguishes between a crime against the state and a religious offense so that homosexual practices, like other sexual practices, are punishable only if performed in public, if they involve violence, or if they are committed with a minor. In England, where in 1886, "acts of gross indecency" became punishable by law, homosexuality as "*peccatum illude horribile, inter Christianos non nominandum*" [the sin so horrible that it must not be mentioned among Christians] made it virtually impossible to present an argument in English (as opposed to Latin) for changing the law that would, itself, not be illegal on the grounds of obscenity.

On the one hand, the German-speaking world produces scientific typologies distinguishing queers from "normal men": Ulrichs' Urning, subdivided into Mannling (butch) or Weibling (femme), and his Uranodioning (bisexual), either conjunctive (active, i.e., sensual) or disjunctive (passive, i.e., romantic); Hirschfeld's hermaphroditism, androgyny, homosexuality, and transvestism; Krafft-Ebing's psychical hermaphroditism, homosexuality, effemination, and hermaphroditism. On the other hand, British men of letters educated in the Greek classics, some specifically in the tradition of "Oxford Hellenism," resort to the evasiveness of literary allusion by referring to same-sex desire as "l'amour de l'impossible" [the impossible love] (John Addington Symonds) or "homogenic love" (Edward Carpenter). In contrast to the ex-coloured man, who as composite type suffers from overgeneralization by needing to represent an entire race, the sexual invert is infinitely classifiable, reduced to an increasingly specific type that comes to stand in for a complex psychological entity. At the same time, the sexual subject who becomes the subject of an autobiography represents an as yet unclassified type: "on the sexual side of life, every individual is *sui generis*" [his own kind].[7] The assumption is that every individual—with the exception of a few sexologists—knows only his own sexual life, refuses to divulge it, and is unable to inquire into the sexual life of others. Sexual inverts neither understand themselves, nor have access to the self-understanding of others like themselves. Thus, there is a need for self-revelation if one is to provide a text that can be read by someone else. If every life is unique, how does one begin to see oneself as conforming to a scientific type? How does the invert acquire the knowledge that enables him to explain the riddle of inversion to himself and other inverts? What status does this autobiographical narrative acquire within the discourse of sexology?

> ii. "It was primarily my object when I began these autobiographical notes to describe as accurately and candidly as I was able a type of character, which I do not at all believe to be exceptional, but which for various intelligible reasons had never yet been properly analysed. I wanted to supply material for the ethical psychologist and student of mental pathology, by portraying a man of no mean talents, of no abnormal depravity, whose life has been perplexed from first to last by passion—natural, instinctive, healthy in his own particular case—but morbid and abominable from the point of view of the society in which he lives—persistent passion for the male sex." (*The Memoirs of John Addington Symonds* [1889], 182)

The *vita sexualis* [sexual life] is not only marked as *sui generis,* but also takes the form of an *apologia pro vita sua* [an apology for one's life]. The *vita sexualis* does not span from birth to the moment of writing, but from the moment when writing first becomes possible to the initial memory of sexual attraction or activity. The chronological narrative that is then recorded, in either the first or third person, vacillates between an autobiographical subject narrating a singular life history and producing himself as sexological type. It is the ability to name the type that makes it possible to offer the story of an anomalous sexuality, even as the taxonomy of the sexologists consists exclusively of individual stories that have been solicited anonymously to function as scientific case histories. Inasmuch as the case histories of the sexologists were classified according to their degree of pathology, the life history requires a self-justification, or apology. To tell the story at all means to reveal that part of oneself has already been classified as vice-ridden or diseased, a part that one has never had to name, or has renamed in order to protect its identity. Unlike Symonds, who invokes his exceptionality as a man of letters to justify his natural, and not depraved, passion for the male sex, Earl Lind protects his middle-class respectability by revealing only the depravity of his sexual life, safely protected behind the veil of three pseudonyms.

If Ellis, in reaction to Krafft-Ebing, refuses to classify his case histories, so as not to pathologize those produced by his friends, Freud makes famous certain case histories by treating them with suspicion, symptoms of the patient's unconscious that can only be deciphered by the psychoanalyst, even if some, like *Dora,* eventually require extensive revision. By contrast, Herzog, in his introduction, refers to *Autobiography of an Androgyne* as Lind's "psychoanalysis of himself." On the one hand, there is "a plain chronological statement of facts." On the other hand, there are symptoms of "pride" and "vanity." On the one hand, drawing attention to a marked masculinity is construed as feminizing, as "vanity," or in James Weldon Johnson's words, "vainglory." On the other hand, psychoanalyzing oneself doesn't depend on the solicitation or interpretation of one's life story by a scientific expert, and thus becomes a form of self-authorization. While Lind mentions having read Ellis and Krafft-Ebing, neither of these texts contains a case history sufficiently similar to his own. Thus, he self-authors both the androgyne as a sexual type situated somewhere between the effeminate man and the transsexual, and the fairy as a sociological type who regularly inhabits military barracks and the Bowery. The autobiography's status as auto-ethnography thus lies in its negotiation of sexological discourse as both sexologist and sexological subject, and of the sexual underworld as both native informant and middle-class ethnographer.

> iii. "Here in the *Phaedrus* and the *Symposium*—in the myth of the Soul and the speeches of Pausanias Agathon and Diotima—I discovered the true *liber amoris* at last, the revelation I had been waiting for, the consecration of a long-cherished idealism. It was just as though the voice of my own soul spoke to me through Plato, as though in some antenatal experience I had lived the life of philosophical Greek lover." (*The Memoirs of John Addington Symonds* [1889], 99)

> iv. "Everyone knows the recumbent marble Hermaphrodite in the Louvre." (Edward Carpenter, *Intermediate Types Among Primitive Folk* [1914], 284)

In Symonds' *vita sexualis,* as in Forster's novel *Maurice* (1914), the scene of reading Plato becomes the *locus classicus* for the recognition of oneself as "Greek lover," for the articulation of one's desire for another man and the legitimation of such a passion prior to either Christianity or the formation of the modern state. The Greek lover is both a soul, in contrast to the body that is English and punishable by law, and prenatal, born not with the body, but with the *vita sexualis.* In *A Problem in Greek Ethics,* Symonds defines Greek love as "a passionate and enthusiastic attachment subsisting between man and youth, recognized by society and protected by opinion, which, though it was not free from sensuality, did not degenerate into mere licentiousness."[8] In other words, even as age is signified by the difference between bodies, the relationship between bodies must aspire to an attachment on the level of souls. The soul of the young man finds its representation originally in sculpture, where corporeal beauty is expressed through feminine grace in the presence of youthful virility.

For Lind, whose concern is less the legitimation of his passion via an epistemology of the Greek lover than the securing of his ontological status as invert, Greek sculpture serves not to embody an ideal form of beauty, but rather, ocular proof of his particular variation on the forms of nature. The Greek statue "Hermaphroditos" (in the Uffizi Gallery in Florence,

Italy) provides a visual representation of an androgyne, with the author serving as "a modern living replica" in the form of a photograph serving as frontispiece. Thus, the androgyne, like the aviatrix, comes into being as simulacrum. But unlike the regendering of the aviator, the androgyne must rename itself in the shift of nomenclature from proper name to scientific type. On the one hand, according to sexologists, hermaphrodites are the least likely to appear in nature of all the "sexual intermediates"; on the other hand, the sheer number of possible combinations of male and female characteristics makes it unlikely that any two will ever replicate each other (Hirschfeld estimates mathematically 43,046,721 combinations.)[9] The original hermaphrodite is not a body with both male and female genitals, but a figure with male genitals and female secondary sexual characteristics. The androgyne embodies what is most visible in terms of what each sex contributes to sexual difference in the form of scopic evidence. Everything except the genitals—"physical structure," "psychical constitution," even "*vita sexualis*"—"approach the female type."[10] Thus, it is not the cross-gender identification that is anomalous, but the genitalia. The sexual organs take on a secondary status in relationship to sexual object choice (young male Irish or Italian immigrant) and sexual object aim (fellatio).

> v. "I'm an unspeakable of the Oscar Wilde sort." (E. M. Forster, *Maurice* [1914], 195)

While Lind credits Ellis' *Sexual Inversion* as the first text to discuss androgynism or male effeminacy, he nevertheless distinguishes between Oscar Wilde as the best known exemplar of one type of homosexual, the psychical hermaphrodite, and himself as an example of the other, the androgyne. In *Autobiography of an Androgyne* he makes the following distinction:

> Homosexuality is due to innate abnormal participation in the mentality of the opposite sex. Whether an active pederast or a passive invert results, depends on the degree of feminization. If slight, the former results, who is also capable of heterosexual love and coitus—a psychical hermaphrodite, as was Wilde, who however had a far stronger leaning toward the homosexual than toward the heterosexual. If the degree is high—for example, almost entirely feminine psychically and even inducing feminesque anatomy—a passive invert results, as in the case of the author.[11]

Homosexuality is the result of sexual inversion, or cross-gender identification, producing the active pederast, attracted to young boys, or the passive invert, attracted to virile men. In *The Female-Impersonators,* where the initial taxonomy involves many more categories, the androgyne, in opposition to various versions of virility, has been subdivided into the "mildly androgynous" and the "ultra-androgyne," of which Wilde is an example of the first and the author of the second.

Sexual instincts resulting in sexual acts can nevertheless extend to physical effects, that is, a feminization of the body. While sexologists characterize androgynes by *gynecomastia,* or mammary glands, in the presence of male genitalia, Lind insists on the enormous physical variation among androgynes (facial hair, mammary glands, skeleton or muscular system, etc.). None of these characteristics guarantee homosexuality. What does is a feminine psyche, characterized by sexual passivity and, above all, the complete divorce of one's male genitalia from one's sexual life. The compulsion of the androgyne is less toward same-sex desire than toward castration.

> vi. "The patient history represents one way of knowing the human body and the human being. It depends for its structure on a codified narrative form that works with the materials of chronicle, ethnography, and biography. The patient history charts an epistemology of the body that is suffused with conventions of the normal." (Julia Epstein, *Altered Conditions,* 59)

Castration guarantees the authentic embodiment of the androgyne by removing the visual marker that serves as disguise: "Your author is really a woman whom Nature disguised as a man."[12] Jay Prosser, in *Second Skins,* returns to those sexological case histories dismissed by gay and lesbian theorists by recognizing inversion as the desire to change sex, rather than as just the desire for the same sex. The transsexual, unlike other queers, avoids sex inasmuch as sex involves the genitals that serve not to authenticate, but to disguise, one's gendered "realness."

Between the androgyne, as *puella sine vagina* [girl without vagina] and the transsexual's vagina formed from penile tissue through surgical intervention, is the case of "eviration" recounted for Krafft-Ebing by a Hungarian physician (Case 129). He was treated like a girl; he wished to be a girl; gradually he begins to feel like a girl, until one day he takes a bath and more than the usual dose of hashish to lessen the pain of his gout, and undergoes a complete transformation:

> All at once I saw myself a woman from my toes to my breast; I felt, as before while in the bath, that the genitals had shrunken, the pelvis broadened, the breasts swollen out, a feeling of unspeakable delight came over me. I closed my eyes, so that at least I did not see the face changed. My physician looked as if he had a gigantic potato instead of a head; my wife had a full moon on her thorax. And yet, I was strong enough to briefly record my will in my note-book when both left the room for a short time.[13]

While the man in him is never fully extinguished but continues to be worn like a mask, he never loses the feeling of being a woman, so that sexual relations with his wife take the form of an *amor lesbicus* [lesbian love]. (He claims that had he been single, he would have undergone castration.) On the one hand, he changes sex before the possibility of transsexualism; on the other hand, sexual inversion embraces not just same-sex object choice, but also transgendered identification. Unlike Orlando, who wakes up a woman having been a man by transcending the flesh, the body in this case experiences the sensations of a woman as she continues to take on the role of a man. While Krafft-Ebing categorizes this case as a "change of sex delusion" that fails to descend into paranoia, its authority stems from the fact that it was written by a physician, relies on notes taken at the time of the event, and takes the form of a first person autobiography rather than a third person case history.

For Prosser, to be transsexual means to become an autobiographical subject, inasmuch as becoming a medico-discursive object depends on the ability to produce a coherent narrative that will result in the desired diagnosis. Once the sex reassignment has taken place, it remains less clear why there persists the desire to publish an autobiography that undoes the passing of the body: "The paradox of transsexual autobiography surely rests here: not one between technology and intersexuality that compromises transsexuality but a paradox between passing as nontranssexual and writing as an autobiographer who wants to be read as transsexual."[14] Inasmuch as the androgyne, in contrast to the transsexual, is not trying to pass as a woman—even once he undergoes castration—but as a "normal man," the central paradox in his life lies between his existence uptown as intellectual worker and his "female impersonation sprees" in downtown Manhattan.

> vii. "And appreciating how tragically sensitive Mark was, June found it easy to understand why he had shrunk from attending the Drag Ball. The very word 'fairy' always brought a flush to his face and pain into his eyes." (Blair Niles, *Strange Brother* [1931], 212–3)

"Female impersonation" refers to the developmental narrative of a fairy, the androgyne not as sexological but as sociological type, that begins to gain currency in the United States in the 1870's. The fairy as flamboyantly effeminate homosexual may or may not get paid for sex by "normal men," that is, adopt the profession of "fille de joie" or "petit jesus," two terms used to refer to prostitution. There is no biography of Earl Lind. George Chauncey's *Gay New York,* the only text to extensively discuss the *Autobiography of an Androgyne,* presents biographical information in a footnote. Chauncey, whose interest is exclusively historical, positions the fairy as follows:

> Much evidence suggests that the fairy, so long as he abided by the conventions of this cultural script, was tolerated in much of working-class society—regarded as an anomaly, certainly, but as more amusing than abhorrent, and only rarely as a threat to the gender order. He was so obviously a "third-sexer," a different species of human being, that his very effeminacy served to confirm rather than threaten the masculinity of other men, particularly since it often exaggerated the conventions of deference and gender difference between men and women. The fairies reaffirmed the conventions of gender even as they violated them: they behaved as no man should, but as any man might wish a woman would. Their representation of themselves as "intermediate types" made it easier for men to interact with them (and even have sex with them) by making it clear who would play the "man's part" in the interaction.[15]

Chauncey suggests further that fairies imitated not so much women as a group, and prostitutes in particular, but that the distinction in the modernist period between queers and "normal men" marks a division less between gay and straight, than between the "normal man," who holds a respectable day job and the queer, who at night leads the life of a fairy.

According to Lind, the term fairy originally referred to the member of a crew on board ship who agreed to fill the role left absent by women and was thus "looked upon as a fairy gift or godsend."[16] In his *apologia pro vita sua,* Lind argues that fairies minister to ultra-virile men between the ages of 18 and 25, that is, until they marry, thereby providing a valuable service to those who would otherwise resort to masturbation or premarital sex. Professional fairies, estimated to be one out of 3,000 men, are able to pursue their career only until they are 30, at which point they no longer seek "husbands" but are ready to "adopt a son," someone whose class status they seek to elevate by financing their education. Because it would be both too shameful and economically disastrous to confide in a man of his own class, Lind is forced to resort to slumming. Thus, during his weekly "nocturnal rambles" in the Bowery he experiences, for the sake of as many pleasurable encounters as possible, theft, blackmail, anal rape, and other violations symptomatic of the "intense loathing by prudes ignorant of abnormal psychology,"[17] who know that no punishment is too cruel for someone who has no recourse to the law.

> viii. "The distinction in my character between an inner and real self and an outer and artificial self, to which I have already alluded, emphasized itself during this period. So separate were the two selves, so deep was my dipsy-

> chia, that my most intimate friends there, of whom I shall soon speak, have each and all emphatically told me that they thought I had passed through school without being affected by, almost without being aware of, its particular vices. And yet those vices furnished a perpetual subject for contemplation and casuistical reflection to my inner self." (*The Memoirs of John Addington Symonds* [1889], 95–6)

The figure of the divided self moves from its physical representation as two gendered bodies in the hermaphrodite or transsexual, to its psychical figuration as two selves residing in the same body. For Symonds, these two selves refer to the split between homosexual and man of letters. The two selves engage in dialogue with each other in the form of diary entries that form the basis of his memoirs, and thus fail to have their existence recognized by anyone else.

For the androgyne, the two selves take the form of two opposing careers, that of religious missionary which Lind abandons, not without regret, and that of *fille de joie,* which comes to its natural end by the age of 30, which also marks the end of the *vita sexualis.* "Female impersonation" refers not only to the sociological role of the fairy, but to playing the private role of a woman in front of a public audience. For the androgyne, the audience is above all the soldier—the most virile and thus most opposite to the passive invert—and the part "she" plays is that of "Baby." Thus, the double life that the androgyne leads is defined not just by the distinction between respectable queer and Bowery fairy, but, in psychoanalytic terms, between the pre-oedipal baby and the oedipal Lind[18]:

> My relations with a coterie of beaux, and particularly with soldiers around the camps and forts, reminded me sometimes of a play. I was, as it were, acting a part. Perhaps it would be nearer the truth to say that another personality was in possession of me. I was conscious that I was the same "I" who was one of the leaders in scholarship at the university and who was there looked upon as a particularly innocent and pure-minded youth. I was also conscious that in the society of my beaux I was not acting as became the sensible, rational, respectable collegian of other occasions. I felt that I had temporarily relinquished my mind and body to the dictates of another spirit, that of a "baby-girl"—a combination of baby and girl. It was however a spirit not alien to me. It was a spirit which had dwelt in my brain from infancy. It was a spirit that had always been called up by the sight of beautiful stalwart males of the proper age. For the work of life I realized that this spirit would not do. If I was to make a name for myself in the world, I must dethrone this baby-spirit in me. When in my study, I sought to forget this baby-spirit. I even turned against it at times with a sort of abhorrence, and asked myself how I could give way to it. Thus I lived a sort of a two-sided life.[19]

The part the androgyne plays as Baby adheres to the same first person pronoun as Earl Lind, even as it seems to belong to a different personality. The second personality takes the form of a "spirit" that dwells in the brain (the "soul" that once medicalized inhabits every cell of the body), that has existed since infancy and takes possession of the "I" by usurping the throne of the person, so to speak. This story of development is thus not about the man who takes the place of the boy, but of the infant replacing the man, in the presence of other men, young men, men of the working classes. The spirit resides in the same body, designated by the "I," by the one who writes, but the difference in gender requires a different name, thus its designation as Jennie June. Jennie June is the one who craves fellatio, who eventually undergoes castration, whose *vita sexualis* this is. Ralph Werther, likewise a pseudonym, is the respectable author who inhabits the study, who reluctantly cohabits with Jennie June, even as she is much more widely known than he is (like Alice, which is her name in France, even though Alice B. is more widely known). Ralph Werther is Jennie June's "real" name, a composite of two historical queers.

> ix. "Like the young men with female breasts and everyone else who entered the domain of the Institute, Christopher had automatically become a museum specimen, subject to Hirschfeld's diagnosis and classification. Karl told him, in due course, that Hirschfeld had classified him as 'infantile.' Christopher didn't object to this epithet; he interpreted it as 'boyish.' You couldn't call him a pretty boy—his head and his nose were too big—but he did look young for his age, with his fresh pink complexion, inherited from Kathleen, bright eyes, and glossy dark-brown hair flopping down over his right cheek. He also had a boyish grin, full of clean white teeth. Far better to be boyish, he thought, than effeminate. He could never join the ranks of Karl's friends and play at nicey-nice third-sexism, because he refused utterly to think of himself as a queen. Wystan was much more mature than Christopher, in this respect. Labels didn't scare him." (Christopher Isherwood, *Christopher and His Kind* [1976], 27)

Ralph Werther is the name the androgyne gives on the street in order to protect his family name when playing the role of Jennie June. Ralph is originally "Raphael," after the Italian Renaissance painter, although later changed to Ralph, because "Raphael sounds too stagey":

> I adopted the name "Raphael" because of its euphony and glorious associations; the name "Werther," because like Goethe's hero I was doomed to great sorrow through the passion of love. During my first two years in college, when I often meditated suicide, and was by far the unhappiest person in the college community, Goethe's "Sorrows of Werther," the romance of suicide, had a peculiar fascination.[20]

By the time Lind returns to the question of names in *The Female-Impersonators,* he offers a somewhat different explanation:

> I named myself after "the Prince of Painters," because he was the greatest ultra-androgyne who ever lived. He was my idol—my ideal. I wished him to pass through the earthly life all over again in my body. I further named myself after "the Prince of Amatory Melancholics" since I was myself such during my teens. Werther was Goethe himself, the most brilliant and most versatile man, "The Prince of Men," born subsequently to the Shakespeare-Author (Francis Bacon).[21]

Like the various versions of how Amelia Earhart became the first woman to fly the Atlantic, these two explanations for the same phenomenon point to the possibility of reinterpretation through retelling. Not only does the fairy need two names, neither of which is authentic, his pseudonym itself is a double name that recasts him as both painter and poet: on the one hand, Raphael as the "most gifted ultra-androgyne the world has ever known," complete with portrait to complement the author's own; on the other hand, the queering of Werther who originally is Goethe's hero, and in the revision Goethe himself, not as writer but as "amatory melancholic." In the second version, it is not the "glorious association" or the "peculiar fascination" that compels the androgyne to choose these names, but the desire to reincarnate two great figures of Western culture.

As for the second name, Jennie June is the penname of Jane Cunnighman Croly (1829–1901), a well-known journalist,[22] although the author claims that Jennie had always been his favorite girl's name and June "was first suggested to me while reading Cooper's novels, where it appears as the name of a gentle, extremely feminine squaw. It was suggested to me secondly by my seeing it appear as a surname on the sign of a business house."[23] Thus, his masculine self re-embodies two examples of European genius, while his feminine personality involves renaming himself as a girl: on the one hand, the girl he might have been; on the other hand, a literary fiction, a squaw, who like the "red-man," offers the only extant example in North America of the androgyne. The Native American berdache serves as legitimation for the androgyne within a national context that lies outside the author's medico-legal jurisdiction. At the same time, the brave condemned to live as a squaw serves as an analogy to the invert doomed to live as a man:

> Suppose in a war between two tribes of red men, a brave is captured, consigned to adopt the dress and occupation of a squaw, and is in every way treated as a squaw. Would this unnatural life be to the brave's tastes? Would he be blamed if he sought to escape where he could live according to his

> masculine inclinations? No more is the passive invert to be blamed for escaping occasionally where he can live according to his quasi-feminine instincts.[24]

Here Lind reverses the cross-gender identification in order to ground his identity in ethnology as opposed to urban sociology, required by an American culture that lacks a Renaissance.

While the name that appears on the title page of *Autobiography of an Androgyne* is Earl Lind ("Ralph Werther"—"Jennie June"), thereby giving the impression that Earl Lind is not a pseudonym in the presence of two others, the authorship of *The Female-Impersonators* is given as Ralph Werther—Jennie June, followed by ("Earl Lind"). Thus, in the second version, Earl Lind requires an explanation: Earl because it rhymes with "girl" and Lind after Jennie Lind, one of his role models. As the result of a court-martial in 1905, it became imperative to change names, at which point Ralph Werther and Jennie June became Earl Lind and Pussie. Thus, the author claims, the need for five aliases. Earl Lind is also the name the author adopts while working for a criminal lawyer and the editor of a legal journal, i.e., Werner Herzog, with whom he attends court as his clerk: "Thus I was, in a sense, a court employee of New York City, while at the same time one of its greatest criminals—according to the statute that is a legacy from the Dark Ages."[25] The names not only keep separate the respectable queer and the Bowery fairy, intellectual worker and Pussie, the genius and the girl, but also the criminal and the criminal lawyer's clerk. Unlike the ex-coloured man who has no name, the one name that is never revealed is the androgyne's legal one. The multiple aliases in the form of proper names replicate the many designations of his type: androgyne, passive invert, fairy, girl-boy, female impersonator, crybaby, aesthete, dilettante, effeminate man, homosexualist, etc. There are many names for one type, just as there are many types who make up the "step-children of nature."

> x. "Hence, what these societies demonstrate is that sexuality between men is a universal possibility *provided that* those involved experience each other as being different; more specifically, *as not being men to the same extent.* But is sexuality between men a universal possibility when they do experience one another as equally male (i.e., not totally equal but in the sense that neither of them is experienced as a 'non-man' or a 'not yet man')?" (Henning Bech, *When Men Meet,* 18)

The narrative of the fairy and the transsexual intersects with that of the transvestite. Hirschfeld, himself one, coins the term "transvestite" in 1910 and places it in the fourth category of "sexual intermediaries." He distinguishes between cross-dressing and transvestism, the latter being a compulsion that can't be driven out of the mind by consciousness and/or made to disappear through treatment. Not visually distinguishable from "normal men," Hirschfeld defines transvestites as "men whose feminine emotions and feelings are reflected in their manner of love, their direction of taste, their gestures and manners, their sensitivity, and many times in the particular way of writing, also men who more or less dress themselves as women or live totally as such. . . ."[26] Transvestites know that they do not belong to the other sex and yet, through clothes, make themselves look as much as possible like the other sex. Unlike fetishists, they love the clothing less on the other person or isolated from the body than on themselves. Transvestites are differentiated from the third category of sexual intermediaries, homosexuals, inasmuch as "the masculine part in the psyche of these people is sexually excited by their feminine side, . . . they feel attracted not only by women themselves, but also more so by the women within themselves."[27] The sexual arousal comes from the stimulation of the other side of the double personality, producing a subject marked by sexual self-sufficiency.

It comes as no surprise, then, that the scene of cross-dressing in *Autobiography of an Androgyne* takes place in front of the mirror:

> Beginning about this time, my twenty-first year, and continuing down to the date when this book goes to press, I have commonly worn in my home an ornamental bathrobe, just like a woman's dress. Clad in it, I have gazed at my reflection in the mirror, imagining I was a woman. Walking in it to and from and up and down the stairs, I have taken pleasure in hearing it rustle like a woman's dress, in feeling it strike against my legs, and in holding it up when ascending the stairs, as a woman her skirts. In my college days, while at home for week-ends, I would occasionally, when alone, put on a sister's hat and gaze at myself in the mirror with rare pleasure, wishing that I might wear that style of hat.[28]

Unlike the homoerotic encounter of the ex-coloured man when he attempts to grasp the epistemological nature of his newly acquired racial identity, this scene addresses the possibility of a different ontological status available to the sexual subject through dress. Inasmuch as the androgyne is more woman than man, putting on women's clothes makes it possible to reestablish an original gender identity, even if only in private. The description moves from the most intimate apparel to the most public, from a bathrobe, worn only in private, to a hat, worn only in public. The bathrobe mediates between public and private by being "like a woman's dress," by producing the sound and sensation of the one item of clothing not permitted to men on the street. With the hat, it is not the item itself, but the style that is perceived as gendered. The mirror serves as a vehicle for the imaginary, whereby the woman can only be seen by the man, the figure in the mirror only by the person in front of it.

The scene in front of the mirror does not constitute the recognition of a public identity, but rather the possibility of authenticating an identity in private. In public, the androgyne is dressed not as a woman, but as a fairy in the attire of a dandy:

> One evening I clad myself so as to present the most attractive appearance possible: a blue suit, with boxplaited, belted coat (Norfolk style); dark red necktie; white gloves; and patent-leather shoes. As a high-class fairie, I sought to dress in a distinctive manner, so as to be more readily recognized by my prey. Therefore unusually large neck bows and white gloves. Fairies are inclined to be loud in their dress. The excessive wearing of gloves and the wearing of a red neck-tie are almost universal with high-class fairies.[29]

Once in public, the "high-class fairie" adopts the signs of a semiotic system that identify him not as a woman, but "as not being a man to the same extent." It is the "loudness" of the dress that identifies it as feminine, rather than any particular item of dress admissible only for women. It is the red tie that announces a sexual interest in men, as in "He got thirty days for wearing a red tie." The same item makes one equally identifiable to one's "prey" and urban policing. Like the tie that marks the aviatrix as (female) flyer, the red tie marks the effeminate man as homosexual. In private, the man is really a woman; in public, the man is really a non-man, in as much as he imagines that his class position makes it impossible for him to dress as a woman on the street.

> xi. "I regard sex as the central problem of life." Havelock Ellis, "General Preface," *Sexual Inversion* [1897], x)

> xii. "There is indeed no worse crippling than the sexual. This is because sex, with all that it implies, is the principal physiological factor in life. Any abnormality of sex is truly the greatest of tragedies." (Earl Lind, *The Female-Impersonators,* 2–3)

The *vita sexualis* is characterized by the proliferation of types rather than a consolidation into a composite type. Thus the conversation among the ultra-androgynes or "avocational female impersonators of the upper and middle classes" who gather as members of the "Cercle Hermaphroditos" is rendered as a composite by Werther of the many confessions heard among those who gather at this particular site of the underworld. The site is Paresis Hall (4th Avenue South of 14th Street) in one of several small rooms rented above a modest bar regularly raided by the police. Like the discussion of race relations in the Jim Crow car that the ex-coloured man enters by passing for white, Werther creates a composite conversation between an androgyne, denounced by a co-worker and fired from his job, and his boss. The conversation begins:

> PLUM: "I confess to being a woman-man and throw myself upon your mercy."
>
> FAIRSEA: "That confession is sufficient, and proves you an undesirable person to have around."
>
> PLUM: "It will be hard to find a new job, since I have been with you for five years and must depend on your recommendation."
>
> FAIRSEA: "Knowing your nature, Plum, I could not recommend you *even to shovel coal into a furnace.*"
>
> PLUM: "But you have steadily advanced me for five years! Why should to-day's discovery make any difference in your opinion of my business ability?"
>
> FAIRSEA with sneer: "An invert ought to leave brain work for others! He ought to exhaust himself on a farm from sunrise to sunset so that the psychic movings would be next to non-existent. He should pass his life in the back woods; not in a city. He has no right in the front ranks of civilization where his abnormality is so out of place!"
>
> PLUM: "You mean that he should commit intellectual suicide and social suicide in obedience to the aesthetic sense of Pharisees!"[30]

Plum does not claim to be something he is not. Rather he uses rational argument to reveal the irrationality of his interlocutor and thereby invoke his sympathy. The employer's arguments are many, ranging from the Bible that teaches that "the invert has no rights," to the nativist discourse in the modernist period proclaiming "race suicide." They include the fact that inverts have always been shunned and should have "unclean" branded on their foreheads, to a final declaration that "bias is justifiable in matters of sex." In each case, Fairsea refigures his own disgust as the problem of the invert's self-loathing and argues against change as counterrevolutionary. Plum responds to each of Fairsea's arguments with a counterargument, arguing against homosexuality as a contagious disease, as jeopardizing the continuation of the human race, as having never been tolerated: "How do you define 'depraved," Mr. Fairsea? If in such a way as to exclude Socrates, Plato, Michael Angelo, and Raphael, then you exclude me also."[31] Once again, he includes himself by placing himself in the company of great homosexuals. His most compelling argument remains: "WHEREAS THE BISEXUALS' BEING AT LIBERTY OCCASIONS NOT THE LEAST DETRIMENT TO ANY INDIVIDUAL, NOR TO THE RACE AS A WHOLE,"[32] the argument of the victimless crime. In other words, the very accusations made against inverts are the effect, not the cause, of the bigotry and bias that produce scorn rather than pity. By not allowing homosexuals to work for a wage, they are forced to become sex workers, the plight of Ralph Werther, or commit suicide, as did Goethe's Werther and many of the female-impersonators. Rather than linking race to sex by imagining a mulatto South, sex is linked to class whereby the invert's threat to the race as a whole requires his elimination from any but the lowest classes.

Lind hopes to change the legal status of the invert by demedicalizing the discourse that constructs him as outlaw. This dialogue replaces the questionnaire of the sexologists as the primary source of knowledge about inversion by presenting itself as steeped in the Socratic tradition. Although the questionnaire used by Symonds and Ellis is no longer extent, Phyllis Grosskurth, in *Havelock Ellis: A Biography,* suggests that a reasonable guess would indicate that the following information was solicited: "data about parents, siblings, and education; relatives who had been inverts; first sexual experience; masturbation; erotic dreams; preferred form of sexual activity; responses to opposite sex; avocations; favourite colour; ability to whistle; and attitude towards their anomaly."[33] Inasmuch as the androgyne is familiar with the genre of the scientific case history, these are the questions informing the developmental narrative of his autobiography. Once Lind frequents the venues haunted by other androgynes, the discourse is no longer determined by the style of the solicited confession, but rather by the contradictions of material conditions generated by outdated laws.

In *The Female-Impersonators,* the androgyne becomes a participant-observer who presents a piece of the sexual underworld to an audience from whom it might elicit sympathy. Werther makes a clear distinction between the audiences of the first two volumes of the trilogy, between the "learned professions" and the "general reader," as well as between two genres: "In my AUTOBIOGRAPHY, I was almost exclusively occupied with a frank exposition of what life meant to me personally. In the two supplements, I have been chiefly occupied with depicting characters with whom I associated in the Underworld."[34] The "Underworld" is approached in the role of neither scientist nor law enforcer, but as amateur detective, someone whose stomping-ground this was as an avocational fairy, who nevertheless belonged to the "overworld" and thus was able to acquire secrets in complete confidentiality. His method for drawing out secrets is to begin by revealing his own.

After a detailed taxonomy of the types that make up abnormal psychology, the second volume begins with a summary of the *Autobiography of an Androgyne,* without the details considered exclusively of medical interest, but including responses to the text after its publication. This takes the form of a "supplement" containing knowledge acquired during the 20 years since the *Autobiography of an Androgyne* was written. *The Female-Impersonators* begins with the description of Paresis Hall in order to render a "typical hour's conversation" of ultra-androgynes speaking among themselves. He then offers two samples of the many confessions to which he was privy, recorded in general outline exclusively from memory, and where memory fails, from "a sea of general memories" based on knowledge gained from personal experience. The autobiographies of Frank-Eunice and Angelo-Phyllis are followed by "Newspaper Accounts of Murders of Androgynes," to impress upon the reader their fairly common occurrence. These accounts are heavily commented on by the author, in brackets, as a way of providing private commentary on public discourse, as a way of illuminating the private lives that enter the public eye only once they are terminated. A newspaper account of a suicide provides an opportunity for the author to amend the *Autobiography of an Androgyne,* in a footnote, by including the story of his own contemplated suicide in the Rockies. Finally, he quotes extensively from "Medical Writers on Androgynism," including his own article "The Biological Sport of Fairieism" and Dr. Robert Schufeldt's "Biography of a Passive Pederast." The very last, and most controversial section, includes examples of his own "Fairie Songs," controversial because this verse is considered of poor literary quality, and because it blurs the boundary between scientific and literary text. Because these songs are written by an androgyne for androgynes and no longer for the "general reader," they are most vulnerable to censorship. The book ends with an announcement for *The Riddle of the Underworld,* "THE CLOSING VOLUME OF THE TRIOLOGY DEPICTING THE LIFE-EXPERIENCE OF A BISEXUAL 'MAN,'" the volume that was never written. Thus, in ways not dissimilar from Earhart's autobiographies, this text serves to both enlighten a general public and reach and recruit potential practitioners.

> xiii. "And how strange and delightful it was to be sitting here, with Turkish smoke tickling his nostrils and German beer faintly bitter on his tongue, writing a story in the English language about an English family in an English country house! It was most unlikely that any people here would be able to understand what he was writing. This gave him a soothing sense of privacy, which the noise of their talk couldn't seriously disturb; it was on a different wave length. With them around him, it was actually easier to concentrate than when he was by himself. He was alone and yet not alone. He could move in and out of their world at will. He was beginning to realize how completely at home one can be as a foreigner. (Christopher Isherwood, *Christopher and His Kind* [1976], 22)

When Christopher Isherwood retells the story of the years between 1929 and 1939, between the time he left England for Berlin and the time he arrives in the United States, he vacillates between the first and third person pronoun, between Christopher the autobiographical subject and Christopher as representative of "his kind," whose homosexuality was not publicly recorded until 1976. Like Isherwood, Symonds, too, resorts to the third person pronoun when at the end of his memoirs he recapitulates his entire life story in an attempt to see it not as anomalous, not as *sui generis,* but as the case history of a sexual type, as though belonging to someone else:

> It is a singular life history; and yet, for aught I know, it may be commoner than I imagine. A town-bred boy, burdened with physical ailments, shy and sensitive, above the average in mental faculty, but ill-adapted to the ordinary course of English education. Emotion wakes in him; and just when the first faint stirrings of sex before the age of puberty are felt, he discerns the masterful attraction of the male.[35]

Likewise with Lind, the autobiographical narrative that begins by relying on diary entries is queered when the third person pronoun enables the autobiographer to look at himself as a queer, not in the mirror, but on the street:

> If the reader had been on Mulberry Street between Grand and Broome on an evening in November of 1892, he would have seen meandering slowly along from one side of the street to the other with a mincing gait, a haggard, tired-looking, short and slender youth between eighteen and nineteen, clad in shabby clothes, and with a skull cap on his head. . . . If we had been able to follow this queer-acting individual for the previous hour before he passed us on Mulberry street, we would have seen him roaming about through all the streets of the then dark and criminal 4th Ward, occasionally halting near the groups of ruffians congregated in front of the bar-rooms, and then failing of courage to speak, pass along.[36]

The *vita sexualis* demands to be read inasmuch as it has finally been told. Because it reveals a secret, it objectifies the autobiographical subject, who, on the one hand, no longer is young, and on the other hand, never really existed. Like Stein, who prefers to write in Paris where she writes in a language no one can read, Isherwood feels at home by writing in his own language while in a foreign country. According to Lind, the acquisition of foreign languages has been scientifically proven as a particular aptitude of the invert, as it was for the cosmopolitan:

> From childhood I have had a craze for the acquisition of foreign languages. I speak two with considerable fluency, and when having frequent occasion to use them, can carry on a conversation in two others. Besides these four,

> I have read quite extensively in the original the literature of about a dozen foreign tongues. For more than a decade, I devoted an average of about ten hours a week to reading in these numerous foreign languages.[37]

Not only does the invert command several languages, but the language of inversion remains Latin, the language of both Hellenism and science, the language used by Lind to guarantee his class status and Ellis refused to use in order to depathologize same-sex desire. Latin is also the language of medico-legal professionals, thereby keeping certain kinds of sexual knowledge within their purview, even as the life story becomes the property of other sexual inverts. To feel the foreignness of being a woman in a man's body, of being a man of letters who, by law, belongs to the criminal classes, of being a storyteller who has to wait until beyond the end of the life for the story to be told. When? In what language? Why?

> xiv. "Autobiography melds together a body narrative in pieces." (Jay Prosser, *Second Skins,* 121)

Coda

In "Queer" by Sherwood Anderson, one of the stories that makes up *Winesburg, Ohio* (1919), subtitled "A Group of Tales of Ohio Small Town Life," Elmer Cowley, the junior member of his father's firm, Cowley and Son's store in Winesburg, "was putting new shoelaces in his shoes. They did not go in readily and he had to take the shoes off. With the shoes in his hand he sat looking at a large hole in the heel of one of his stockings."[1] Elmer Cowley's unmended stocking suggests his marital state as much as his economic status, even as that is not the primary source of his queerness, as he continues to walk around town with only one shoe. His father sold the farm to become a merchant, where he stands behind the counter in a long Prince Albert coat. It is not what people wear that makes them queer, but rather their relationship to buying and selling: "The store itself was indescribable. Will Henderson once said of it that it sold everything and nothing."[2] It is not that Ebenezer Cowley doesn't make money, but that he is afraid of entering into an economy of exchange: "He was afraid, first that he would stubbornly refuse to buy and thus lose the opportunity to sell again; second that he would not be stubborn enough and would in a moment of weakness buy what could not be sold."[3] What he is being sold by a traveling salesman is "a small flat metal substitute for collar buttons," a simulacrum that promises to make money. At this point his son brandishes a revolver he has taken from the store and cries: "We ain't going to buy any more stuff until we begin to sell. We ain't going to keep on being queer and have folks staring and listening."[4]

What makes people queer is not that they wear an outmoded coat or fail to be sold, or sell, a new-fangled button, but other people "staring and listening," and laughing like the newspaper reporter, George Williard, whom Elmer identifies as the representative of public opinion. "The spirit of the town" condemns one to queerness, even as queerness is also something one inherits: "Father is queer and mother was queer, too."[5] But not to know one is queer, like his parents, is not to be queer. Knowing one is queer means imagining that others are thinking one is queer because one hasn't made any friends. Sometimes one is so queer, one can't speak; sometimes one seeks out another queer one, like Mook, the halfwit, who still lives on the farm. On the farm there was no one else, so one didn't notice other people looking and listening; in the city there are so many others, one becomes indistinguishable; but in a small town, it is impossible not to be singled out. Williard is ready to be Elmer's friend, but Elmer is only able to imagine telling him, "I will not be queer."[6] His father's failure as a merchant becomes his son's failure to "declare his determination not to be queer."[7] By the end of the story, Elmer has stolen money from his father and beaten the reporter unconscious at the train station on his way out of town: "I guess I showed him. I ain't so queer. I guess I showed him I ain't so queer."[8]

To be queer is to be the offspring of queer parents, to have shoes with shoelaces untied, like Poll in Woolf's "A Society." It means to be paralyzed by buying and selling, not being able to enter economies of money or sex. It means not just being single, but being made suspect by members of one's own sex. It produces the disavowal of homosexuality against which male homosociality must defend itself through violence. Queerness means other people identifying one as not being like others, as being odd. Not wanting to be queer requires one not just to say so. It means, in 1919 in a small town in the Midwest, taking the train elsewhere.

Modernism cannot be understood as simply the withdrawal from the sphere of a common culture in which the public no longer plays a significant part. These memoirs negotiate the public within a consumer culture by providing their own publicity. The making of an identity for the first time means going public as queer subject and queering those who seek to pass in the public sphere. Queerness allows the subject to pose as, provide the portrait of, or perform the role provided by, an imaginary ideal. Cross-gender and cross-racial identifications make representable, through circuitous forms of self-representation involving transportation, translation, and transmigration, the culturally unimaginable. The culturally imaginable enters modernity not as ideal, but as reproducible image. The memoir, like the photograph, makes us believe that the private has been made public, even as the public becomes that which we consume in private.

Notes

Notes for Prologue

1. See Ross Chambers, *Loiterature* (Lincoln: U Nebraska P, 1999) for an immensely illuminating guide to reading for digression.
2. Virginia Woolf, "A Society," *The Complete Shorter Fiction of Virginia Woolf,* ed. Susan Dick (New York: Harcourt, 1985) 118.
3. See Eve Sedgwick, *Between Men: English Literature and Male Homosocial Desire* (New York: Columbia UP), 1985.
4. Elizabeth Gaskell, *Mary Barton* (1848; New York: Penguin, 1996) 155.
5. Virginia Woolf, *A Room of One's Own* (1929; New York: Harcourt, 1957) 13.
6. Woolf, *A Room of One's Own* 89.
7. Woolf, *A Room of One's Own* 40–1.
8. Nella Larsen, *Quicksand and Passing,* ed. Deborah E. McDowell (1929; New Brunswick: Rutgers UP, 1986) 227.
9. Michael Warner, introduction, *Fear of a Queer Planet: Queer Politics and Social Theory* (Minneapolis: U Minnesota P, 1993) xxvi.
10. Elspeth Probyn, "Queer Belongings: The Politics of Departure," *Sexy Bodies: The Strange Carnalities of Feminism,* eds. Elizabeth Grosz and Elspeth Probyn (New York: Routledge, 1995) 9.
11. Diana Fuss, *Identification Papers* (New York: Routledge, 1995) 3.
12. Fuss, 69.
13. Gertrude Stein, *Paris France* (1940; New York: Liveright, 1970) 24–5.
14. Virginia Woolf, "Mr. Bennett and Mrs. Brown" (1924) in *The Captain's Deathbed and Other Essays* (New York: Harcourt, 1950) 96–7.
15. Roland Barthes, *Camera Obscura: Reflections on Photography,* trans. Richard Howard (New York: Hill and Wang, 1981) 98.
16. George Chauncey, *Gay New York: Gender, Urban Culture, and the Making of the Gay Male World 1890–1940* (New York: BasicBooks, 1994) 23.

Notes for Amelia Earhart

1. Charles Lindbergh, "*WE*" (New York: G. P. Putnam's Sons, 1927) 265.

2. Laurence Goldstein, *The Flying Machine and Modern Literature* (London: Macmillan, 1986) 98.
3. Lindbergh 301–2.
4. Lindbergh 230.
5. Lindbergh 231.
6. Lindbergh 232.
7. Lindbergh 302–3.
8. Lindbergh 276.
9. Lindbergh 277.
10. Lindbergh 266.
11. Lindbergh 236.
12. Mayor Walker quoted in *Chicago Tribune,* 21 June 1932, p. 9 (qtd. in Susan Ware, *Still Missing: Amelia Earhart and the Search for Modern Feminism* [New York: Norton, 1993] 19).
13. Mary S. Lovell, *The Sound of Wings: The Life of Amelia Earhart* (New York: St. Martin's) 94.
14. Amelia Earhart, *20 Hrs. 40 Min.* (1928; Salem, NH: Ayer Company, 1992) 11.
15. Hilton H. Railey, "Finding a Woman to Fly the Atlantic," *Philadelphia Evening Bulletin* 10 September 1938 (qtd. in Doris Rich, *Amelia Earhart: A Biography* [New York: Dell, 1989] 46–7).
16. *Lantern* July-August 1928 (qtd. in Lovell 111).
17. Amelia Earhart, "Amelia Earhart Flies Atlantic; First Woman To Do It," *New York Times* 19 June 1928: 1.
18. Earhart, *20 Hrs. 40 Min.* 100.
19. Earhart, "Flying the Atlantic—and selling sausages have a lot of things in common," *The American Magazine* August 1932: 17.
20. Earhart, *Last Flight* (1937; New York: Crown, 1988) 4–5.
21. Doris Rich, *Queen Bess: Daredevil Aviator* (Washington: Smithsonian Institution P, 1993) 47.
22. See Mary Loeffelholz, *Experimental Lives: Women and Literature 1900–1945* (New York: Twayne, 1992) 191.
23. Rich, *Amelia Earhart* 77.
24. Susan Ware, *Still Missing: Amelia Earhart and the Search for Modern Feminism* (New York: Norton, 1993) 109.
25. Anne Morrow Lindbergh, *North to the Orient* (New York: Harcourt, Brace and Company, 1935) 135.
26. Earhart, *New York Times* 20 June 1928: 2.
27. Allen Raymond, *New York Times* 20 June 1928: 2.
28. Earhart, *New York Times* 19 June 1928: 2.
29. Earhart, *New York Times* 20 June 1928: 2.
30. Earhart, *New York Times* 21 June 1928: 1.
31. Earhart, *New York Times* 22 June 1928: 1.
32. Ray Long, editorial, *Cosmopolitan* November 1928: 33.
33. Earhart, "Why Are Women Afraid to Fly?" *Cosmopolitan* July 1929: 71.

34. Earhart, "Why Are Women Afraid to Fly?" 138.
35. Joseph Corn, *The Winged Gospel: America's Romance with Aviation, 1900–1950* (New York: Oxford UP, 1983) 89.
36. Jane Addams, *Twenty Years at Hull-House* (1910; New York: Signet, 1981) 98.
37. Earhart, "Try Flying Yourself," *Cosmopolitan* November 1928: 33.
38. Earhart, *New York Times* 22 June 1928: 2.
39. George Palmer Putnam, *Soaring Wings: A Biography of Amelia Earhart* (New York: Harcourt, Brace and Company, 1939) 41.
40. Earhart, *20 Hrs. 40 Min.* 112.
41. See Karla Jay, "No Bumps, No Excrescences: Amelia Earhart's Failed Flight into Fashions," *On Fashion,* eds. Shari Benstock and Suzanne Ferriss (New Brunswisk, NJ: Rutgers UP, 1994) 76–94.
42. Rich, *Amelia Earhart* 82.
43. Ware 168.
44. Terry Castle, *The Apparational Lesbian: Female Homosexuality and Modern Culture* (New York: Columbia UP, 1993) 62.
45. Ware 170.
46. Ware 171;173.
47. See Lovell 165–6.
48. Elizabeth Wilson, *Adorned in Dreams: Fashion and Modernity* (London: Virago, 1985) 162.
49. Earhart, "Flying the Atlantic" 72.
50. Wilson 180.

Notes for Beryl Markham

1. "Ghost Story," Editorial, *New York Times* 29 August 1993.
2. Editorial. *News Chronicle* 3 September 1936.
3. Theodore Roosevelt, *African Games Trails* (New York: Scribners, 1909) 381–2.
4. Honorable Mrs. Victor Bruce, *The Bluebird's Flight* (London: Chapman and Hall, 1931) 7.
5. Bruce 57.
6. See Donna Haraway, "Teddy Bear Patriarchy: Taxidermy in the Garden of Eden, New York City, 1908–1936," *Cultures of United States Imperialism,* eds. Amy Kaplan and Donald E. Paese (Durham: Duke UP, 1993).
7. Roosevelt 570.
8. Isak Dinesen, *Out of Africa* (New York: Vintage, 1937) 205–6.
9. Beryl Markham, *West With the Night* (San Francisco: North Point Press, 1983) 102.
10. Mary S. Lovell, *Straight on Till Morning: The Biography of Beryl Markham* (New York: St. Martin's, 1987) xxiv.
11. Errol Trzebinski, *The Lives of Beryl Markham: "Out of Africa's" Hidden Free Spirit and Denys Finch Hatton's Last Great Love* (New York: Norton, 1993) 185.

12. Trzebinski 46.
13. Lovell 120–21.
14. Trzebinski 93.
15. Molly Castle, *Daily Mirror* 16 January 1940.
16. Scott O'Dell, Letter, *Vanity Fair* March 1987: 24.
17. Lovell xix.
18. James Fox, "The Beryl Mystery," *Vanity Fair* October 1984: 90; 111.
19. Fox 112.
20. Martha Gelhorn, introduction, *West With the Night,* by Beryl Markham (London: Virago, 1984) vii.
21. Thomas R. Knipp, "Kenya's Literary Ladies and the Mythologizing of the White Highlands," *South Atlantic Review* 88 (1990): 3.
22. Knipp 4.
23. See Judith Halberstam, *Female Masculinity* (Durham: Duke UP, 1998).
24. Markham 137.
25. Markham 108–9.
26. Markham 110.
27. Markham 111–12.
28. Markham 77.
29. Markham 268.
30. Markham 152–3.
31. Markham 207.
32. Markham 208.
33. Markham 212.
34. Markham 211.
35. Markham 8.
36. Anne McClintock, *Imperial Leather: Race, Gender and Sexuality in the Colonial Contest* (New York: Routledge, 1995) 242.
37. Roosevelt 95.
38. Markham 234.
39. Markham 235.
40. Markham 235.
41. Markham 12.
42. Markham 283
43. Sidonie Smith, "The Other Woman and the Racial Politics of Gender: Isak Dinesen and Beryl Markham in Kenya," *De/Colonizing the Subject: The Politics of Gender in Women's Autobiography,* eds. Sidonie Smith and Julia Watson (Minneapolis: Minnesota UP, 1992) 421.
44. Laura Doan, "Passing Fashion: Reading Female Masculinities in the 1920s" *Feminist Studies* 24 (1998): 670.

Notes for Virginia Woolf

1. Hermione Lee, *Virginia Woolf* (New York: Knopf, 1997) 748.
2. Lee 291.

3. Lee 457.
4. See Gillian Beer, "The Island and the Airplane: The Case of Virginia Woolf," *Nation and Narration,* ed. Homi K. Bhabha (New York: Routledge, 1990) 265–290.
5. Lytton Strachey, "Letter to Roger Senhouse," 9 February, 1919 (qtd. in Holroyd, *Lytton Strachey: The New Biography* [New York: Farrar, Straus, and Giroux, 1994] 569).
6. See Leslie Kathleen Hankins, "*Orlando* :'A Precipice Marked V': Between 'A Miracle of Discretion' and 'Lovemaking Unbelievable: Indiscretions Incredible,'" *Virginia Woolf: Lesbian Readings,* eds. Eileen Barrett and Patricia Cramer (New York: New York UP, 1997) 180–202.
7. Virginia Woolf, "To Hugh Walpole," 28 December 1932, *Letters of Virginia Woolf,* eds. Nigel Nicolson and Joanne Trautmann, 6 vols. (New York: Harcourt, 1979) 5: 142.
8. See Laura Marcus, "Bringing the Corpse to Life: Woolf, Strachey and the Discourse of the 'New Biography,'" in *Auto/biographical Discourses* (Manchester: Manchester UP, 1994) 90–134.
9. Woolf, "The New Biography," *Granite and Rainbow* (New York: Harcourt, 1958) 153–4.
10. Maurizia Boscagli and Enda Duffy, "Joyce's Face," *Marketing Modernisms: Self-Promotion, Canonization and Rereading,*" eds. Kevin J.H. Dettmar and Stephen Watt (Ann Arbor: U Michigan P, 1996) 152.
11. Boscagli and Duffy 151.
12. Lytton Strachey, *Eminent Victorians* (New York: Harcourt, 1918) vii.
13. Woolf, *A Room of One's Own* (New York: Harcourt, 1929) 5.
14. Woolf, "The Art of Biography," *The Death of the Moth and Other Essays* (New York: Harcourt, 1942) 194–5.
15. Walter Pater, *The Renaissance.* (1910; Chicago: Academy, 1977) 2.
16. Oscar Wilde, "The Portrait of Mr. W. H.," *The Complete Works of Oscar Wilde* (New York: Harper, 1966) 1174.
17. Walter Pater, qtd. in Gerald Cornelius Monsman, *Pater's Portraits: Mythic Pattern in the Fiction of Walter Pater* (Baltimore: Johns Hopkins UP, 1967) 37.
18. Strachey, *Elizabeth and Essex* (New York: Harcourt, 1928) 10.
19. Strachey 10.
20. Woolf, *Orlando* (New York: Harcourt, 1928) 137.
21. Strachey 29.
22. See Susan M. Squier, "Tradition and Revision in Woolf's *Orlando:* Defoe and the 'The Jessamy Brides,'" *Women's Studies* 12 (1986): 167–178.
23. See Joanne Trautmann, "The Jessamy Brides: The Friendship of Virginia Woolf and V. Sackville-West," *Pennsylvania State University Studies* 36 (1973); Louise A. DeSalvo, "Lighting the Cave: The Relationship between Vita Sackville-West and Virginia Woolf," *Signs* 8.2 (1982): 194–214; Sherron E. Knopp, "'If I Saw You Would You Kiss Me?': Sapphism and the Subversiveness of Virginia Woolf's *Orlando, PMLA* 103 (1988): 24–34.

24. Perry Meisel, *The Absent Father: Virginia Woolf and Walter Pater* (New Haven: Yale UP, 1980) 45.
25. Woolf, *Moments of Being* (New York: Harcourt, 1976) 160.
26. Woolf, "Moments of Being: 'Slater's Pins Have No Points,'" *The Complete Shorter Fiction of Virginia Woolf,* ed. Susan Dick (New York: Harcourt, 1985) 210.
27. Woolf, "'Slater's Pins Have No Points'" 210.
28. Woolf, "'Slater's Pins Have No Points'" 214.
29. Pater, *The Renaissance* 236.
30. Woolf, 21 December 1925 of *The Diary of Virginia Woolf,* ed. Anne Olivier Bell, 5 vols. (New York: Harcourt, 1980) 3: 53.
31. Woolf, *Diary,* 18 December 1928, 3:212.
32. Suzanne Raitt, *Vita and Virginia: The Work and Friendship of V. Sackville-West and Virginia Woolf* (Oxford: Oxford UP, 1993) 5;9;167.
33. Woolf, *Orlando* 65.
34. Woolf, *Orlando* 119.
35. Woolf, *Orlando* 119.
36. Woolf, *Orlando* 312.
37. Woolf, *Orlando* 219.
38. Woolf, *Orlando* 219.
39. Woolf, *Orlando* 219.
40. Woolf, *Orlando* 220.
41. Woolf, *Orlando* 187.
42. Woolf, *Orlando* 188.
43. Woolf, *Orlando* 189.
44. Buscagli and Duffy 152.
45. Woolf, "From V. Sackville-West to Virginia Woolf," 11 October 1928, *Letters* 3: 574.
46. "From V. Sackville-West to Virginia Woolf," 574.
47. Woolf, "To Vita Sackville-West," 27 April 1927, *Letters* 3: 487.
48. Woolf, *Diary,* 11 March 1935, 4: 287.
49. Woolf, *Orlando* 304–5.
50. Woolf, *Orlando* 307.

Notes for Gertrude Stein

1. Gertrude Stein, "A Transatlantic Interview 1946," *A Primer for the Gradual Understanding of Gertrude Stein,* ed. Robert Bartlett Haas (Los Angeles: Black Sparrow, 1973) 19.
2. Stein, *Everybody's Autobiography* (New York: Random House, 1937) 40.
3. Stein, *Everybody's,* 309.
4. Stein, *Narration; Four Lectures* (1935; New York: Greenwood, 1969) 52–3.
5. Stein, *The Autobiography of Alice B. Toklas* (New York: Knopf, 1933) 70.
6. Stein, *The Autobiography* 70.
7. Stein, *The Autobiography* 240.

8. Stein, *The Autobiography* 249.
9. Stein, *Lectures in America* (1935; London: Virago, 1988) 205.
10. Stein, "A Transatlantic Interview 1946," 19.
11. Stein, *Narration* 57.
12. S.C. Neuman, *Gertrude Stein: Autobiography and the Problem of Narration* (University of Victoria: English Literary Studies, 1979) 26. See also Paul Akron, "Visual Rhetoric in *The Autobiography of Alice B. Toklas,*" *Critical Inquiry* 1 (1975): 849–81.
13. Charles Caramello, *Henry James, Gertrude Stein, and the Biographical Act* (Chapel Hill: U North Carolina P, 1996) 123.
14. See Wayne Koestenbaum, "Stein Is Nice," *Parnassus Review* 20.2–3 (1995): 297–319.
15. Stein, *The Autobiography* 252.
16. See Priscilla Wald, *Constituting Americans: Cultural Anxiety and Narrative Form* (Durham: Duke, 1995) 237–98.
17. Ulla E. Dydo, "*Stanzas in Meditation:* The Other Autobiography," *Chicago Review* 32.2 (1985): 14.
18. Dydo 16.
19. See Diana Souhani, *Gertrude and Alice* (London: Pandora, 1991) 38–44.
20. Stein, *The Autobiography* 85.
21. Stein, *Everybody's* 1.
22. Stein, *Everybody's* 104.
23. Caramello 162.
24. Stein, *The Autobiography* 12.
25. Stein, *The Autobiography* 57.
26. Stein, *The Autobiography* 53; 57.
27. Michael North, *The Dialect of Modernism: Race, Language and Twentieth Century Literature* (New York: Oxford UP, 1994) 61.
28. Stein, *The Autobiography* 49.
29. Stein, *The Autobiography* 50.
30. Alice B. Toklas, *What is Remembered* (New York: Holt, Rinehart, Winston, 1963) 139.
31. Stein, *Everybody's* 171.
32. Stein, *Everybody's* 174.
33. Stein, *What Are Masterpieces?* (1940; New York: Pitman, 1970) 90–91.
34. Stein, *What Are Masterpieces?* 86.
35. Stein, *Everybody's* 180.
36. Stein, *Everybody's* 288–89.
37. Stein, *How Writing is Written,* ed. Robert Bartlett Haas (Los Angeles: Black Sparrow, 1974) 71.
38. Stein, *How Writing is Written* 71.
39. Bryce Conrad, "Gertrude Stein in the American Marketplace," *Journal of Modern Literature* 19.2 (1995): 231.
40. Stein, *How Writing is Written* 72.
41. Stein, *Everybody's* 225.

42. See Corinne E. Blackmur, "Selling Taboo Subjects: The Literary Commerce of Gertrude Stein and Carl Van Vechten," *Marketing Modernisms,* eds. Kevin J.H. Dettmar and Stephen Watt (Ann Arbor: U Michigan P, 1996) 221–52.
43. Stein, *Everybody's* 324.
44. Stein, *The Geographical History of America* (New York: Random House, 1936) 112–3.

Notes for James Weldon Johnson

1. Frances E.W. Harper, *Iola Leroy or Shadows Uplifted* (1892; Boston: Beacon, 1987) 245.
2. Hortense Spillers, "Mama's Baby, Papa's Maybe: An American Grammar Book," *Diacritics* 17.2 (1987): 80.
3. See Marlon Ross, "Folkways of Desire: Patronage, Sex, and Same-Sexuality in the New Negro Renaissance," Working Paper #19, Center for Afroamerican and African Studies, University of Michigan, 1996. Forthcoming in *The Color of Manhood: Racial Imaging and Sexual Politics in the Civil Rights Era.*
4. W. E. B. Du Bois, *The Souls of Black Folk* (1903; New York: Signet, 1982) 44.
5. James Weldon Johnson, *Along This Way* (1933; New York: Penguin, 1990) 169.
6. Johnson, *Along this Way* 166.
7. Spillers 78.
8. Du Bois 45.
9. Johnson, *The Autobiography of an Ex-Coloured Man* (1927; New York: Vintage, 1989) 21–2.
10. See Eric Lott, *Love and Theft: Blackface Minstrelsy and the American Working Class* (New York: Oxford UP, 1993).
11. Johnson, "Double Audience Makes Road Hard for Negro Authors," *Philadelphia Tribune* 29 November 1928 rpt. *The Selected Writings of James Weldon Johnson* vol. 2, ed. Sondra Kathryn Wilson (New York: Oxford UP, 1995) 409.
12. Johnson, "Double Audience" 411.
13. Barbara Christian, *Black Women Novelists: The Development of a Tradition, 1892–1976* (Westport, CT: Greenwood, 1980) 45.
14. Hazel Carby, introduction, *Iola Leroy,* by Frances E. W. Harper (Boston: Beacon, 1987) xxi-xxii.
15. Gertrude Stein, *Three Lives* (1909; New York: Vintage, 1939) 86.
16. Stein 103.
17. Stein 97.
18. Stein 97; 100; 101.
19. Stein 100.
20. Carl Van Vechten, *Nigger Heaven* (New York: Knopf, 1928) 149.

21. See Marlon Ross, "Some Glances at the Black Fag: Race, Same-Sex Desire and Cultural Belonging," *Canadian Review of Comparative Literature* 21.1–2 (1994): 193–219.
22. Van Vechten 57.
23. Van Vechten 223.
24. See Eric Garber, "A Spectacle of Color: The Lesbian and Gay Subculture of Jazz Age Harlem," *Hidden from History: Reclaiming the Gay and Lesbian Past,*" eds. Martin Bauml Duberman, Martha Vicinus, and George Chauncey, Jr. (New York: New American Library, 1989) 318–31 and Joseph Boone, "Queer Sites in Modernism: Harlem/The Left Bank/Greenwich Village in the 1920s and 1930s" in *Libidinal Currents: Sexuality and the Shaping of Modernism* (Chicago: U Chicago P, 1998).
25. Richard Bruce, "Smoke, Lilies and Jade," *Voices From the Harlem Renaissance,* ed. Nathan Irvin Huggins (New York: Oxford UP, 1995) 105.
26. Bruce 102.
27. Bruce 106.
28. Wallace Thurman, *Infants of the Spring* (1932; Boston: Northeastern UP, 1992) 114.
29. Thurman 45.
30. Thurman 47.
31. Thurman 263–4.
32. Steven Watson, *The Harlem Renaissance: Hub of African-American Culture 1920–1930* (New York: Pantheon, 1995) 9.
33. See Henry Louis Gates, "The Trope of the New Negro and the Reconstruction of the Image of the Black," *Representations* 24 (1988) 129–55.
34. See Deborah Nord, "The Social Explorer as Anthropologist: Victorian Travellers Among the Urban Poor," *Visions of the Modern City: Essays in History, Art and Literature,* eds. William Sharp and Leonard Wallock (New York: Columbia UP, 1983) 118–130.
35. See James Buzzard, "Mass-observation, Modernism and Auto-Ethnography," *Modernism/Modernity* 4.3 (1977): 93–122.
36. Van Vechten, introduction, Johnson, *The Autobiography* xxxiii-xxxiv.
37. The Publishers, preface, *The Autobiography,* by Johnson (1912): xi.
38. Mary Louise Pratt, *Imperial Eyes: Travel Writing and Transculturation* (New York: Routledge, 1992) 7.
39. Johnson, *Along* 327.
40. Johnson, *Along* 238–9.
41. Booker T. Washington, *Up From Slavery* (1901; New York: Penguin, 1986) 23–4.
42. Johnson to Towns, 2 February 1913, in Jackson, Miles, ed. "Letters to a Friend: Correspondence from James Weldon Johnson to George A. Towns," *Phylon* 29 (1968): 182–98 qtd. Eugene Levy, *James Weldon Johnson: Black Leader Black Voice* (Chicago: U Chicago P, 1973) 146–7.
43. Johnson, *The Autobiography* 17–19; 33.
44. Johnson, *The Autobiography* 17.

45. Johnson, *Along* 391.
46. Johnson, *Along* 76.
47. Johnson, *Along* 241.
48. See Cheryl Clarke, "Race, Homosocial Desire, and 'Mammon' in *Autobiography of an Ex-Coloured Man,*" *Professions of Desire: Lesbian and Gay Studies in Literature,* eds. George E. Haggerty and Bonnie Zimmerman (New York: MLA, 1995) 84–96.
49. Phillip Brian Harper, *Are We Not Men?: Masculine Anxiety and the Problem of African-American Identity* (New York: Oxford UP, 1996) 110.
50. Harper 111.
51. Johnson, *The Autobiography* 144–5.
52. Johnson, *The Autobiography* 148.
53. Johnson, *Along* 95.
54. Johnson, *Along* 59.
55. See Julia Stern, "Spanish Masquerade and the Drama of Racial Identity in *Uncle Tom's Cabin,*" *Passing and the Fictions of Identity,* ed. Elaine Ginsberg (Durham: Duke UP, 1966) 103–30.
56. Johnson, *The Autobiography* 163.
57. Johnson, *Along* 47.
58. Johnson, *Along* 136.
59. Johnson, *The Autobiography* 3.

Notes for Earl Lind

1. See Siobhan B. Somerville, "Scientific Racism and the Invention of the Homosexual Body," *Sexology in Culture: Labelling Bodies and Desires,* eds. Lucy Bland and Laura Doan (Chicago: U Chicago P, 1998) 60–76.
2. *The Medico-Legal Journal* 36.1 (1919).
3. See James D. Steakley, *The Homosexual Emancipation Movement in Germany* (New York: Arno, 1975). See also John Lauritsen and David Thorstad, *The Early Homosexual Rights Movement (1864–1935)* (New York: Times Change, 1974).
4. Carl Heinrich Ulrichs, *"Memnon": Die Geschlectsnatur des mannliebenden Urnings* in *Forschungen über das Rätsel der Mannmännlichen Liebe* (1898; New York: Arno, 1975) 10.
5. Havelock Ellis and John Addington Symonds, *Sexual Inversion* (1897; New York: Arno, 1975) 1.
6. See Magnus Hirschfeld, "Sexuelle Zwischenstufen: Das Männliche Weib und der weibliche Mann" in *Sexualpathologie: Ein Lehrbuch für Ärzte und Studierende* (Bonn: A. Marcus & E. Webers, 1918).
7. Ralph Werther—Jennie June ("Earl Lind"), *The Female-Impersonators* (1922; New York: Arno, 1975) 168.
8. John Addington Symonds, *A Problem in Greek Ethics,* Appendix A in Havelock Ellis and John Addington Symonds, *Sexual Inversion* (1897; New York: Arno, 1975) 173.

9. Magnus Hirschfeld, *Transvestites: The Erotic Drive to Cross-Dress,* trans. Michael A. Lombardi-Nash (1910; Buffalo: Prometheus, 1991) 227.
10. Earl Lind ("Ralph Werther"—"Jennie June"), *Autobiography of an Androgyne* (1918; New York: Arno, 1975) 6.
11. Lind 258–9.
12. Lind 14.
13. Richard von Krafft-Ebing, *Psychopathia Sexualis: With Especial Reference to the Antipathic Sexual Instinct. A Medico-Forensic Study* [1886], trans. Franklin S. Klaf from the 12th German edition, (1886; New York: Stein and Day, 1965) 205.
14. Jay Prosser, *Second Skins: The Body Narratives of Transsexuality* (New York: Columbia UP, 1998) 130.
15. George Chauncey, *Gay New York: Gender, Urban Culture, and the Making of the Gay Male World 1890–1940* (New York: BasicBooks, 1994) 57.
16. Lind 7.
17. Werther 138.
18. See Francette Pacteau, "The Impossible Referent: Representations of the Androgyne," *Formations of Fantasy,* eds. Victor Burgin, James Donald, and Cora Kaplan (London: Methuen, 1986) 62–84.
19. Lind 119.
20. Lind 26.
21. Werther 93.
22. See Chauncey 387.
23. Lind 26.
24. Lind 137.
25. Werther 93.
26. Hirschfeld, *Transvestites* 222.
27. Hirschfeld, *Transvestites* 140.
28. Lind 103.
29. Lind 122.
30. Werther 159–60.
31. Werther 160–61.
32. Werther 161.
33. Phyllis Grosskurth, *Havelock Ellis: A Biography* (New York: Knopf, 1980) 186.
34. Werther 4.
35. *The Memoirs of John Addington Symonds: The Secret Homosexual Life of a Leading Nineteenth Century Man of Letters,* ed. Phyllis Grosskurth (Chicago: U Chicago, 1984) 281–82.
36. Lind 71.
37. Lind 17.

Notes for Coda

1. Sherwood Anderson, *Winesburg, Ohio* (1919; Oxford: Oxford UP, 1997) 155.

2. Anderson 155.
3. Anderson 156.
4. Anderson 157.
5. Anderson 160.
6. Anderson 161.
7. Anderson 162.
8. Anderson 164.

Bibliography

Works Cited and Consulted

Prologue

Barthes, Roland. *Camera Obscura: Reflections on Photography.* Trans. Richard Howard. New York: Hill and Wang, 1981.

Butler, Judith. *Gender Trouble: Feminism and the Subversion of Identity.* New York: Routledge, 1990.

——. *Bodies that Matter: On the Discursive Limits of 'Sex'.* New York: Routledge, 1993.

Chambers, Ross. *Loiterature.* Lincoln: U Nebraska P, 1999.

Chauncey, George. *Gay New York: Gender, Urban Culture, and the Making of the Gay Male World 1890–1940.* New York: BasicBooks, 1994.

Cleto, Fabio, ed. Introduction. *Camp Aesthetics and the Performing Subject: A Reader.* Ann Arbor: U Michigan P, 1999. 1–36.

Fuss, Diana. *Identification Papers.* New York: Routledge, 1995.

Gaskell, Mary. *Mary Barton.* 1848. New York: Penguin, 1996.

Jagose, Annamarie. *Queer Theory: An Introduction.* New York: New York UP, 1996.

Larsen, Nella. *Quicksand and Passing.* Ed. Deborah E. McDowell. 1929. New Brunswick: Rutgers UP, 1986.

Phelan, Peggy. *Unmarked: The Politics of Performance.* New York: Routledge, 1993.

Probyn, Elspeth. "Queer Belongings: The Politics of Departure." *Sexy Bodies: The Strange Carnalities of Feminism.* Ed. Elizabeth Grosz and Elspeth Probyn. New York: Routledge, 1995. 1–18.

Sedgwick, Eve Kosofsky. *Between Men: English Literature and Male Homosocial Desire.* New York: Columbia UP, 1985.

——. *Epistemology of the Closet.* Berkeley: U California P, 1990.

——. *Tendencies.* New York: Routledge, 1994.

Stein, Gertrude. *Paris France.* 1940. New York: Liveright, 1970.

Warner, Michael. Introduction. *Fear of a Queer Planet: Queer Politics and Social Theory.* Minneapolis: U Minnesota P, 1993. xii-xxxi.

Woolf, Virginia. *A Room of One's Own.* 1929. New York: Harcourt, 1957.

——. "Mr. Bennett and Mrs. Brown." *The Captain's Deathbed and Other Essays.* New York: Harcourt, 1950. 94–119.

——. "A Society." *The Complete Shorter Fiction of Virginia Woolf.* Ed. Susan Dick. New York: Harcourt, 1985. 118–130.

Amelia Earhart

Adams, Jane and Margaret Kimball. *Heroines of the Sky.* New York: Doubleday, 1942.

Addams, Jane. *Twenty Years at Hull-House.* 1910. New York: Signet, 1981.

Anderson, Allison. *Hidden Latitudes: A Novel.* New York: Scribners, 1996.

Anderson, Mark M. *Kafka's Clothes: Ornament and Aestheticism in the Habsburg Fin de Siècle.* Clarendon: Oxford UP, 1992.

Batten, Jean. *Alone in the Sky.* 1938. Shrewsbury: Airlife Publishing, 1979.

Berger, John. "The Suit and the Photograph" in *About Looking.* New York: Pantheon. 27–36.

Bird, Nancy. *Born to Fly.* London: Angus and Robertson, 1962.

Brooks-Pazmany, Kathleen. *United States Women in Aviation 1919–1929.* Washington DC: Smithsonian Institution P, 1991.

Castle, Terry. *The Apparitional Lesbian: Female Homosexuality and Modern Culture.* New York: Columbia UP, 1993.

Cochran, Jacqueline. *The Stars at Noon.* Boston: Little, Brown and Company, 1954.

Coombe, Rosemary. "The Celebrity Image and Cultural Identity: Publicity Rights and the Subaltern Politics of Gender." *Discourse* 14.3 (1992): 59–88.

Corn, Joseph. *The Winged Gospel: America's Romance with Aviation, 1900–1950.* New York: Oxford UP, 1983.

Earhart, Amelia. *20 Hrs. 40 Min.* 1928. Salem, NH: Ayer Company, 1992.

——. *The Fun Of It.* 1932. Chicago: Academy Publishers, 1977.

——. *Last Flight.* 1937. New York: Crown Publishers, 1988.

Fritzsche, Peter. *A Nation of Fliers: German Aviation and the Popular Imagination.* Cambridge: Harvard UP, 1992.

Goldstein, Laurence. *The Flying Machine and Modern Literature.* London: Macmillan, 1986.

Gower, Pauline. *Women with Wings.* London: John Long, 1938.

Lady Heath and Stella Wolfe Murray. *Women and Flying.* London: John Long, 1929.

Hollander, Anne. *Sex and Suits: The Evolution of Modern Dress.* New York: Knopf, 1994.

Humphreys, Helen. *Leaving Earth: A Novel.* New York: Henry Holt, 1997.

Jay, Karla. "No Bumps, No Excrescences: Amelia Earhart's Failed Flight into Fashions." *On Fashion.* Eds. Shari Benstock and Suzanne Ferriss. New Brunswick: Rutgers UP, 1994. 76–94.

Johnson, Amy. *Sky Roads of the World.* London: W & R Chambers, 1939.

Lindbergh, Anne Morrow. *North to the Orient.* New York: Norton, 1935.

Lindbergh, Charles. "*WE.*" New York: G.P. Putnam's Sons, 1927.

Loeffelholz, Mary. *Experimental Lives: Women and Literature 1900–1945.* New York: Twayne Publishers, 1992.

Lomax, Judy. *Women of the Air.* London: John Murray, 1986.

Lovell, Mary S. *The Sound of Wings: The Life of Amelia Earhart.* New York: St. Martin's, 1989.

Marcus, Jane. "Invincible Mediocrity: The Private Selves of Public Women." *The Private Self: Theory and Practice of Women's Autobiographical Writings.* Ed. Shari Benstock. Chapel Hill: North Carolina UP, 1988. 114–146.

Mendelsohn, Jane. *I Was Amelia Earhart.* New York: Knopf, 1996.

Nichols, Ruth. *Wings for Life.* Philadelphia: J.B. Lippincott, 1957.

Oakes, Claudia M. *United States Women in Aviation 1930–1939.* Washington DC: Smithsonian Institution P, 1991.

Planck, Charles E. *Women with Wings.* New York: Harper, 1942.

Powell, William J. *Black Wings.* Los Angeles: Ivan Deach, 1934.

Putnam, George Palmer. *Soaring Wings: A Biography of Amelia Earhart.* New York: Harcourt, 1939.

Quinby, Lee. *Freedom, Foucault and the Subject of America.* Boston: Northeastern U, 1991.

Rich, Doris. *Amelia Earhart: A Biography.* New York: Dell, 1989.

——. *Queen Bess: Daredevil Aviator.* Washington, DC: Smithsonian Institution P, 1993.

Russo, Mary. "Up There, Out There: Aerialism, the Grotesque, and Critical Practice" in *The Female Grotesque: Risk, Excess and Modernity.* New York: Routledge, 1994. 17–51.

Schivelbusch, Wolfgang. *The Railway Journey: Trains and Travel in the Nineteenth Century.* Trans. Anselm Hollo. New York: Urizen, 1979.

Schnapp, Jeffrey T. "Propeller Talk." *Modernism/Modernity* 1.3 (1994): 153–178.

Smith, Sidonie. *A Poetics of Women's Autobiography.* Bloomington: Indiana UP, 1987.

——. *Subjectivity, Identity and the Body: Women's Autobiographical Practices in the Twentieth Century.* Bloomington: Indiana UP, 1993.

Thaden, Louise. *High, Wide and Frightened.* New York: Stackpole Sons, 1938.

Verrill, Dorothy. *The Sky Girl.* New York: The Century Company, 1930.

Ware, Susan. *Still Missing: Amelia Earhart and the Search for Modern Feminism.* New York: Norton, 1993.

Whyte, Edna Gardner. *Rising Above It: An Autobiography.* New York: Orion, 1991.

Wilson, Elizabeth. *Adorned in Dreams: Fashion and Modernity.* London: Virago, 1985.

Wohl, Peter. "The Bards of Aviation: Flight and French Culture, 1909–1939." *Michigan Quarterly Review* 29:3 (1990): 303–327.

——. *A Passion for Wings: Aviation and the Western Imagination 1909–1918.* New Haven: Yale UP, 1994.

Beryl Markham

Barrie, J.M. *Peter Pan.* 1911. New York: Bantam, 1985.

Bederman, Gail. *Manliness and Civilization: A Cultural History of Gender and Race in the United States, 1880–1917.* Chicago: U Chicago P, 1995.

Bruce, Honorable Mrs. Victor. *The Bluebird's Flight.* London: Chapman and Hall, 1931.

Chow, Rey. *Writing Diaspora: Tactics of Intervention in Contemporary Cultural Studies.* Bloomington: Indiana UP, 1993.

Churchill, Winston S. *My African Journey.* 1908. London: Holland Press, 1962.

Crary, Jonathan. *Techniques of the Observer: On Vision and Modernity in the Nineteenth Century.* Boston: MIT P, 1990.

Dinesen, Isak. *Out of Africa.* New York: Vintage, 1937.

Doan, Laura. "Passing Fashion: Reading Female Masculinities in the 1920s." *Feminist Studies* 24 (1998): 663–700.

Fox, James. "The Beryl Mystery." *Vanity Fair* March 1987: 88–113.

Frawley, Maria H. *A Wider Range: Travel Writing by Women in Victorian England.* Cranbury, NJ: Associated University Presses, 1994.

Freud, Sigmund. *Civilization and its Discontents.* Trans. James Strachey. New York: Norton, 1961.

Fussell, Paul. *Abroad: British Literary Traveling Between the Wars.* New York: Oxford UP, 1980.

Gelhorn, Martha. Introduction. *West With the Night.* By Beryl Markham. London: Virago, 1984. vii– xii.

Halberstam, Judith. *Female Masculinity.* Durham: Duke UP, 1998.

Haraway, Donna. "Teddy Bear Patriarchy: Taxidermy in the Garden of Eden, New York City, 1908–1936." *Cultures of United States Imperialism.* Eds. Amy Kaplan and Donald E. Paese. Durham: Duke UP, 1993. 237–291.

Hemingway, Ernest. *Green Hills of Africa.* 1935. New York: Touchstone, 1996.

Horton, Susan R. *Difficult Women, Artful Lives: Olive Schreiner and Isak Dinesen, In and Out of Africa.* Baltimore: Johns Hopkins UP, 1995.

Hulme, Peter. *Colonial Encounters: Europe and the Native Caribbean, 1492–1797.* London: Methuen, 1986.

Huxley, Elsbeth. *White Man's Country: Lord Delamere and the Making of Kenya.* 2 vols. 1935. New York: Praeger, 1967.

——. *The Flame Trees of Thika: Memories of an African Childhood.* London: Chatto and Windus, 1959.

Knipp, Thomas R. "Kenya's Literary Ladies and the Mythologizing of the White Highlands." *South Atlantic Review* 88 (1990): 1–16.

Lovell, Mary S. *Straight On Till Morning: The Biography of Beryl Markham.* New York: St. Martin's, 1987.

Lowe, Lisa. *Critical Terrains: French and British Orientalisms.* Ithaca: Cornell UP, 1991.

Markham, Beryl. *West With the Night.* 1942. San Francisco: North Point Press, 1983.

——. *The Splendid Outcast: African Stories.* New York: Dell, 1987.

McClintock, Anne. *Imperial Leather: Race, Gender and Sexuality in the Colonial Contest.* New York: Routledge, 1995.

Mudimbe, V.Y. *The Invention of Africa: Gnosis, Philosophy and the Order of Knowledge.* Bloomington: Indiana UP, 1988.

Nixon, Rob. "'Out of Africa.'" *Grand Street* 5 (1986): 216–27.

O'Dell, Scott. Letter. *Vanity Fair* March 1987: 24–26.

Roosevelt, Theodore. *African Game Trails.* New York: Scribners, 1909.

Shaw, Carolyn Martin. *Colonial Inscriptions: Race, Gender and Class in Kenya.* Minneapolis: U Minnesota P, 1995.

Smith, Sidonie. "The Other Woman and the Racial Politics of Gender: Isak Dinesen and Beryl Markham in Kenya." *De/Colonizing the Subject: The Politics of Gender in Women's Autobiography.* Eds. Sidonie Smith and Julia Watson. Minneapolis: U Minnesota P, 1992. 410–435.

Spurr, David. *The Rhetoric of Empire: Colonial Discourse in Journalism, Travel Writing and Imperial Administration.* Durham: Duke UP, 1993.

Thomas, Nicolas. *Colonialism's Culture: Anthropology, Travel and Government.* Princeton: Princeton UP, 1994.

Torgovnick, Marianna. "Loving Africa: Memoirs by European Women" in *Primitive Passions: Men, Women and the Quest for Ecstasy.* Chicago: U Chicago P, 1997. 61–87.

Trzebinski, Errol. *The Lives of Beryl Markham: "Out of Africa's" Hidden Free Spirit and Denys Finch Hatton's Last Great Love.* New York: Norton, 1993.

Van Den Abbele, Georges. *Travel as Metaphor: From Montaigne to Rousseau.* Minneapolis: U Minnesota P, 1992.

Ward, David. "Elspeth Huxley: *The Flame Trees of Thika*" in *Chronicles of Darkness.* New York: Routledge, 1989. 56–60.

Virginia Woolf

Adams, James Eli. *Dandies and Desert Saints: Styles of Victorian Masculinity.* Ithaca: Cornell UP, 1995.

Barrett, Eileen and Patricia Cramer, eds. *Virginia Woolf: Lesbian Readings.* New York: New York UP, 1997.

Barthes, Roland. *A Lover's Discourse: Fragments.* Trans. Richard Howard. New York: Farrar, Straus, Giroux, 1978.

Beer, Gillian. "The Island and the Airplane: The Case of Virginia Woolf" in *Nation and Narration.* Ed. Homi K. Bhaba. New York: Routledge, 1990. 265–290.

Brake, Laurel and Ian Small, eds. *Pater in the 1990s.* Greensboro, NC: ELT, 1991.

Cooley, Elizabeth. "Revolutionizing Biography: *Orlando, Roger Fry,* and the Tradition." *South Atlantic Review.* 55.2 (1990): 71–83.

Corbett, Mary Jean. *Representing Femininity: Middle-Class Subjectivity in Victorian and Edwardian Women's Autobiographies.* Oxford: Oxford UP, 1992.

Cucullu, Lois. "Retailing the Female Intellectual." *differences* 9.2 (1998): 25–68.

Dahl, Christopher. "Virginia Woolf's *Moments of Being* and Autobiographical Tradition in the Stephen Family." *Journal of Modern Literature* 10.2 (1983): 175–196.

Dellamora, Richard. *Masculine Desire: The Sexual Politics of Victorian Aestheticism.* Chapel Hill: U North Carolina P, 1990.

DeSalvo, Louise. "Lighting the Cave: The Relationship between Vita Sackville-West and Virginia Woolf." *Signs* 8.2 (1982): 194–214.

Dettmar, Kevin J.H. and Stephen Watt, eds. *Marketing Modernisms: Self-Promotion, Canonization and Rereading.* Ann Arbor: U Michigan P, 1996.

Dowling, Linda. *Hellenism and Homosexuality in Victorian Oxford.* Ithaca: Cornell UP, 1994.

Elliott, Bridget and Jo-Ann Wallace. *Women Artists and Writers: Modernist (Im)positionings.* New York: Routledge, 1994.

Felski, Rita. *The Gender of Modernity.* Cambridge: Harvard UP, 1995.

Gagnier, Regina. *Idylls of the Marketplace: Oscar Wilde and the Victorian Public.* Stanford: Stanford UP, 1986.

——. *Subjectivities: A History of Self-Representation in Britain, 1832–1920.* Oxford: Oxford UP, 1991.

Heilbrun, Carolyn. "Non-Autobiographies of 'Privileged' Women: England and America." *Life/Lines: Theorizing Womens' Autobiography.* Eds. Bella Brodzki and Celeste Schenck. Ithaca: Cornell UP, 1988. 62–76.

Holroyd, Michael. *Lytton Strachey: The New Biography.* New York: Farrar, Straus, Giroux, 1994.

Hovey, Jaimie. "'Kissing a Negress in the Dark': Englishness as a Masquerade in Woolf's *Orlando.*" *PMLA* 112 (1997): 393–404.

Jones, Ellen Carol. "The Flight of a Word: Narcissism and the Masquerade of Writing in Virginia Woolf's *Orlando.*" *Women' Studies* 23 (1994): 155–174.

Knopp, Sherron E. "'If I Saw You Would You Kiss Me?': Sapphism and the Subversiveness of Virginia Woolf's *Orlando. PMLA* 103 (1988): 24–34.

Lawrence, Karen. *Penelope Voyages: Women and Travel in the British Literary Tradition.* Ithaca: Cornell UP, 1994.

Lee, Hermione. *Virginia Woolf.* New York: Knopf, 1997.

Levenson, Michael. *A Geneology of Modernism: A Study of English Literary Doctrine 1908–1922.* Cambridge: Cambridge UP, 1984.

Marcus, Laura. *Auto-biographical Discourses: Theory, Criticism, Practice.* Manchester: Manchester UP, 1994.

Matlock, Jann. "Masquerading Women, Pathologized Men: Cross-Dressing, Fetishism, and the Theory of Perversion, 1882–1935." *Fetishism as Cultural Discourse.* Eds. Emily Apter and William Pietz. Ithaca: Cornell UP, 1993. 31–61.

Meisel, Perry. *The Absent Father: Virginia Woolf and Walter Pater.* New Haven: Yale UP, 1980.

Monsman, Gerald Cornelius. *Pater's Portraits: Mythic Pattern in the Fiction of Walter Pater.* Baltimore: Johns Hopkins UP, 1967.

Nicolson, Harold. *Some People.* 1927. New York: Oxford UP, 1934.

——. *The Development of English Biography.* New York: Harcourt, 1928.

Nicolson, Nigel. *Portrait of a Marriage: V. Sackville-West and Harold Nicolson.* New York: Atheneum, 1973.

Nussbaum, Felicity. *The Autobiographical Subject: Gender and Ideology in Eighteenth Century England.* Baltimore: Johns Hopkins UP, 1989.

Pater, Walter. *The Renaissance.* 1910. Chicago: Academy, 1977.

——. *Imaginary Portraits.* London: Macmillan, 1912.

——. *Selected Writings of Walter Pater.* Ed. Harold Bloom. New York: Signet, 1974.

Raitt, Suzanne. *Vita and Virginia: The Work and Friendship of V. Sackville-West and Virginia Woolf.* Oxford: Clarendon, 1993.

Sackville-West, Vita. *Passenger to Teheran.* 1926. New York: HarperPerennial, 1990.

——. *The Land.* London: William Heinemann, 1926.

——. "Appendix A: From Vita Sackville-West to Harold Nicolson." "Virginia Woolf's *Orlando:* an Edition of the Manuscript." Ed. Madeline Moore. *Twentieth Century Literature* 25.3–4 (1979): 351–352.

——. *The Letters of Vita Sackville-West to Virginia Woolf.* Eds. Louise DeSalvo and Mitchell A. Leaska. New York: William Morrow, 1985.

Shaffer, Talia. "Posing *Orlando.*" *Genders 19: Sexual Artifice: Persons, Images, Politics.* New York: New York UP, 1994. 26–63.

Silver, Brenda. "What's Woolf Got To Do With It? Or, The Perils of Popularity." *Modern Fiction Studies* 38.1 (1992): 21–60.

Squier, Susan. "Tradition and Revision in Woolf's *Orlando:* Defoe and 'The Jessamy Brides.'" *Women's Studies* 12 (1986): 167–178.

Stansky, Peter. *On or About December 1910: Early Bloomsbury and Its Intimate World* Cambridge: Harvard UP, 1996.

Stimpson, Catherine. "The Female Sociograph: The Theater of Virginia Woolf's Letters." *The Female Autograph: Theory and Practice of Autobiography from the Tenth to the Twentieth Century.* Ed. Domna Stanton. Chicago: U Chicago P, 1984. 168–179.

Strachey, Lytton. *Eminent Victorians.* New York: Harcourt, 1918.

——. *Elizabeth and Essex.* New York: Harcourt, 1928.

Trautmann, Joanne. "The Jessamy Brides: The Friendship of Virginia Woolf and V. Sackville-West." *Pennsylvania State University Studies* 36 (1973).

Vanita, Ruth. "Biography as Homoerotic Fiction: Freud, Pater and Woolf" in *Sappho and the Virgin Mary: Same-Sex Love and the English Literary Tradition.* New York: Columbia UP, 1996. 165–186.

Wharton, Edith. *A Motor-Flight Through France.* New York: Scribners, 1908.

Wilde, Oscar. *The Complete Works of Oscar Wilde.* New York: Harper, 1966.

Woolf, Leonard. *Downhill All the Way: An Autobiography of the Years 1919 to 1939.* New York: Harcourt, 1967.

Woolf, Virginia. *Orlando: a Biography.* New York: Harcourt, 1928.

——. *A Room of One's Own.* New York: Harcourt, 1929.

——. *The Death of the Moth and Other Essays.* New York: Harcourt, 1942.

——. "Flying Over London" in *The Captain's Deathbed and Other Essays.* New York: Harcourt, 1950. 203–210.

——. *Granite and Rainbow.* New York: Harcourt, 1959.

——. *Moments of Being: Unpublished Autobiographical Writings.* New York: Harcourt, 1976.

——. *Letters of Virginia Woolf.* Ed. Nigel Nicolson and Joanne Trautmann. 6 vols. New York: Harcourt, 1979.

——. *The Diary of Virginia Woolf.* Ed. Anne Olivier Bell. 5 vols. New York: Harcourt, 1980.

——. *The Complete Shorter Fiction of Virginia Woolf.* Ed. Susan Dick. New York: Harcourt, 1985.

Wussow, Helen. "Virginia Woolf and the Problematic Nature of the Photographic Image." *Twentieth Century Literature* 40.1 (1994): 1–14.

Gertrude Stein

Abraham, Julie. *Are Girls Necessary?: Lesbian Writing and Modern Histories.* New York: Routledge, 1996.

Adams, Timothy Dow. *Telling Lies in Modern American Autobiography.* Chapel Hill: U North Carolina P, 1990.

Akron, Paul. "Visual Rhetoric in *The Autobiography of Alice B. Toklas.*" *Critical Inquiry* 1 (1975): 849–881.

Anderson, Sherwood. "Four American Impressions. *The New Republic.* 11 October 1922: 171–173.

Berry, Ellen. *Curved Thought and Textual Wandering: Gertrude Stein's Postmodernism.* Ann Arbor: U Michigan P, 1992.

Blackmur, Corrine E. "Selling Taboo Subjects: The Literary Commerce of Gertrude Stein and Carl Van Vechten." Kevin J. H. Dettmar and Stephen Watt, eds. *Marketing Modernisms.* Ann Arbor: U Michigan P, 1996.

Bridgman, Richard. *Gertrude Stein in Pieces.* Oxford: Oxford UP, 1970.

Caramello, Charles. *Henry James, Gertrude Stein, and the Biographical Act.* Chapel Hill: U North Carolina P, 1996.

Chessman, Harriet Scott. *The Public Is Invited to Dance: Representation, the Body, and Dialogue in Gertrude Stein.* Stanford: Stanford UP, 1989.

Conrad, Bryce. "Gertrude Stein in the American Marketplace." *Journal of Modern Literature* 19.2 (1995): 215–233.

Cowley, Malcolm. *Exile's Return: A Literary Odyssey of the 1920s.* 1934. New York: Penguin, 1956.

DeKoven, Marianne. "Gertrude Stein and Modern Painting: Beyond Literary Criticism." *Contemporary Literature* 22.1 (1981): 81–95.

——. *A Different Language: Gertrude Stein's Experimental Writing.* Madison: U Wisconsin P, 1983.

Doane, Janice. *Silence and Narrative: The Early Novels of Gertrude Stein.* Westport, CT: Greenwood, 1986.

Dydo, Ulla E. "*Stanzas in Meditation:* The Other Autobiography." *Chicago Review* 32.2 (1985): 4–20.

——. "*Landscape is Not Grammar:* Gertrude Stein in 1928." *Raritan* 7.1 (1987): 97–113.

——. "Composition as Meditation." *Gertrude Stein and the Making of Literature.* Eds. Shirley Neuman and Ira B. Nadel. Boston: Northeastern UP, 1988.

DuPlessis, Rachel Blau. "Woolfenstein." *Breaking the Sequence: Women's Experimental Fiction.* Eds. Ellen G. Friedman and Miriam Fuchs. Princeton: Princeton UP, 1989. 99–114.

Eakin, John Paul. *Fictions of Autobiography: Studies in the Art of Self-Invention.* Princeton: Princeton UP, 1985.

Fifer, Elizabeth. "Is Flesh Advisable: The Interior Theater of Gertrude Stein." *Signs* 1 (1979): 472-483.

——. *Rescued Readings: A Reconstruction of Gertrude Stein's Difficult Texts.* Detroit: Wayne State UP, 1992.

Folkenflick, Robert, ed. *The Culture of Autobiography: Constructions of Self-Representation.* Stanford: Stanford UP, 1993.

Gallup, Donald. "Carl Van Vechten's Gertrude Stein." *Yale University Library Gazette.* New Haven: Yale U Library, 1953. 77–86.

Gambrell, Alice. *Women Intellectuals, Modernism, Difference: Transatlantic Culture: 1919–1945.* Cambridge: Cambridge UP, 1997.

Gilmore, Leigh. "A Signature of Lesbian Autobiography: 'Gertrude/Altrice.'" *Autobiography and Questions of Gender.* Ed. Shirley Neuman. London: Frank Cass, 1991. 56–75.

Goodwin, James. *Autobiography: The Self-Made Text.* New York: Twayne, 1993.

Hemingway, Ernest. *A Moveable Feast.* New York: Bantam, 1964.

Koestenbaum, Wayne. "Stein is Nice." *Parnassus Review* 20.2–3 (1995): 297–319.

Matthews, T.S. "Gertrude Stein Comes Home." *The New Republic* 5 December 1934: 100–101.

Meyer, Steven J. "Gertrude Stein Shipwrecked in Bohemia: Making Ends Meet in the *Autobiography* and After." *Southwest Review* 77.1 (1992): 12–33.

Neuman, S.C. *Gertrude Stein: Autobiography and the Problem of Narration.* University of Victoria: English Literary Studies, 1979.

North, Michael. *The Dialect of Modernism: Race, Language and Twentieth Century Literature.* New York: Oxford UP, 1994.

Perloff, Marjorie. "(Im)personating Gertrude Stein." *Gertrude Stein and the Making of Literature.* Eds. Shirley Neuman and Ira B. Nadel. 61–80.

Ruddick, Lisa. *Reading Gertrude Stein: Body, Text, Gnosis.* Ithaca: Cornell UP, 1990.

Schmitz, Neil. "Portrait, Patriarchy, Mythos: The Revenge of Gertrude Stein." *Salmagundi* 40 (1978): 68–91.

Schultz, Susan. "Gertrude Stein's Self-Advertisement." *Raritan* (1992): 71–87.

Stanley, Liz. *The Auto/biographical I: The Theory and Practice of Feminist Auto/biography.* Manchester: Manchester U, 1992.

Stein, Gertrude. *The Autobiography of Alice B. Toklas.* New York: Knopf, 1933.

——. *Lectures in America.* 1935. London: Virago, 1988.

——. *Narration; Four Lectures.* 1935. New York: Greenwood, 1969.

——. *The Geographical History of America.* New York: Random House, 1936.

——. *Everybody's Autobiography.* New York: Random House, 1937.

——. *Picasso.* 1938. Boston: Beacon, 1959.

——. *What Are Masterpieces?.* 1940. New York: Pitman, 1970.

——. *Four in America.* New Haven: Yale UP, 1947.

——. *A Primer for the Gradual Understanding of Gertrude Stein.* Ed. Robert Bartlett Haas. Los Angeles: Black Sparrow, 1973.

——. *How Writing Is Written.* Ed. Robert Bartlett Haas. Los Angeles: Black Sparrow, 1974.

Steiner, Wendy. *Exact Resemblances to Exact Resemblances: The Literary Portraiture of Gertrude Stein.* New Haven: Yale UP, 1978.

Stendhal, Renate, ed. *Gertrude Stein: In Words and Pictures.* Chapel Hill: Algonquin Books, 1994.

Souhani, Diana. *Gertrude and Alice.* London: Pandora, 1991.

Stimpson, Catherine. "Gertrude/Altrude: Stein, Toklas, and the Paradox of the Happy Marriage." *Mothering the Mind: Twelve Studies of Writers and Their Silent Partners.* Eds. Ruth Perry and Martina Watson Brownley. New York: Holmes and Meier, 1984. 123–166.

——. "Gertrude Stein and the Transposition of Gender." *The Poetics of Gender.* Ed. Nancy K. Miller. New York: Columbia UP, 1986. 1–18.

——. "The Mind, the Body and Gertrude Stein." 1977. *Modern Critical Views: Gertrude Stein.* Ed. Harold Bloom. New York: Chelsea House, 1986. 131–144.

Toklas, Alice B. *What Is Remembered.* New York: Holt, Rinehart, Winston, 1963.

Wagner, Linda. *"Favored Strangers": Gertrude Stein and Her Family.* New Brunswick: Rutgers UP, 1994.

Wald, Priscilla. *Constituting Americans: Cultural Anxiety and Narrative Form.* Durham: Duke UP, 1995.

Weininger, Otto. *Sex and Character.* 1903. London: W. Heinemann, 1906.

Williams, Raymond. *The Politics of Modernism: Against the New Conformists.* London: Verso, 1989.

Wineapple, Brenda. *Sister Brother: Gertrude and Leo Stein.* New York: Putnam, 1996.

James Weldon Johnson

Baker, Houston A. *Modernism and the Harlem Renaissance.* Chicago: U Chicago P, 1987.

Boone, Joseph. *Libidinal Currents: Sexuality and the Shaping of Modernism.* Chicago: U Chicago P, 1988.

Buzzard, James. "Mass-observation, Modernism and Auto-Ethnography." *Modernism/Modernity* 4.3 (1997). 93–122.

Carby, Hazel. Introduction. *Iola Leroy.* By Frances W.E.Harper. Boston: Beacon, 1987. ix-xxvi.

Chestnutt, Charles, W. *The House Behind the Cedars.* 1900. New York: Penguin, 1993.

Christian, Barbara. *Black Women Novelists: The Development of a Tradition, 1892–1976.* Westport, CT: Greenwood, 1980.

Clarke, Cheryl. "Race, Homosocial Desire, and 'Mammon' in *Autobiography of an Ex-Coloured Man.*" *Professions of Desire: Lesbian and Gay Studies in Literature.* Eds. George E. Haggerty and Bonnie Zimmerman. New York: MLA, 1995. 84–96.

Clifford, James. *The Predicament of Culture: Twentieth Century Ethnography, Literature and Art.* Cambridge: Harvard UP, 1988.

De Jongh, James. *Vicious Modernism: Black Harlem and the Literary Imagination.* Cambridge: Cambridge UP, 1990.

Douglas, Ann. *Terrible Honesty: Mongrel Manhattan in the 1920's.* New York: Farrar, Straus, Giroux, 1995.

Du Bois, W.E.B. *The Souls of Black Folk.* 1903. New York: Signet, 1982.

Fanon, Frantz. *Black Skin, White Masks: The Experiences of a Black Man in a White World.* New York: Grove, 1967.

Fauset, Jessie Redmon. *Plum Bun: A Novel Without a Moral.* 1928. Boston: Beacon, 1990.

——. *Comedy: American Style.* 1933. New York: G.K. Hall, 1995.

Garber, Eric. "A Spectacle of Color: The Lesbian and Gay Subculture of Jazz Age Harlem." *Hidden from History: Reclaiming the Gay and Lesbian Past.* Eds. Martin Bauml Duberman, Martha Vicinus and George Chauncey Jr. New York: New American Library, 1989. 318–331.

Gates, Henry Louis. "The Trope of the New Negro and the Reconstruction of the Image of the Black." *Representations* 24 (1988): 129–155.

Ginsberg, Elaine K., ed. *Passing and the Fictions of Identity.* Durham: Duke UP, 1996.

Gubar, Susan. *Racechanges: White Skin, Black Face in American Culture.* New York: Oxford UP, 1997.

Harper, Frances E.W., *Iola Leroy or Shadows Uplifted.* 1892. Boston: Beacon, 1987.

Harper, Phillip Brian. *Are We Not Men?: Masculine Anxiety and the Problem of African-American Identity.* New York: Oxford UP, 1996.

Huggins, Nathan Irvin. *Harlem Renaissance.* New York: Oxford UP, 1971.

——. ed. *Voices from the Harlem Renaissance.* New York, Oxford, 1995.

Hughes, Langston. *Selected Poems.* 1959. New York: Vintage, 1987.

——. *The Big Sea: An Autobiography.* 1940. New York: Hill and Wang, 1993.

Hurston, Zora Neale. *Dust Tracks on the Road: An Autobiography.* 1942. New York: HarperPerennial, 1991.

Hutchinson, George. *The Harlem Renaissance in Black and White.* Cambridge: Harvard UP, 1995.

Johnson, James Weldon. *The Autobiography of an Ex-Coloured Man.* 1927. New York: Vintage, 1989.

——. *Black Manhattan.* New York: Knopf, 1930.

——. *Along This Way.* 1933. New York: Penguin, 1990.

——. *Selected Writings of James Weldon Johnson.* vol 2. Ed. Sondra Kathryn Wilson. New York: Oxford UP, 1995.

Kawish, Samira. *Dislocating the Color Line: Identity, Hybridity, and Singularity in African-American Identity.* Stanford: Stanford UP, 1997.

Lemke, Sieglinde. *Primitivist Modernism: Black Culture and the Origins of Transatlantic Modernism.* New York: Oxford UP, 1998.

Levy, Eugene. *James Weldon Johnson: Black Leader Black Voice.* Chicago: U Chicago P, 1973.

Lewis, David Levering. *When Harlem Was In Vogue.* New York: Oxford UP, 1981.

Lionnet, Françoise. *Autobiographical Voices: Race, Gender, Self-Portraiture.* Ithaca: Cornell UP, 1989.

Locke, Alain, ed. *The New Negro: Voices of the Harlem Renaissance.* 1925. New York: Simon and Shuster, 1992.

Lott, Eric. "Racial Cross-Dressing and the Construction of American Whiteness." *Cultures of United States Imperialism.* Eds. Kaplan and Paese. 474–495.

——. *Love and Theft: Blackface Minstrelsy and the American Working Class.* New York: Oxford UP, 1993.

McKay, Claude. *Home to Harlem.* 1928. Boston: Northeastern UP, 1987.

——. *A Long Way From Home.* 1937. New York: Harcourt, 1970.

Michaels, Walter Benn. "The Souls of White Folk." *Literature and the Body: Essays On Populations and Persons.* Ed. Elaine Scarry. Baltimore: Johns Hopkins UP, 1988. 185–209.

——. *Our America: Nativism, Modernism, and Pluralism.* Durham: Duke UP, 1995.

Nord, Deborah Epstein. "The Social Explorer as Anthropologist: Victorian Travellers Among the Urban Poor." *Visions of the Modern City: Essays in History, Art and Literature.* Eds. William Sharp and Leonard Wallock. New York: Columbia UP, 1983. 118–130.

——. *Walking the Victorian Streets: Women, Representation, and the City.* Ithaca: Cornell, 1995.

Pratt, Mary Louise. *Imperial Eyes: Travel Writing and Transculturation.* New York: Routledge, 1992.

Robinson, Amy. "It Takes One to Know One: Passing and Communities of Common Interest." *Critical Inquiry* 20 (1994): 715–736.

Rogin, Michael. "Blackface, White Noise: The Jewish Jazz Singer Finds His Voice." *Critical Inquiry* 18 (1992): 418–453.

Ross, Marlon. "Folkways of Desire: Patronage, Sex and Same-Sexuality in the New Negro Renaissance." Working Paper #19, Center for Afroamerican and African Studies, University of Michigan, 1996.

——. "Some Glances at the Black Fag: Race, Same-Sex Desire and Cultural Belonging." *Canadian Review of Comparative Literature* 21.1–2 (1994): 193–219.

Schuyler, George. *Black No More.* 1931. Boston: Northeastern UP, 1989.

Stein, Gertrude. *Three Lives.* 1909. New York: Vintage, 1939.

Stern, Julia. "Spanish Masquerade and the Drama of Racial Identity in *Uncle Tom's Cabin.*" *Passing and the Fictions of Identity.* Ed. Elaine Ginsberg. 103–130.

Stovall, Tyler. *Paris Noir: African Americans in the City of Light.* New York: Houghton Mifflin, 1996.

Thurman, Wallace. *Infants of the Spring.* 1932. Boston: Northeastern UP, 1992.

Torgovnick, Marianna. *Gone Primitive: Savage Intellects, Modern Lives.* Chicago: U Chicago P, 1990.

Tyler, Carole-Anne. "Passing: Narcissism, Identity, and Difference." *differences* 6.2–3 (1994): 210- 248.

Van Vechten, Carl. *Nigger Heaven.* New York: Knopf, 1928.

——. Introduction. *The Autobiography of an Ex-Coloured Man.* By Johnson. xxxiii-xxxviii.

Washington, Booker T. *Up From Slavery.* 1901. New York: Penguin, 1986.

Watson, Steven. *The Harlem Renaissance: Hub of African-American Culture 1920–1930.* New York: Pantheon, 1995.

Weinberg, Jonathan. "'Boy Crazy': Carl Van Vechten's Queer Collection." *The Yale Journal of Criticism* 7.2 (1994): 25–49.

Wintz, Cary D. *Black Culture and the Harlem Renaissance.* Houston: Rice UP, 1988.

Earl Lind

Ackerley, J.R. *My Father and Myself.* New York: Poseidan, 1968.

Bartlett, Neil. *Who Was That Man?: A Present for Oscar Wilde.* London: Serpent's Tail, 1988.

Bech, Henning. *When Men Meet: Homosexuality and Modernity.* Trans. Teresa Mesquit and Tim Davies. 1987. Chicago: U Chicago P, 1997.

Bland, Lucy and Laura Doan. *Sexology in Culture: Labelling Bodies and Desires.* Chicago: U Chicago P, 1998.

——. *Sexology Uncensored: The Documents of Sexual Science.* Chicago: U Chicago P, 1998.

Bravman, Scott. *Queer Fictions of the Past: History, Culture and Difference.* Cambridge: Cambridge UP, 1997.

Bristow, Joseph. *Sexuality.* New York: Routledge, 1997.

Carpenter, Edward. *Selected Writings: Sex.* Vol 1. London: Gay Male Press, 1984.

Cohen, William A. *Sex Scandal: The Private Parts of Victorian Fiction.* Durham: Duke UP, 1996.

Craft, Christopher. *Another Kind of Love: Male Homosexual Desire in English Discourse, 1850–1920.* Berkeley: U California P, 1994.

Edelman, Lee. *Homographesis: Essays in Gay Literary and Cultural Theory.* New York: Routledge, 1994.

Ellis, Havelock and John Addington Symonds. *Sexual Inversion.* 1897. New York: Arno, 1975.

Epstein, Julia. *Altered Conditions: Disease, Medecine and Storytelling.* New York: Routledge, 1995.

Ford, Charles and Parker Tyler. *The Young and Evil.* 1933. New York: Arno, 1975.

Forster, E.M. *Maurice.* 1914. New York: Quality Paperback Book Club, 1971.

Gosse, Edmund. *Father and Son: A Study of Two Temperaments.* 1907. New York: Penguin, 1983.

Grosskurth, Phyllis. *The Woeful Victorian: A Biography of John Addington Symonds.* New York: Holt, Rinehart and Winston, 1964.

——. *Havelock Ellis: A Biography.* New York: Knopf, 1980.

Hirschfeld, Magnus. *Transvestites: The Erotic Drive to Cross Dress.* 1910. Trans. Michael A. Lombardi-Nash. Buffalo: Prometheus, 1991.

——. *Sexualpathologie: Ein Lehrbuch für Ärzte und Studierende.* Bonn: A. Marcus & E. Webers, 1918.

Kennedy, Hubert. *Ulrichs: The Life and Works of Karl Heinrich Ulrichs: Pioneer of the Modern Gay Movement.* Boston: Alyson, 1988.

Koestenbaum, Wayne. *Double Talk: The Erotics of Male Literary Collaboration.* New York: Routledge, 1989.

Kopelson, Kevin. *The Queer Afterlife of Vaslav Nijinsky.* Stanford: Stanford UP, 1997.

Krafft-Ebing, Richard von. *Psychopathic Sexualis: With Especial Reference to the Antipathic Sexual Instinct. A Medico-Forensic Study.* Trans. Franklin S. Klaf from the 12th German Edition. 1886. New York: Stein and Day, 1965.

Lauritsen, John and David Thorstad. *The Early Homosexual Rights Movement (1864–1935)*. New York: Times Change, 1974.

Lind, Earl ("Ralph Werther"—Jennie June"), *Autobiography of an Androgyne.* 1918. New York: Arno, 1975.

Miller, D.A. *Bringing Out Roland Barthes.* Berkeley: U California P, 1992.

Niles, Blair. *Strange Brother.* 1931. New York: Arno, 1975.

Pacteau, Francette. "The Impossible Referent: Representations of the Androgyne." *Formations of Fantasy.* Eds. Victor Burgin, James Donald, and Cora Kaplan. London: Methuen, 1986.

Prosser, Jay. *Second Skins: The Body Narratives of Transsexuality.* New York: Columbia UP, 1998.

Robinson, Paul. *Gay Lives: Homosexual Autobiography from John Addington Symonds to Paul Monette.* Chicago: U Chicago P, 1999.

Santner, Eric L. *My Own Private Germany: Daniel Paul Schreber's Secret History of Modernity.* Princeton: Princeton UP, 1996.

Sinfield, Alan. *The Wilde Century: Effeminacy, Oscar Wilde and the Queer Moment.* New York: Columbia UP, 1994.

Steakely, James D. *The Homosexual Emancipation Movement in Germany.* New York: Arno, 1975.

The Memoirs of John Addington Symonds: The Secret Homosexual Life of a Leading Nineteenth Century Man of Letters. Ed. Phyllis Grosskurth. Chicago: U Chicago P, 1984.

Trask, Michael. "Merging With the Masses: The Queer Identity Politics of Leftist Modernism." *differences* 8.8 (1996): 94–131.

Tsuzuki, Chushichi. *Edward Carpenter 1844–1929: Prophet of Human Fellowship.* New York: Cambridge UP, 1980.

Ulrichs, Carl Heinrich. *Forschungen über das Rätsel der Mannmännlichen Liebe.* 1898. New York: Arno, 1975.

Weeks, Jeffrey. *Coming Out: Homosexual Politics in Britain, from the Nineteenth Century to the Present.* London: Quartet, 1977.

Werther, Ralph—Jennie June ("Earl Lind"). *The Female-Impersonators.* 1922. New York: Arno, 1975.

Wolff, Charlotte. *Magnus Hirschfeld: A Portrait of a Pioneer in Sexology.* London: Quartet, 1986.

Coda

Anderson, Sherwood. *Winesburg, Ohio.* 1919. Oxford: Oxford UP, 1997.

Index

Italics indicate photo